Pittsburgh and the Urban League Movement

Pittsburgh and the Urban League Movement

A Century of Social Service and Activism

Joe William Trotter Jr.

UNIVERSITY PRESS OF KENTUCKY

Scholarly publisher for the Commonwealth,
serving Bellarmine University, Berea College, Centre
College of Kentucky, Eastern Kentucky University,
The Filson Historical Society, Georgetown College,
Kentucky Historical Society, Kentucky State University,
Morehead State University, Murray State University,
Northern Kentucky University, Transylvania University,
University of Kentucky, University of Louisville,
and Western Kentucky University.
All rights reserved.

Editorial and Sales Offices: The University Press of Kentucky
663 South Limestone Street, Lexington, Kentucky 40508-4008
www.kentuckypress.com

Library of Congress Cataloging-in-Publication Data

Names: Trotter, Joe William, 1945– author.
Title: Pittsburgh and the Urban League movement : a century of social service
    and activism / Joe William Trotter Jr.
Description: Lexington : The University Press of Kentucky, [2020] |
    Series: Civil rights and the struggle for black equality in the twentieth century |
    Includes bibliographical references and index.
Identifiers: LCCN 2020022804 | ISBN 9780813179919 (hardcover) |
    ISBN 9780813180700 (paperback) | ISBN 9780813179933 (pdf) |
    ISBN 9780813179940 (epub)
Subjects: LCSH: Urban League (Pittsburgh, Pa.) | African
    Americans—Pennsylvania—Pittsburgh—Societies, etc. |
    African Americans—Pennsylvania—Pittsburgh—Social conditions. |
    African Americans—Civil rights—Pennsylvania—Pittsburgh—
    History. | Working class—Pennsylvania—Pittsburgh—History—
    20th century. | Pittsburgh (Pa.)—Race relations—History. |
    Pittsburgh (Pa.)—Social conditions.
Classification: LCC F159.P69 N484 2020 | DDC 305.8009748/86—dc23

To Esther L. Bush and the Urban League of Greater Pittsburgh, in appreciation for a century of social service and activism

Contents

Prologue   1

Part I: Founding and Early History

1. Quest for Jobs and Housing   9

2. Promise and Limits   41

Part II: The Depression and World War II

3. Surviving the Depression   71

4. Establishing a New Social Service Regime   93

Part III: The Modern Black Freedom Movement and Beyond

5. Combating Inequality in the Postwar City   115

6. Navigating Civil Rights and Black Power Struggles   137

7. Confronting Decline and Facilitating Renaissance   159

Epilogue   180

Acknowledgments   183

Notes   185

Selected Bibliography   225

Index   227

Prologue

This history of the Urban League of Pittsburgh (ULP) examines the organization's century of social service and activism in the Greater Pittsburgh metropolitan area. It complements existing studies of the Urban League movement and deepens our understanding of the Urban League as a national phenomenon. Most important, this book addresses the debate over the Urban League movement's impact on the lives of poor and working-class blacks as they made the transition from farm to city. Some scholars and popular writers argue that the Urban League movement was largely a conservative force that rarely improved the lives of the black poor. Others defend the Urban League as a progressive interracial social movement that eased the painful impact of migration, labor exploitation, and poor living conditions on thousands of southern black newcomers to the city.

Important class and gender biases punctuated the Urban League movement in Pittsburgh and elsewhere across twentieth-century America and called into question some of its approaches to helping the poor. In the years after World War II, the Urban League's determination to expand the ranks of black professionals reinforced its popular image as a middle-class organization that had lost touch with the grass roots. Even so, this book shows that the Urban League of Pittsburgh supported and sometimes led militant social justice and civil rights struggles designed to eradicate class and racial inequality in the larger political economy of the region and the nation.

Based on a corpus of both primary and secondary sources—including the branch files of the National Urban League, the black weekly newspaper the *Pittsburgh Courier*, and oral histories—this book examines the Urban League movement's century-long quest for social science research into race and class relations, social justice, and professional social services

1

for poor and working-class black families in Pittsburgh and western Pennsylvania.[1] Founded in New York City in 1911, the National Urban League (originally the National League on Urban Conditions among Negroes) was formed by the merger of several preexisting social service organizations assisting blacks in the city—namely, the National League for the Protection of Colored Women, the Committee for Improving the Industrial Condition of Negroes in New York, and the Committee on Urban Conditions among Negroes. During and immediately after World War I, the number of Urban League branches increased dramatically to nearly thirty in major cities such as Chicago, Detroit, Milwaukee, Cleveland, and Pittsburgh.

Following its establishment in 1918, the Urban League of Pittsburgh played a key role in transforming the city's African American community under industrial and later postindustrial capitalism. As a result of the Great Migration, the city's black population increased from more than 25,600 (about 5 percent of the total) to nearly 105,000 (20 percent) in 1970. In the larger metropolitan area, the African American population grew from about 3 percent to more than 6 percent of the total (see the accompanying table). From the outset of this massive black migration, newcomers to Pittsburgh saw the local branch of the Urban League as a great resource to help them make the adjustment to life in the urban-industrial city. Writing for himself and other blacks seeking jobs in the industrial North, one southerner wrote to the ULP, "We Southern Negroes want to come to the north . . . [southern whites] ain't giving a man nothing for what he do . . . they is trying to keep us down."[2] Throughout the interwar years, the organization served as a mediator between black workers and employers, landlords, schools, and correctional institutions. Local courts sometimes employed Urban League staffers to investigate alleged criminal misconduct by southern newcomers and helped curtail the number of African Americans incarcerated for certain crimes.

The Urban League intensified its social service and social justice work under the influence of the Great Depression, World War II, and the emergence of the modern black freedom movement in the 1950s and 1960s. Through a variety of occupational, economic, educational, and social service programs, the agency connected African Americans to a broad range of New Deal programs, but it was an uphill climb. The ULP documented

Table 1. African American Population of Greater Pittsburgh, 1910–2010

Year	Pittsburgh		Allegheny County		Six-County Metropolitan Area	
	Number	%	Number	%	Number	%
1910	25,623	4.8	34,217	3.3	51,712	3.0
1920	37,200	6.4	53,517	4.5	74,789	3.6
1930	54,983	8.2	83,326	6.0	117,530	5.1
1940	62,251	9.3	90,060	6.3	122,767	5.1
1950	82,453	12.2	113,643	7.5	145,776	5.8
1960	100,692	16.6	134,122	8.2	170,067	6.3
1970	104,904	20.1	144,545	9.0	176,979	6.5
1980	101,813	24.0	150,077	11.6	182,261	7.0
1990	95,362	25.7	149,550	11.0	179,700	8.1
2000	93,904	28.7	159,000	12.4	190,511	8.0
2010	79,710	26.0	161,861	13.2	198,074	8.6

Source: US Decennial Census Reports, 1910–2010.

widespread discrimination against blacks in federal housing and employment programs. Works Progress Administration (WPA) projects, it pointedly noted, "proved a handicap to the employment of Negroes" in Pittsburgh and Allegheny County.[3]

In the years after World War II, new Urban League programs fueled the growth and expansion of the city's black middle class. In relatively rapid succession, the Pittsburgh branch launched initiatives designed to open doors for black professionals and businesspeople—the Pilot Placement Project (1948), the Defense Manpower Project (1951), and the Management Council (1958), to name a few. Together, these efforts resulted in blacks moving into new jobs as engineers and chemists and as journalists for the city's leading newspapers, including the *Pittsburgh Post-Gazette*. Beginning with the March on Washington movement during World War II, the ULP also joined forces with grassroots civil rights organizations to fight segregation and discrimination at public parks and swimming pools, as well as in employment, education, and health services.

As the city's African American community increased its assaults on Jim Crow, it gradually reaped the benefits of the modern black freedom movement. The ULP not only helped Pittsburgh take advantage of the gains achieved by the civil rights and black power struggles but also shaped African American responses to the simultaneous loss of industrial jobs, the creation of a new renaissance city (graphically symbolized by expansion of the downtown "Golden Triangle"), and the growing white resistance to local, state, and federal affirmative action programs during the final decades of the twentieth century. Near the turn of the twenty-first century, according to branch president and CEO Esther L. Bush, for too many African Americans, Pittsburgh's Golden Triangle was more akin to an "Iron Circle—a never-ending cycle of glass ceilings, revolving doors and broken ladders."[4] At the same time, the local Urban League struggled to survive as a social service and social justice organization amid budget cuts and staff reductions.

At the dawn of the new century, and against immense odds, the ULP resolved to address the subtle and not so subtle manifestations of the color line in the socioeconomic and institutional life of the region. Against the backdrop of deep racial and class divisions, and while engaged in a fight for its own survival, the ULP developed new social programs aimed at reducing unemployment, homelessness, and poverty following the aggressive onslaught of deindustrialization. Late-twentieth-century and early-twenty-first-century programs included state-funded projects to help able-bodied men and women prepare for the new workforce, a federal bonding placement program to assist ex-offenders reenter the workforce, a new Urban League charter school to enhance the opportunities for young blacks, and a Black Male Leadership Development Institute, among others.

This book is divided into three closely interrelated parts. Part I (chapters 1 and 2) discusses how an "interracial band" of urban reformers established the Pittsburgh branch of the Urban League and set the organization's social service agenda—specifically, the quest for jobs, housing, health care, and education—for most of the twentieth century. These chapters underscore the class and gender biases of Urban League programs, despite the ULP's otherwise stellar achievements on behalf of the city's African American community.

Part II (chapters 3 and 4) covers the impact of the Depression and World War II. It illuminates the transformation of Urban League programs under the influence of a variety of New Deal social, labor, and public works initiatives, including low-income housing projects, efforts to professionalize domestic service employment, and workers' rights. Chapters 3 and 4 also underscore the Urban League's role in the development of grassroots movements such as the "Don't Buy Where You Can't Work" and March on Washington movements.

Part III (chapters 5–7) analyzes the transformation of the Urban League's ideas and social practices during the intensification of the modern black freedom movement and its aftermath. Specifically, these chapters document how the Pittsburgh branch sometimes initiated activities and sometimes followed the lead of other, more militant grassroots movements to erase the color line in jobs, housing, education, health care, and public accommodations, particularly swimming pools. These chapters also illustrate how, following a brief period of success before the collapse of the manufacturing sector, the ULP addressed the challenges of the emerging postindustrial economy. Although it achieved uneven results, the Pittsburgh branch worked to move African Americans from the periphery to the center of the city's new health, education, hospitality, and computer technology firms. Perhaps most important, part III documents the Urban League's growing involvement in grassroots efforts to combat police brutality, mobilize poor and working-class black voters, and ensure that the established political process worked in the interest of Pittsburgh's African American community.

Finally, the epilogue reflects on the ULP's history through a national perspective. As elsewhere—and perhaps even more strongly than elsewhere—I conclude that the Urban League of Pittsburgh consistently merged social science research and professional social services with grassroots social justice, workers' rights, civil rights, and black power struggles.

Part I

Founding and Early History

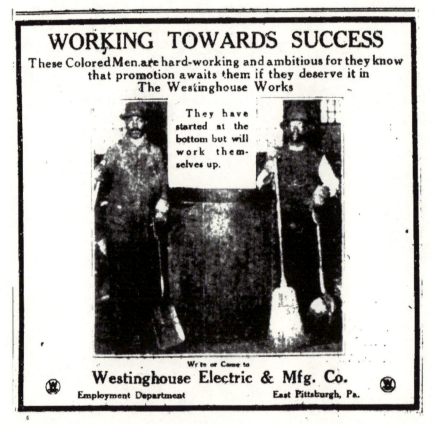

The Urban League of Pittsburgh encouraged not only steel mills to employ southern black workers but also a broad range of other companies, including Westinghouse. (*Pittsburgh Courier*, 16 June 1923)

1

Quest for Jobs and Housing

The fight to obtain much-needed social services for Pittsburgh's poor and working-class black families had deep roots in the prewar years. But this struggle intensified during and after World War I with the formation and development of the Urban League of Pittsburgh (ULP). An affiliate of the National Urban League (NUL), the ULP built on significant prewar efforts and, like its parent body, resolved to aid southern black migrants through the creation of interracial professional social service networks. Following the lead of national headquarters in New York City, the Steel City's small band of reformers placed the provision of migration, employment, housing, and health services at the core of its mission in Pittsburgh and western Pennsylvania. After a brief moment of extraordinary success working with wartime employers and social service providers to create jobs, find homes, and improve the living and working conditions of black people, the ULP's programs dissipated as the demand for labor declined, unemployment increased, and corporate support of the organization dropped during the postwar economic downturn. As the economy gradually recovered during the mid-1920s, the ULP placed increasing pressure on corporate leaders to remove racial barriers to professional and skilled occupations and employ African Americans. It also urged the organized labor movement to open union membership to black workers on an equal footing with their white counterparts. At the same time, the agency exhorted African Americans to train themselves for skilled, managerial, and professional positions. Pittsburgh branch leaders were cautiously optimistic that the color bar would eventually fall as the black freedom struggle intensified.

This chapter and the one that follows cover the wartime beginnings and postwar efforts of the ULP before the onset of the Great Depression and World War II transformed the national Urban League movement, the city, the state, and the nation.

Establishing the Pittsburgh Branch

The Urban League of Pittsburgh emerged out of the socioeconomic and political struggles of World War I and its aftermath, but prewar urban reformers established the foundation for its development. By the early twentieth century, western Pennsylvania was a major site of innovative social work. The famous *Pittsburgh Survey,* a massive six-volume study of the Pittsburgh industrial region published between 1909 and 1914, fueled research on the lives of immigrant, poor, and working-class whites; stimulated the creation of the Pittsburgh Associated Charities; and influenced the professionalization of social work on a national scale.[1]

Although the first generation of professional social workers focused primarily on the plight of poor and working-class whites, an interracial group of social reformers launched the Association for the Improvement of Social Conditions in the Hill District in 1914. Closely intertwined with the work of the Associated Charities, the Hill District organization aimed to promote and execute measures designed to correct "all conditions" that endangered "the social life of the community"—poor housing, lack of leisure-time facilities, delinquency, and injustice before the law. The organization's officers included president G. B. Howard, pastor of the city's African American Central Baptist Church; Samuel R. Morsell, director of the Hill District Centre Avenue YMCA; and Dr. Charles R. Zahniser, Presbyterian minister and head of the Pittsburgh Council of Churches.[2] A year later, the city's Associated Charities spearheaded the formation of the Pittsburgh Council for Social Service among Negroes (PCSSN) and hired its first black social worker, Edith Spurlock (Sampson). Like its predecessor, the new organization unfolded under interracial leadership that included Walter May, president of a major pharmaceutical company; Robert L. Vann, editor of the nationally circulated black weekly the *Pittsburgh Courier;* Francis Tyson, professor of economics at the University of Pittsburgh; and YMCA director Samuel R. Morsell.[3]

As the Great Migration intensified during the war years, the PCSSN transformed itself into a local chapter of the National Urban League. In Pittsburgh and elsewhere, black leaders of the social work movement and their white allies articulated the belief that although "individual action" could best counter color "prejudice," sustained organization among black and white residents could effect significant material changes, or "racial progress," in the lives of black people. Formed in New York City in 1911, the NUL represented the merger of three earlier organizations serving the needs of Empire City blacks: the National League for the Protection of Colored Women, the Committee for Improving the Industrial Condition of Negroes in New York, and the Committee on Urban Conditions among Negroes.[4]

As historian Nancy Weiss notes, the creation of the National Urban League charted distinctly new paths in the provision of social services for urban blacks. Most important, the NUL anchored its programs in "*research for facts*" about the movement of white and black populations into cities and the impact on living and working conditions among African Americans. The new agency sought "*educational opportunities*" for the professional training of black social workers and "*social science education*" for black community leaders. It proposed to "*secure*" jobs for professional black social workers in existing welfare agencies and, at the same time, induce all-white organizations to include blacks among the constituents they served. Finally, the NUL pledged to "survey and coordinate social agencies already at work and to create new organizations where necessary" to address the broad range of challenges confronting the expanding black population.[5]

The Urban League of Pittsburgh emerged during the explosive wartime expansion of National Urban League chapters across the Northeast and Midwest. During the war years alone, the organization added thirteen new affiliates, and by war's end, the NUL reported twenty-seven branch offices in major cities such as Newark, Chicago, Cleveland, St. Louis, Detroit, and Milwaukee.[6]

In the summer and fall of 1917, University of Pittsburgh student Abraham Epstein was conducting research for his BS thesis "The Negro Migrant in Pittsburgh" (1918), under the supervision of Professor Tyson. With support from the PCSSN, Epstein interviewed some 500 black migrants on virtually every aspect of their experiences in the city of Pittsburgh, including the conditions and quality of their work, housing, health, education, and access to social services. As Epstein pursued his research, the PCSSN moved to establish a local branch of the National Urban League in Pittsburgh.[7] After receiving a letter of inquiry from Tyson, the national office wrote to S. R. Morsell, "We are ready to send a worker to Pittsburgh on October first to help place the Pittsburgh organization on a substantial basis financially and otherwise." Shortly thereafter, John T. Clark was dispatched to Pittsburgh to undertake a survey of the city's black population. The *Pittsburgh Courier* later described Clark as "a man of broad views with a thorough knowledge of the general conditions of our people" and substantial experience "doing uplifting work" among black people.[8]

Originally from Louisville, Kentucky, Clark was a graduate of Ohio State University and had been employed at NUL headquarters for four and a half years before arriving in Pittsburgh. In New York City he had worked extensively on labor issues at Brooklyn's Busch Terminal, where he helped integrate black dockworkers into the labor force. Though pushing for equal employment opportunities for black workers, he was critical of Brooklyn's southern blacks, describing them as somewhat unreliable due to "irregular old habits acquired in the lazy industrial system of the South and the islands."[9] Building on Epstein's research on black newcomers to the city, Clark produced a detailed report and "work plan" for the establishment of the Pittsburgh branch. His recommendations covered a wide range of housing, job, health, policing, leisure-time, and other issues confronting the city's growing black population. In January 1918 the Associated Charities accepted Clark's recommendations and dissolved the PCSSN and established the Urban League of Pittsburgh. The branch's constitution declared that the "objects of this organization are first, to bring co-ordination and co-operation among existing agencies and organizations working especially for the betterment of the Pittsburgh Negro; secondly to assist and encourage all agencies and organizations working for the general welfare, to render a fuller and more sympathetic service to Negroes; thirdly, to promote any work not adequately being done by other agencies, for the industrial, economic and social welfare of the Negro in Pittsburgh and its environs."[10] The new agency selected Walter A. May as its president, G. B. Howard as first vice president, the Reverend C. Y. Trigg as second vice president, Samuel R. Morsell as secretary, John D. Fraser of the Monongahela National Bank as treasurer, and John T. Clark as executive director.

Economist Francis Tyson served as director of the organization's most active unit, the industrial relations department, and later became president of the ULP board of trustees. *Pittsburgh Courier* editor Robert Vann joined the executive board and "handled its publicity." The *Courier* publicized the organization's travelers' aid program, room registry, home and school visitor program, and work with the courts, as well as its employment and job placement services.[11] Working closely with May, Tyson, Vann, and other board members, Clark and the ULP carefully navigated Pittsburgh's ongoing conflicts between capital and labor. Industrial Pittsburgh remained exceedingly hostile to organized labor throughout the war and into the 1920s. According to a member of the Pittsburgh League for Social Justice, the city's corporate elites detested the labor movement and were determined to squash it by any means necessary, including the denial of free speech. "You can talk all you want to in Pittsburgh . . . except when you get to the subject of organized labor." In a special report on the capital-labor conflict in Pennsylvania during this period, the American Civil Liberties Union described the violation of workers' rights as "the shame of Pennsylvania," particularly in the coalfields of Pittsburgh and western Pennsylvania, where victims of police violence carried "scars on their faces and head from the rough treatment they received."[12]

Clark served the ULP for eight years before leaving the city to take charge of the St. Louis Urban League in July 1926. Contentious labor and race relations played a major role in Clark's departure, although Urban League files are largely silent on the conflict that led to his dismissal. In a letter to T. Arnold Hill of the national office, however, Clark put matters simply: "It appears that the situation here has been brought to a head over our industrial work. I suppose it is necessary for somebody to be sacrificed when policies conflict as they have in this case."[13] But Urban Leaguers Arthur Edmunds and Esther Bush note that "Clark was responsible for getting AFL organizer William Z. Foster (who later became a Communist leader and three-time Presidential candidate) together with black workers in the steel mills," and "it was because of this that he was forced out of Pittsburgh."[14] Nonetheless, Clark's comprehensive blueprint guided the city's Urban League movement through the mid-twentieth century.

Building on Clark's initial survey of conditions among black migrants to Pittsburgh, the ULP placed migration, jobs, and housing at the core of its agenda. Clark had sought detailed information on the social and political conditions in the principal regions of the South from which Pittsburgh's new black residents had migrated. For instance, Paul F. Mowbray, field secretary for the Nashville Public Welfare League, responded to Clark's request for data on black migration from his area. Mowbray informed Clark that

Tennessee tried to discourage black migration through antienticement legislation. But despite state and local authorities' requirement that labor recruiters secure licenses to operate in their jurisdictions, these recruiters had succeeded in mobilizing large numbers of black residents to leave the South for jobs in the urban North, including Pittsburgh.[15]

The branch documented heartrending stories of the mistreatment of migrants during their travels to Pittsburgh: "Mrs. Birch an aged widow of Birmingham Alabama came North three weeks ago. . . . A Negro man coming North from Mobile, Ala. was helping the old lady in changing trains and he walked off with her suit case which contained all her clothes. She arrived in Pittsburgh almost penniless and without her clothes."[16] Thus, Clark had urged the Pittsburgh community to establish "traveller's aid assistance" at railroad stations to direct migrants to reliable jobs, houses, and neighborhoods and "protect them from unfavorable surroundings." The ULP hired Sadie Bond to coordinate aid for newcomers at Union Station (the largest of the city's five railroad stations) in downtown Pittsburgh. Sadie, the daughter of Mary Peck Bond, was a member of an old nineteenth-century Pittsburgh family. She reported serving more than 600 newcomers during the first three months of her employment with the ULP. Nearly 300 of those cases involved girls and women who had come to the city "without jobs, money, or friends." Bond not only helped migrant men and women find homes and jobs but also helped them avoid pretenders who offered assistance as a means to "take advantage of them."[17]

Industrial Employment, Economic Downturn, and Recovery

In addition to helping migrants find their way from Union Station to homes in the city, the ULP established an industrial relations department to assist migrants' search for jobs. With funding from the Carnegie Steel Company, the ULP hired Tom Barton, a recent graduate of the University of Pittsburgh, as its first industrial secretary to direct job-placement services. He was assisted by Elizabeth Elliott, the women's employment secretary. The placement service received job applications from 1,200 black workers during its first six months of operation (200 whites also applied). The ULP placed 569 of these applicants, more than 85 percent of them in semiskilled or unskilled positions. Hired in June 1918, Barton later reported a 71 percent placement rate during his first year on the job. From January to October 1918, the ULP recorded more than 2,600 job listings. It screened at least 1,500 applicants for these jobs and placed more than 1,100 black workers in industrial plants within the city and the region. In May 1920 the ULP reported that it had placed 1,099 workers out of a total applicant pool of 2,357.[18]

As the placement of black workers proceeded apace, the ULP pledged to ensure that this labor force was "properly treated" by employers and "given opportunities for advancement." In forging this agenda, the branch developed a strong relationship with the state of Pennsylvania, and in 1920 the State Department of Labor moved its "Colored Branch" into the Urban League's office at 518 Wylie Avenue in the Hill District. This was an extraordinarily fruitful arrangement for the fledgling branch. In exchange for running the state's placement service for black workers, the state covered the salary of the ULP's industrial secretary, including clerical assistance, and paid rent for use of the facility. The executive director "supervised this work, made reports and handled the situation" to the "apparent satisfaction" of the state employment service. Thus, the Pittsburgh branch "became widely known as related to and co-operative with the public placement service" of the state.[19]

The ULP's job-placement efforts encountered stiff resistance from a number of industrial employers, including the Pittsburgh Railway Company, Westinghouse, and the Heinz Pickle Factory. In May 1920 the ULP facilitated a meeting of black Westinghouse employees at the Rodman Street Church. According to one board member, the "low wages" paid by Westinghouse was a major grievance among black workers. Some companies justified these low wages by noting that these unskilled employees had ample opportunities to increase their pay by working "two shifts if they desired." The ULP's advocacy on behalf of black workers was not limited to those with little formal education or training in skilled crafts. During the ULP's first six months of service, it reported the placement of "3 foremen, 9 machinists, 1 lathe hand, 14 chippers, 5 moulders, 41 experienced mill hands, 2 pipe fitters, 1 tin repairman, [and] 5 painters." In November 1919 the organization sought to place a group of skilled black chain makers at Westinghouse. These men were eager to find employment using the skill they had learned and practiced in the Tidewater area of Virginia. The ULP was also placing black women in a variety of jobs in the manufacturing and trade sectors, in addition to jobs in domestic service. The industrial secretary reported the placement of "21 girls in Department Stores—stock girls, sheet writers, filing clerks and general office assistants—7 girls for manufacturing parts of gas stoves, 14 as operators in Burlap and Raincoat Factories, etc., 12 in Bakery, 55 domestics, etc." Throughout urban industrial America, black women used their slowly expanding access to jobs in the manufacturing sector to demand higher wages for domestic service. In Pittsburgh, wages for domestic workers gradually increased from less than $5 per day to between $5 and $8 per day and occasionally as high as $10.[20]

From its inception, the ULP met with skilled black workers to forge strategies to combat racial barriers in the workplace. Following a meeting at the YMCA with black cement masons, hoisting engineers, plumbers, and plasterers, the ULP made several recommendations: that the building and construction trade unions provide detailed accounts of their policies and practices toward skilled black workers, that unions discriminating against blacks be denied exclusive closed-shop agreements on building projects, and that temporary work permits be issued to blacks excluded from all-white and racially discriminatory unions. In its campaign to upgrade black workers, the ULP compiled and disseminated profiles of capable black men who hoped to move up from unskilled jobs into skilled, clerical, and supervisory positions. In an article on the steel industry, the organization challenged the notion that black men classified as "unskilled" lacked useful knowledge or know-how: "We are inclined to consider any man skilled who daily protects himself where thousands of tons of steel and iron are carried over head, with sparks, smoke, gas fumes, dust, molten and red-hot iron on every hand, and who so quickly learns to synchronize his movements with machine operations so as not to slow up their normal capacity of production."[21] In a letter to H. M. Reed, assistant general manager at the Standard Sanitary Manufacturing Company, Clark submitted the names of several black men deemed "good material" for advancement up the occupational ladder:

Earnest McKinney, #435, is a Trucker in your lower shake-out. McKinney is an exceptionally intelligent young Negro. He was recently married and is now working in your plant. . . . He has had experience in the Y.M.C.A. work directing boys and in directing a Soldier and Sailor Club after the armistice.

Earnest Leech, #349 is a Moulder in the Foundry and has been working for the plant for one year. He is another very intelligent Negro; a man capable of being advanced.

There are two other men: William Alexander and M. Moore who are ex-soldiers. They served for six years in the Twenty-Fourth U.S. Infantry. Moore was an Exchange Sargeant and has a very fine personality. He is an excellent man to advance.[22]

College students figured prominently in the ULP's effort to advance black workers. Several firms in the area recruited black students from southern schools and colleges for summer jobs in their manufacturing plants. These companies—most notably the Pittsburgh Plate Glass Company and the Standard Sanitary Manufacturing Company—paid the travel costs for their student employees. Although these costs were later deducted from the students' earnings, the employers promised to refund the students' transportation expenses contingent on a record of steady employment for the entire three months of summer vacation. In its campaign to support black workers, the ULP strongly urged firms to promote black students. Clark wrote to Reed, "There are quite a number of young men students in your plant: Johnson from Knoxville College; George Ashton from Storer College and Isaiah Woodson. These are a few men whom you might [advance]."[23]

Urban League social services expanded well beyond the municipal boundaries of Pittsburgh and into a variety of industrial towns in western Pennsylvania and parts of West Virginia. The agency took a strong and abiding interest in the welfare of black workers at Homestead, Donora, Johnstown, Braddock, New Castle, and other steel centers in the larger Pittsburgh region (see the accompanying map). In particular, the experiences of black workers in New Castle attracted Clark's attention. During the war and in the early postwar years, the town proudly claimed to have the largest concentration of industrial firms among American cities of comparable size. New Castle's major employers—the Carnegie Steel Company, the American Sheet and Tin Plate Mill, and the Standard Steel Car Company—hired a significant number of black workers during the

Pittsburgh metropolitan area, 1919. (Map by Dick Gilbreath; reproduced from Peter Gottlieb, *Making Their Own Way: Southern Blacks' Migration to Pittsburgh, 1916–20* [Urbana: University of Illinois Press, 1987], 41, courtesy of University of Illinois Press)

war years. After the war, Clark traveled to New Castle to ascertain the status of black workers there. In November 1921 he also sought information on black workers in the steel mills of Johnstown, located some seventy miles east of Pittsburgh. "I have little or no acquaintance with the Mills in Johnstown," Clark wrote to John Johnson, but "would like to get an idea of how big your [race] problem is up there." On another occasion, he refuted charges that the ULP paid little attention to outlying mill towns such as Braddock. In a letter to Miss J. A. Gruber, a welfare worker at Carnegie Steel, Clark reported, "We made an investigation of the situation in Port Perry [in Braddock] and made recommendations to your company but no definite steps have been taken." The ULP's work also extended across the state line into Wheeling, West Virginia, where Clark observed conditions at the Wheeling Mold and Foundry Company and recommended the hiring of a trained welfare worker to help black employees transition into the company's industrial labor force.[24]

Wartime labor recruitment efforts included a focus on farming and coal mining, as well as work in steel mills and other manufacturing firms. In his May 1920 report to the ULP's executive board, Clark observed that a number of applicants were "farm hands or from the rural districts." He believed that some of these newcomers should be encouraged to pursue farmwork, "after having met some difficulties in the Mills and manufacturing districts." Thus, the Pittsburgh branch took steps to secure information on "farms for sale or rent." ULP president May also suggested that the State College of Agriculture could provide advice along these lines. In March 1923 the executive director reiterated the league's "efforts to connect up many of these Southern migrants with opportunities to work on the farms" of western Pennsylvania. In the meantime, according to the US Census of Occupations, the number of black bituminous coal miners in the entire state of Pennsylvania stood at about 2,288 in 1920. These men worked almost exclusively in the mines of western Pennsylvania. Their numbers and engagement with the ULP would accelerate during the mid to late 1920s.[25]

In the years after World War I, the demand for labor declined, and the ULP documented the spread of unemployment among black workers. The minutes of a January 1922 meeting reported that "the biggest problem facing Colored people" was unemployment. According to ULP social worker Aluvia Stoner, domestic service advertisements for "colored girls" rapidly dissipated. At the same time, Clark reported that many black workers had returned to the South but would return "if opportunities open up before the Spring time Planting; otherwise they are likely to remain in the South." The executive director also noted substantial bitterness among black workers due to discriminatory layoff practices during the downturn. They complained that the foremen of mill towns did not "recognize the length or character of the service rendered by Negroes in comparison to their white workers." Moreover, as the war wound down and the economy skidded in the postwar years, Tom Barton enlisted in the US Army and left the ULP without an industrial relations department. Although Barton returned briefly after his military service, he left again to enroll in law school at the University of Pittsburgh.[26]

During the economic downturn, the ULP reiterated its philosophy "to refrain from relief giving." "Not Alms, but Opportunity" was the organization's motto. However, the suffering became "so serious" that the ULP "felt justified in organizing sources of emergency relief, and then referring cases to the recognized relief giving agencies." It received and dispensed clothing, shoes, and coal to the poor. Moreover, African American workers at Kaufman's Department Store held a dance to raise money for the league's relief efforts. The ULP's January 1920 report emphasized "the alarming amount of poverty throughout the city among the Colored people." At its November 1921 meeting, the executive board took up the issue of homelessness among Pittsburgh's poor and working-class blacks. It referred African Americans to the city's hotel for poor and homeless people operated by the Association for the Improvement of the Poor, but the agency rejected black referrals on the premise that "blacks and whites could not possibly mix in their hotel."[27]

Pittsburgh's industrial economy slowly rebounded during the mid-1920s, as it did elsewhere in the country. As early as June 1922, the ULP reported a gradual resumption of black migration into the city and the region. It received a growing number of letters from prospective black migrants from the South requesting help finding jobs and homes in Pittsburgh. The same year, Tyson encouraged the local board to add an industrial secretary to the staff to "link the League more closely with industries as well as give Mr. Clark a much needed assistant." In 1923 the travelers' aid office urged the branch to extend its hours to 9:30 p.m. "to help distribute many of the Negroes who reach the city on the night train." Three years later, the agency called attention to "a new need for travelers aid work at the station, due to the number of Negro families coming in." As the economy recovered, the ULP's home economics worker reported a "falling off of cases for relief" and a "picking up of employment throughout her district." The branch reopened its dormant job-placement office and registered an increasing number of men and women seeking work. This included thirty men and thirty-eight women in June 1922, thirty-nine men and fifty women in July, and forty-five men and fifty women in August.[28]

The era of recovery presented a mixed picture for the city's black population and the Urban League's efforts on behalf of poor and working-class residents. Salary reductions and delays persisted well into the mid-1920s. In an August 1924 letter to Edwin C. May, who served as ULP president between 1924 and 1926, Clark declared that he had not "until this time become discouraged with our efforts to finance" the organization's work. In early September, after pondering Clark's bleak portrait of the ULP's finances, May informed the board that a series of events over the summer had "shaken the Urban League to its foundation." Consequently, the local branch arranged a meeting with E. K. Jones of the national office "to go over some of our problems [and] . . . take action on several matters that will determine the future policy of the [organization] if it is to continue in existence." In the wake of this financial crisis, the Advisory Committee, a community-wide roster of Urban League supporters, recommended that the ULP change its name to the "Negro Welfare Association of Pittsburgh" to blend the "new with the old," retain its affiliation with the NUL, but strike out on a more vigorous publicity and fund-raising campaign to salvage the organization and acknowledge important changes in the agency's staff and personnel.[29]

The branch ultimately rejected the name change, gradually rebounded, and deepened its work as an affiliate of the National Urban League. It placed increasing emphasis on the experiences of skilled black workers and the destructive impact of technological changes on those at the bottom of the occupational ladder. Many of the skilled black men who migrated to the region had experience in the building and construction trades, but nearly all of them worked as common laborers and hod carriers for skilled white craftsmen. Moreover, the ULP documented the negative influence of technological changes on black workers' employment prospects. New machinery increasingly displaced "common labor." In a ten-year study of blacks in key industries covering the period between 1917 and 1927, the ULP received replies from forty firms employing an estimated 54,000 workers, including about 9,000 blacks. Over the first half of the study, eleven industries increased the number of black employees, thirteen reported a decline in the number of black workers, and the remainder stayed about the same.

Between June and August 1927, when more than 200 black men and women sought employment through the ULP, it placed only 32 women and 7 men. Employment in the coal mines partially compensated for losses in the manufacturing sector, but even the mines were soon operating at no more than half their capacity.[30]

By the mid-1920s, as suggested by the rising number of "Negro families" arriving at Union Station, both ULP and corporate leaders emphasized the recruitment of married rather than single men for jobs in the manufacturing sector. T. Arnold Hill, the NUL's industrial secretary, and other national officers regularly visited Pittsburgh to address employment inequality and promote other local programs.[31] During a December 1928 visit to Pittsburgh, Hill conducted an exceedingly fruitful round of interviews with corporate leaders, underscoring both the opportunities for black workers and the limitations they faced. Hill and local branch officers met with W. G. Marshall, personnel director at the Philadelphia Company, a utilities firm operating in Pittsburgh. From the outset of the interview, Marshall made it clear that the firm employed blacks almost exclusively in a limited range of general labor jobs, but Alonzo Thayer (Clark's successor), Hill, and other Urban League staffers carefully outlined the many heretofore all-white areas in which the company could employ black workers. They forcefully argued that, "in the gas and electric light companies [colored] men could be used in the power plants as electricians, that automobile repairmen could be found to work on the busses of the company, that women as demonstrators of electrical and gas appliances could be found, that men as skilled and semi-skilled repairmen could be obtained for repairs on the surface cars, and that a more liberal policy of granting positions in keeping with the fitness of colored people should be adopted by the company." Despite these persuasive arguments for expanding the jobs available to black workers, Marshall gave "no indication" that he was moved by them.[32]

The Joseph Horne Department Store employed an estimated 200 black workers "as sheetwriters, store girls, maids, janitors, and work of this type." F. C. Schatz, the assistant manager, declared his support for expanding and upgrading the black workforce, but he urged the ULP to prepare black workers for promotion through attention to their "personality" and "conduct." When asked "if it would be possible to try to change the sentiment of a few of his [white] managers or department heads while we were at the same time trying to improve the personal efficiency of the colored employees, Mr. Schatz thought this was advisable, but offered no way by which it could be done." At the Carnegie Steel Company, vice president L. H. Burnett declared that black workers were "eminently proficient in all operations at which they have worked." He even noted that the problem of turnover had improved because many of the southern black workers were beginning to adopt "northern methods rather than those they have been brought up under in the South." Burnett referred to a negative "hanging over" from the South—a racially biased perspective on southern black work habits that in fact varied considerably from place to place in the South and among different groups of workers. Nonetheless, when asked whether he would consider hiring a black metallurgist at his company, Burnett said he would "momentarily hesitate" but ultimately not object.[33]

In its research on the labor process in the steel industry, the ULP underscored the skills deployed by black workers in some of the most dangerous and difficult jobs, "from the mining of coal to the melting, pouring and handling of the iron and steel products." According to one branch research report, the so-called unskilled worker displayed considerable technical knowledge in the "conserving of his health and strength, personally avoiding burns or other accidents and protecting his fellow workman from same." Such know-how, the report suggested, explained why some immigrant "leaders of Negro gangs" were "gradually being displaced by Negro straw-bosses." Some companies employed black bosses even when black workers made up less than a third of the gang. In one plant, 35 black straw bosses directed the labor of 883 men, including 273 immigrant workers. Among the twenty-three mills studied in this report, there were eleven black foremen, working mostly in blast furnaces, open hearths, and power facilities and on labor gangs.[34]

Branch leaders consistently celebrated the accomplishments of black industrial workers as a way to open the door to promotion and advancement up the occupational ladder. For instance, the ULP enthusiastically reported that in one large steel mill, a black man headed the transportation department and had "complete direction of the trains, handling incoming raw materials and out-going steel products." At the Park Works of the Crucible Steel Company and the Clark Mills of the Carnegie Steel Company, African Americans had first entered the firms as strikebreakers nearly three decades earlier and had increased their numbers during the Great Migration. Blacks now made up about 25 and 40 percent of the workforce in these two companies, respectively, and occupied a broad range of jobs, including grinders, heaters, chippers, rollers, millwrights, and crane operators. Moreover, Crucible's Park Works employed a black chemist, draftsman, and civil engineer before the downturn of the early 1920s. At Carnegie's Clark Mills, a black worker nicknamed "Daddy Clay" became known as "one of the greatest experts on shaft steel" and earned from $15 to $40 per day. During the period of economic recovery, black college students continued to work during the summer months, and the ULP called attention to it: "More and more of our college men are entering the mills during summer vacations. Contact of mill officials with this type of young Negro is aiding materially in opening new departments to Negro labor." Branch officials underscored the work ethic of these young men, as illustrated by this elaborate example:

> Last June, a young Cornell student, son of a prominent Negro attorney drove up to an employment office in his father's new Jordan Sedan asking for any kind of available job, was put to work in the fitting department of a mill which heretofore had never as much as had a Negro porter in it. He never missed a day in 2½ months, was advanced three times, and when he was ready to return to school, drove down after his pay check. The General Superintendent sent for him, complimented him and assured him that a job in the Engineering Department would be waiting him when he finished.[35]

In 1928 the ULP printed extensive excerpts about the promotions of black workers. These comments reflected the league's interest in the upward movement, however modest, of black workers from general labor positions to semiskilled and skilled jobs:

> Have advanced from laborers to second helpers at the open hearth.
> Have advanced from laborers to machinery and locomotives.
> From laborers to drawers of cold steel.
> From laborers to grinders and machine molders.
> Have advanced from laborers to foremen.

In some cases, these promotions included increases in pay:

> From laborers to drawers of copper wire with an advancement of
> $.44 to $.87 per hour.
> From laborers to machine operators—$.44 to $.80 and as high as
> $1.00 per hour, piece work.
> From laborers to machine operators with an advancement of
> $11.00 per week.
> One firm declared, "We have promoted one Negro as superin-
> tendent of our warehouse because of his work; another as a
> receiving clerk; another Negro who works for us owns and
> operates seven delivery trucks."[36]

Whereas the vast majority of black workers continued to be employed in the industrial sector of Pittsburgh and the surrounding mill towns, the mid-1920s witnessed an upsurge in the recruitment of black coal miners across western Pennsylvania, most notably in the mines at Library, Imperial, George, and Moon Run. Between 1924 and 1927 the number of black coal miners increased by an estimated 6,000 men. Some 25 percent of the new miners were recruited from the city of Pittsburgh, and another 25 percent came from West Virginia. One coal company in the Pittsburgh district employed 2,800 black miners. Although coal mining towns offered few employment opportunities for black women, the mining industry somewhat offset the preference for married men in the manufacturing sector and offered expanding employment opportunities for young single men. Moreover, cyclical swings in the steel industry sent unemployed black mill hands into the mines. Work among the coal miners added another layer of diversity and complexity to the ULP's mission.[37]

Recruitment of intact black families (husband, wife, and children) would presumably help resolve the problem of turnover, increase production, and improve living conditions in the larger black community. Indeed, blacks increased their average length of employment in the mills from one month during World War I to three and a half months by the early to mid-1920s.[38] Even so, the challenges of labor turnover persisted. In a letter to James Hemphill, employment manager at Carnegie

Steel's Duquesne Works, Clark suggested convening a special conference to discuss the problem. He pointed out that even though local industries had recruited "a much better set of men now than ever . . . the same difficulty of holding men still exists." Moreover, while the hiring of men with families may have increased, the ULP continued to focus on the labor and living conditions of single men. In a letter to Jones and Laughlin Steel, Clark relayed the grievances of several black workers at the company. "A group of Colored men came into our office on Saturday morning," he wrote, "and two more men came this morning who claim to have worked at Jones and Laughlin's plant in Woodlawn, but quit after an incident which happened a few nights ago in the camp." League officials interviewed the black workers and documented their mistreatment at gunpoint by company guards. Some seventy-five black workers had quit Jones and Laughlin and sought employment elsewhere, but the company refused to fully compensate the men for work rendered up to that time.[39]

Partly to offset black workers' precarious place in the industrial labor force, the ULP promoted, applauded, and celebrated black entrepreneurship. Entrepreneurial pursuits were integral to southern blacks' migration to Pittsburgh and other northern industrial centers. In 1924 a group of southern blacks informed the ULP that they hoped to export watermelon to the northern market, claiming that they could "begin shipping about June 15th [1924], two car loads a week of the best melons. Our terms are ($25.00) a carload."[40]

In an article on industry, the ULP noted the "successful operation of about a dozen mines by thrifty Negroes" in western Pennsylvania. The Iron Valley Coal Company, for example, operated a mine in Shinnston, West Virginia, and produced 200 tons of coal per day for shipment to markets in Toledo, Cleveland, Pittsburgh, and other nearby towns and cities. In Jeanette, Pennsylvania, another black miner, G. M. Johnson, perfected, manufactured, and sold mine safety equipment. Although women were excluded from the coal mining workforce, an African American woman "purchased some valuable coal land near Pittsburgh," employed a "Negro mining engineer," and sunk her "first mining shaft."[41]

From the outset of the Great Migration, the ULP's first executive director lamented the dearth of employment for black women. "Pittsburgh's industry has truly been unfair to Colored women," Clark observed. Accordingly, he strongly urged Heinz and other companies to employ black women as a "purely patriotic duty," since many of their husbands, sons, brothers, and other male relatives had enlisted in the army, leaving the women to take care of themselves and their families. Mrs. Scully, a member of the ULP board, noted that white women had aggravated the employment prospects of black women by organizing against "the policy of paying street car fare for day's work." Pittsburgh's white female employers believed that the low wage paid to household workers was sufficient for black women. At the same time, ULP president May suggested that the growing number of women immigrating from Ireland, China, and Mexico would undercut the position of black women in the domestic labor market. Thus, he suggested creating a mechanism for tracking this trend and communicating this information to prospective black women employees.[42]

In its survey of a wide variety of manufacturing, utility, commercial, and hospitality firms, the ULP paid close attention to the employment status of black women. Grace Lowndes, the ULP's civic and industrial secretary, launched a comprehensive survey of the social and economic conditions of black women, partly as a way to sum up her eight years of service as a Morals Court worker.[43] Under her direction, the branch analyzed the distribution of black women employees in apartment buildings, cigar factories, hotels, laundries, installment houses, business houses, and hospitals, to name a few. The 1927 report cited numerous restrictions on the employment of black women, including in laundries—a traditional occupational stronghold for African American women. As the report put it, "The Negro woman in spite of traditions, is no longer mistress of the laundry situation. In Pittsburgh, it has passed into the hands of white men." Only two laundries employed more than five women. And as commercial laundries moved toward the use of white labor, employers increasingly described black women as a "health hazard," ignoring their long history as skilled washerwomen. Further, "not one baking company in Pittsburgh uses Negro women in any capacity," although they did employ a few black male janitors, porters, and truck drivers. The Standard Cigar Factory employed forty black women, and one of them had been with the company for twenty years. Another cigar maker had replaced many of its black female employees with white women because "Negro women will not strip tobacco when they can get day's work." Black women also lost ground in so-called high-class apartment houses. Although King Edward Apartment House employed a black manager and several black maids, whites were gaining greater access to such jobs. "The dining room was at one time under Negro management, but it is now in the hands of a white woman, who employs only three colored women in the kitchen." The ULP noted that although two of four high-class apartment houses employed black women, the other two would not even consider hiring blacks.[44]

Opening up new job opportunities for black women was even more difficult than placing black men in the manufacturing sector. Employers' rationales for excluding black women ranged from previous experiences with black women who were presumably "inefficient" and "unprepared" to a traditional reliance on white help and a refusal to change employment policies and practices. As employers replaced blacks with whites, they expressed a firm determination to keep it that way. As the manager of one apartment house put it, "We have gotten away from that [employing black workers], and we certainly do not wish to go back to it." Lowndes suggested, however, that claims about the "inefficiency and unpreparedness" of black girls might be "well founded, for the average girl has little or no incentive for preparation in the face of the occupational proscription that she sees on every hand. . . . In all the stores there is always a goodly sprinkling of Negro shopper (the detectives ought to be able to tell the exact number daily, for they are always carefully watched) but whenever a dark face appears as an employee, it must always be accompanied by the uniform of a maid and a broom. Nothing else is to be considered . . . the decision to narrow the economic horizon of the Negro girl is determined."[45]

Welfare Workers, the Labor Movement, and Living Conditions

As part of its program of promoting and upgrading black workers, both men and women, the Urban League of Pittsburgh increased pressure on corporate leaders to remove the racial job ceiling and hire professional black "welfare workers." Only by employing a staff of black social workers, the league emphatically argued, could industrial employers effectively "coordinate and implement" a program of social services to improve the housing, health, work, and living conditions of African American employees and their families. Black welfare workers, the branch promised, would help "reduce the large Negro labor turnover in the various industrial plants by noon-day and Sunday talks, by distributing literature among the men and by assisting corporations in getting the most reliable type of Negro labor." Furthermore, Clark promised that "vagrancy" would not be tolerated, "especially when work is so plentiful."[46] Administered in collaboration with the University of Pittsburgh, the ULP developed a fellowship program to train professional black social workers.

Social work fellowships broadened the opportunities for professional training and jobs in firms employing large numbers of black workers. In February 1921 the *Pittsburgh Gazette Times* reported the ULP's placement of "14 Negro Welfare Workers in Industrial Plants" across the region. The Lockhart Iron and Steel Company, located in McKees Rocks, hired W. P. Young from East Orange, New Jersey, to develop programs for its black employees. Young, a graduate of Lincoln University near Philadelphia, not only persuaded the company to establish modern laundry facilities (with steam dryers, irons, and ironing boards) for the use of its black workers and their families but also coached the company's Negro Industrial League baseball team. Lockhart's welfare worker also spearheaded the formation of McKees Rocks' first race relations committee to address the influence of southern black migration on the workplace and community life. While the ULP recruited most of these early black social work fellows and welfare workers from outside of western Pennsylvania, it later enthusiastically announced the appointment of Gerald E. Allen as an Urban League fellow with roots in Pittsburgh. Allen graduated from the University of Pittsburgh and later took a job as executive secretary of the Canton, Ohio, Urban League. Under his leadership, the Canton branch looked forward to a bright future "without a cent of indebtedness."[47]

By hiring their own black welfare workers, employers relieved the pressure on the Urban League's small staff and allowed the organization to focus on expanding the black professional middle class at a time when few employers hired blacks for white-collar jobs. As such, the ULP served as a launching pad for young black professionals who hoped to obtain jobs in previously all-white organizations. In 1920, for example, the Traveler's Aid Society recognized Sadie Bond's work as "indispensable" to its mission and added her to its staff.[48] Similarly, Margaret Mann, a home economist and nutritionist, moved from the ULP to full-time employment at Carnegie Steel. The company eventually hired an assistant to help Mann manage the expanding workload as she provided services to Pittsburgh's black workers and their families.[49] These transitions were never easy or unproblematic, however. In a letter to board member Mary E. Bakewell, Clark lamented that the ULP had to wage "quite a fight" with the Traveler's Aid Society before it officially hired Bond. And once she was hired, she encountered problems with the Traveler's Aid staff. At its March 1920 meeting, the ULP reported that white staffers had shown "indifference" though not outright hostility toward her, and Clark had advised her "to do everything to show that she wanted to co-operate with them." Bond routinely turned cases over to the white workers at Union Station when they came in, but her white counterparts "had not turned over a single case to her."[50]

The Urban League of Pittsburgh developed an extensive network of professional black social workers. Early on, in March 1918, Clark sought the names of social welfare workers at various plants as part of a larger effort to organize black social workers into a cohesive group. In addition to maintaining close contact with past employees, volunteers, and fellows, the ULP regularly organized special meetings and conferences to address the challenges confronting black welfare workers. In collaboration with the Employers' Association of Pittsburgh, the organization convened a two-day Conference on Negro Industrial Welfare Workers at the city's Morgan Community House in 1920. The conference brought together representatives of nearly fifty plants employing some 17,500 black workers. Before adjourning, the gathering established a seven-member subcommittee charged with developing a plan for hiring "competent," university-trained African American welfare workers in all plants with 100 or more black employees. The group also called for the creation of "shop training" classes for black workers and exhorted new employees to "eliminate irregularity, establish their family life, and further demonstrate to [white] capital and labor their determination to hold a permanent and indispensable position in Northern Industrial Life." According to Edmunds and Bush, Urban League professionals became "daybreakers." In the words of Harlem Renaissance poet Arna Bontemps— they beat "a way for the rising sun" and helped "open doors for themselves and for those who followed them."[51]

The annual conferences of the National Urban League became a cornerstone in the building of strong networks of black social workers across the nation. ULP officers and members regularly attended and participated in these yearly meetings. In November 1920 the NUL held its fifth annual industrial conference in Newark, New Jersey. Attendees heard not only lectures and papers presented by local and national leaders of the Urban League movement and other social welfare organizations but also talks by "representatives of capital and labor" and proponents of union and nonunion shops. The ULP's John T. Clark spoke at the opening session of the gathering. He "outlined the general program of the League" and set the stage for subsequent presentations by branch executives from across the nation, including John T. Dancy of Detroit, Mrs. S. W. Layton and A. L. Manley of Philadelphia, James H. Hubert of New York City, Robert J. Elizy of Brooklyn, William R. Cannors of Cleveland, George W. Buckner of St. Louis, and Matthew Bullock of Boston. At the third annual meeting of the ULP in late January 1921, NUL president L. H. Hollingsworth Wood delivered the keynote address at Pittsburgh's Carnegie Lecture Hall. He encouraged local white elites to cooperate in building a better life for the African American community. "The world crisis today, if there is one," Wood declared, involved a lack of harmonious interracial relations. "We have our hands [firmly] together in groups" among whites, he stated, but with "minority groups," the grasp "grows limp and cold." Clark, Tyson, and the Reverend J. C. Anderson of the Bethel African Methodist Episcopal Church also addressed the gathering. On the same day, Oswald Garrison Villard, editor of the *Nation* magazine and national officer of the NAACP, presented an encouraging talk to social workers gathered at the YWCA.[52]

Despite extensive reliance on corporate sponsorship of its fellowship and work programs, the Pittsburgh branch was by no means hostile to the organized labor movement. Steel mills routinely hired blacks to operate blast furnaces and open hearths during the hot summer months, but these men were dismissed when the cold weather set in and white men took over these coveted inside jobs during the winter. In addition, white farmers and farmhands often moved into the city during the slow winter season, taking inside jobs away from black workers. The Urban League applauded black workers' protests against such workplace injustices: "Last

August the writer met with a group of Negro blast furnace men who drafted a petition requesting plant officials not to permit their jobs to be taken from them when cold weather comes, which indicates a fine group expression of the inherited law of self-preservation as well as another means of checking the aforementioned practice."[53]

When the ULP opened for business in 1918, only about sixty black men belonged to the building trade unions, most of them in "common labor unions" with small numbers of skilled craftsmen. Half a decade later, that figure had jumped to 400 blacks in the building trade unions, including many carpenters, brick masons, painters, and plasterers. As the number of black union members increased, however, hostility toward blacks working on large commercial, governmental, and industrial construction projects became "more firmly entrenched." Thus, most skilled black construction workers were employed on small residential building projects outside the city. White workers dominated the large commercial and residential projects in the city and the region. By the mid-1920s, the ULP reported only one relatively successful black-owned building and construction company, suggesting that entrepreneurial initiatives had not produced significant results. Hence, the ULP continued to push for black membership in labor unions. As late as 1928, executive director Alonzo Thayer met with bricklayers and plasterers and visited white "union heads to get them to take these men into the union." But this proved to be a slow process, and some of the men became "discouraged."[54]

The ULP firmly opposed the use of black strikebreakers in the early postwar steel strike and the widespread coal strikes of the mid-1920s. During the steel strike, the ULP informed corporate Pittsburgh that it would not supply African American labor to firms looking for strikebreakers. At the same time, Clark intensified pressure on the organized white labor movement to open membership to African Americans on an equal basis with their white counterparts. Only by challenging low wages and poor working conditions across the color line, the ULP argued, could the labor movement stop the use of black strikebreakers during labor-management disputes. Clark played a key role in arranging a meeting between black steel mill workers and radical white labor leader and American Federation of Labor (AFL) organizer William Z. Foster. Citing NUL historians Guichard Parris and Lester Brooks, Edmunds and Bush described Clark as perhaps "the first man in the League to come to grips with the problems of the black worker and organized labor."[55]

Strikes in the coalfields of western Pennsylvania intensified in 1924 when the largest producer in the region, the Pittsburgh Coal Company, closed its union mines and reopened on an open-shop basis, employing a largely nonunion black and white labor force. By the mid-1920s, the coal companies were closing numerous small mines and consolidating their holdings. For instance, the Pittsburgh Coal Company operated 108 mines in 1909, but that number had dropped to only 20 mines between 1925 and 1928. By the late 1920s, the number of black miners in the region had increased to more than 3,500 men. Striking members of the United Mine Workers of America (UMWA), which had moved to forge a broader and more inclusive interracial labor movement since the late nineteenth century, included a small number of black miners. The ULP's Tyson reported that black workers were in good standing in UMWA locals.

The ULP decried the labor policies of the Pittsburgh Coal Company. It discouraged black workers from crossing the picket lines of striking workers and "refused to send job applicants to the mines where union miners were on strike." At the Houston mines of the Pittsburgh Coal Company, black miners with at least ten years' experience joined their white counterparts in resisting the use of southern black newcomers as strikebreakers. Older union men reported that "the finest feelings have always existed between the white and colored citizens and Negroes worked at whatever jobs in the mines which they were capable of holding; coal-cutters, check-weighmen, motor drivers, etc." However, when a mob of some hundred union miners attacked a group of six newcomers, the new men fought back with knives, killing one man and injuring four others. Authorities arrested two of the newcomers and threw them in jail in Washington, Pennsylvania. Clark's efforts on behalf of workers and the labor movement precipitated his dismissal as the ULP's executive director. He departed Pittsburgh to head the St. Louis Urban League in 1926.[56]

Clark's departure intersected with two significant events in the early history of the Pittsburgh branch and its relationship to the parent body, the city, and the state of Pennsylvania. First, in April 1926, the NUL's industrial relations department announced plans to produce a monthly bulletin on labor conditions in major industrial centers across the nation.

Covering some 100 cities, this document promised to provide an authoritative overview of the black worker in America. The NUL asked each affiliate to supply monthly reports on the status of black labor in its city. Clark readily agreed to join the effort to address five basic questions about black employment: (1) significant gains, (2) issues or barriers encountered, (3) changes in relations between blacks and organized labor, (4) movement of blacks into or away from the city, and (5) any other developments of consequence for black labor. But Clark left Pittsburgh before he was able to comply.

At about the same time, the Department of Labor terminated its agreement with the branch and moved out of the Urban League offices on Wylie Avenue. The state centralized all its employment-related work in Pittsburgh, "regardless of sex and color," and moved into a new office on Grant Street between Sixth and Seventh Avenues. In the wake of this separation from the state employment service, the ULP moved to resume its job-placement work under the auspices of its own independent industrial relations department. However, according to acting executive director Christina Jeffries, the ULP put its plans on hold after Clark's departure, awaiting the appointment of a new executive director.[57]

Alonzo Thayer, Clark's successor, also supported the labor movement. Originally from Charleston, South Carolina, Thayer was a graduate of Avery Normal Institute and Fisk University. He had pursued postgraduate studies at the University of Chicago and gained valuable research experience as an "industrial investigator" for the Chicago Commission on Race Relations following the bloody Chicago race riot of 1919. Before coming to Pittsburgh in 1927, he had served as executive director of the Atlanta Urban League. Shortly after his arrival, the coal strikes in western Pennsylvania intensified, and union miners in New Kensington, Pennsylvania, advised Thayer to warn African Americans against taking jobs in that district "because of race violence between union and nonunion whites and blacks." Thayer carefully evaluated the situation from the vantage point of black union and nonunion workers: "Here are miners who have been working, and have agreed not to work. Another group of men come up who need bread and butter, and say they will take a chance on their lives in order to get bread and butter. Is it the sphere of the League to advise these men even against their own wishes not to go in . . . or should it be the sphere of the League to stay out of it altogether and let it work its way out?"[58]

Thayer implored the Urban League's board to establish a committee to address the interests of black workers in the deepening capital-labor divide. The board not only revived its defunct industrial committee but also approved the hiring of a University of Pittsburgh social work fellow, Sterling Spero, to conduct a thorough study of black coal miners in western Pennsylvania. In December 1927 the president of the Pittsburgh Terminal Coal Company, where African Americans made up about 30 percent of the workforce, invited the Urban League to conduct a survey of its black employees. Based on conditions in the coal towns, the ULP recommended the hiring of black welfare workers, as it had done in the region's steel plants. In the meantime, class and racial conflict continued to mount. In early October 1928 a group of miners visited the branch office, complaining about an effort "to rid the Mollenauer mines of the Pittsburgh Terminal Coal Company of all the Negroes in the camp." Although Thayer contacted the company's president, Templeton Smith, to address the issue, the matter was largely ignored. One prominent scholar of Pittsburgh's black working class concluded that ULP representatives "remained several steps removed from the shop floors [and mines] where the formation of the industrial work experience took place," but this evidence of the league's role in the region's coal and steel industries suggests that the organization was much closer to workplace issues than previously thought.[59]

Thayer's tenure with the ULP was exceedingly short-lived. In December 1929 Urban League staffers staged a farewell event for Thayer as he prepared to leave the city for a new job as head of the Chicago Urban League's industrial relations department.[60] Before his departure, the *Pittsburgh Courier* enthusiastically reported that the local branch had "reached its height in efficiency and popularity." The work of the ULP was attracting increasing attention not only within Pittsburgh and western Pennsylvania but "all over the country." Moreover, under Thayer's leadership, the ULP had conducted major studies of African Americans in the coal mines and the iron and steel mills of the region. Based on this research, Thayer recommended and the ULP board approved the creation of a new full-time industrial relations secretary to advance "work opportunities for Negroes and better treatment on their jobs." Furthermore, during his time in Pittsburgh, Thayer served on the executive committee of the local branch of the NAACP and helped strengthen the link between the ULP's social service work and the larger social justice struggles of the African American community.[61]

In addition to jobs, the local branch developed a vigorous program to address the desperate housing needs of African American migrants. Whether well educated, poor, or working class, African Americans "had great difficulty either renting or buying good houses in non-segregated areas." Seeking extraordinary returns on their investment in dilapidated rental properties, the city's real estate agents pressed every conceivable structure—railroad boxcars, basements, and alley shacks—into service for southern black tenants, charging exorbitant rents. Overcrowding in African American neighborhoods led to the creation of small enclaves that followed Pittsburgh's tortuous terrain: hollows, ravines, hilltops, riverbanks, rail lines, and a plethora of mill yards and manufacturing establishments. In a letter to the Donora Steel Company, the ULP described living conditions among a cluster of black families from Louisville, Kentucky. These families, Clark declared, "are living in a very disreputable and congested environment . . . and are thoroughly disgusted at the limited opportunities for getting better houses." In its New Castle report, the organization underscored the barriers to African Americans renting and buying homes "in the more respectable communities" in town. "The houses occupied by Negroes are the oldest and most run down as usual." In a May 1919 report, the home economics worker declared that the deplorable housing conditions were "fast driving" the very best traits "out of the newcomers." The ULP also regularly urged the city to enforce existing municipal housing codes "to prevent rent exploitation" and clean up and repair unsanitary and unsafe properties inhabited by black residents.[62]

The ULP nonetheless documented significant variations in housing quality from neighborhood to neighborhood. It even praised the Carnegie Steel Company's housing policies: "In the matter of housing and general welfare, the same opportunities were open to his colored employees as his white employees share. The real estate corporations of the company have made loans to colored workers, both in their purchase of company houses and in houses owned privately." At the same time, Carnegie Steel admitted that it "had not done enough for colored men in the housing situation." However, management espoused support for the ULP's housing campaign and endorsed efforts to improve black workers' housing conditions and community life.[63]

The ULP's home economics unit provided detailed reports on housing and neighborhood conditions among the city's black workers. In June 1919 the home economics worker reported on housing and living conditions on Fifth and Second Avenues as well as in the North Side, Oakland, Lawrenceville, and Soho communities. Specifically, the report described the Negley Run East End community as "a deplorable place in which to live, it is a deep hollow and is sadly neglected by the city. The people living on the hill tops on either side of the hollow dump their garbage, rubbish and any refuse that they wish to be rid of over the hill. The rains wash it down into the hollow and make it very unsanitary as the drainage is merely a gutter and this rubbish stops it up and floods the families [living in the area]." Moreover, the report stated, "The garbage men and rubbish men do not visit this district at all; yet [it] is part of the city. A petition has been put out that Mr. Sauer have the sanitary police to investigate conditions there. The homes are very poor and unsanitary with few exceptions, and almost the entire population of this district are Negroes and Foreigners. The North Side districts are mostly in good neighborhoods." The ULP also regularly reported on housing and health conditions in the mill towns surrounding the city. In April 1923 it reported on crowded and unsanitary conditions in Duquesne and agreed to set up a committee— comprising chairperson Daisy Lampkin, Walter Buchanan, and the Reverend C. B. Allen—to investigate the matter.[64]

The ULP repeatedly appealed to the city's real estate developers, public officials, and corporate leaders to improve the rental housing available to working-class black tenants, build affordable new "family homes" for African American occupancy, and create opportunities for African Americans to establish their own building and loan firms and construct their own family-owned homes—in the face of strict racial barriers, including new zoning laws delineating where African Americans could live. The ULP not only encouraged white real estate developers to expand housing opportunities for black workers and their families but also promoted the creation of black-owned real estate firms. Before his departure in the early 1920s, for example, Tom Barton helped found the Union Construction Company. Financed exclusively by black stockholders, the venture faced an uphill battle in its attempt to gain a footing in the real estate market and collapsed within a year of its founding. In a 1929 report, the home economics unit recommended the teaching of "home financing and accounting" to reinforce both individual self-help and entrepreneurial initiatives.[65]

By the mid-1920s, the ULP reported an increasing number of black real estate developers entering the housing field. In 1925 one black developer finished three of ten homes targeted for "colored people." Another group of black residents purchased "cheap land" on a high hill and built between 75 and 100 homes, while another black-owned construction firm planned to erect even "cheaper houses" for poor and working-class black families in the city. Better housing conditions for black workers, the ULP firmly and repeatedly argued, would reduce the turnover rate among black workers and increase the bottom line of industrial firms. In his correspondence with the Donora Steel Company, Clark carefully tied the quest for better housing to the productivity of black workers. "The husbands of some of these families are working at your mills," he noted. "I am sure these men could render more regular service if [healthier] accommodations were afforded near your plant." Clark made the same point in a letter to Robert E. Newcomb, a manager at the Worthington Pump and Machinery Corporation. Some attention, he wrote, "must be given to the [housing and] community life of the workers to help them develop permanency and steadiness."[66]

The Pittsburgh branch of the Urban League also took an abiding interest in the housing available to black workers in nearby coal towns. In a 1927 study the organization offered an extensive assessment of African American homes in the coalfields of western Pennsylvania. Despite substantial variation from place to place, the report accented the good quality of many homes—including an adequate water supply, good sanitation, and even fair rents—compared with many of the homes in the steel towns and in Pittsburgh itself. Still, the ULP found that the coal camps were racially segregated, with "whites together" and "Negroes together." Thus, as elsewhere, the ULP advocated the hiring of a welfare worker to carry out broad social programs among black workers in the coalfields. It declared that a welfare worker "would be worth ten times his pay in the order which could be worked out of the chaos which sometimes prevailed" in the coal towns, particularly during strikes by union workers. Similarly, the ULP was engaged in housing issues that crossed the boundary into West Virginia, and in February 1920 Clark wrote to Cameron, a foreman at the Wheeling Mold and Foundry Company, "I am advising that you build houses of from three to five rooms each with bath accommodations and modern conveniences; and that these houses be available for families only and that single men be accommodated in separate dormitories. An effort should be made to locate these houses within walking distance of your plant."[67]

Although the Urban League of Pittsburgh built on the wartime and prewar work of the city's interracial reformers, it dramatically expanded the scope of social services provided to the African American community during the early years of the Great Migration. From its inception, and following the lead of the national office, the ULP underscored its commitment to improve the lives of poor and working-class black residents, while simultaneously advancing the interests of educated, middle-class, and elite blacks. The Urban League's fellowship program enabled the training of an expanding roster of professional black social workers. At the same time, its industrial labor campaign increased the number of blacks in the manufacturing sector and gradually gave them access to jobs defined as "skilled" and "semiskilled" as opposed to "general" or "unskilled" labor. Despite its heavy dependence on corporate sponsorship of its programs, the branch carefully navigated the ongoing conflicts between capital and labor. It offered much more support to the organized labor movement and efforts to bring black workers into unions than is usually acknowledged. Although the branch developed a variety of programs designed to address the needs of women, African American women did not share equally in the modest gains achieved at either end of the occupational hierarchy. Most important, before the advent of the Great Depression, the ULP increasingly merged its social service activities with broader civil rights, social justice, and equal rights movements and advanced the fight against Jim Crow in all areas of the city's life.

The Urban League of Pittsburgh worked hard to improve African American home and community life. This photograph of participants in a "baby show" underscores the league's ongoing efforts to address the health and welfare needs of black families. (Urban League of Pittsburgh, Manuscript Collection, ca. 1930–1940, Archives Service Center, University of Pittsburgh)

2

Promise and Limits

The Urban League of Pittsburgh not only exposed inequality in the labor and housing markets and worked to strengthen the economic foundation of the black community. It also revealed the depths of racial disparities across virtually every aspect of the city's institutional life and vigorously pushed to improve African Americans' access to all categories of human and civic resources and social services. Accordingly, the Pittsburgh branch increasingly merged its civil, human rights, and social service agenda. It joined forces with the NAACP and other social justice organizations to desegregate schools, hospitals, and public accommodations; curtail police brutality; and prevent the arrest of migrants as vagrants and prostitutes, including the transport of some newcomers back to "the flames of the torturing South."[1] As such, the organization sought to expand the black middle class through the training of social workers, teachers, and health care professionals for employment in the public schools, social service organizations, and health care institutions. At the same time, as was true elsewhere in the Urban League movement, the ULP experienced its own class and gender blind spots in the treatment of its clients and volunteers.

Health, Education, and Vocational Training

Along with economic and neighborhood conditions, the ULP documented alarming disparities in the health and medical care of blacks and whites both within and beyond the city limits. Drawing on the pioneering research of Abraham Epstein, the Urban League reported a 200 percent increase in pneumonia deaths among African Americans during the early years of the Great Migration (1910–1920), although the black population rose by only 45 percent. In 1917 the city reported 70 deaths for every 100 births among Pittsburgh's white population, compared with 148 deaths for every 100 African Americans born. Moreover, by the mid-1920s, the ULP reported that 102 "colored infants out of every 1,000" died before the age of one, compared with 82 per 1,000 white infants. The ULP regularly reported on the day-to-day health challenges confronting newcomers and their families: "a seriously ill" girl on Spruce Street; a boy "with running glands playing in the street"; an orphaned girl who "needed the removal of her tonsils and adenoids"; an "underweight" fourteen-year-old boy who required help with "a cardiac condition."[2] In coal mining towns, the ULP documented insufficient treatment of mine-related injuries and inadequate physician visits to treat ill women and children in the home.[3]

The branch developed a variety of strategies to address the health needs of urban black workers and their families. First and foremost, it launched an energetic public health education program in collaboration with municipal health officials, educators, public schools, physicians, nurses, and a plethora of African American and interracial social, cultural, educational, religious, and social justice organizations, as well as the nationally circulated black weekly newspaper the *Pittsburgh Courier*. The branch and its partners conducted recurring "cleanup movements" to combat unsanitary neighborhood conditions, "Better Baby Contests" to fight infant mortality, and observances of National Negro Health Week. Established in 1914 under the leadership of Booker T. Washington and expanded during the 1920s, National Negro Health Week provided special occasions for disseminating information on the health hazards of patent medicines, improper dress and diet, and poor housing ventilation, among other ordinary aspects of daily life in an urban environment.[4]

Health education programs took place in churches and public schools across the city. The *Courier* regularly published a schedule of health events, including health education parades through different parts of the African American community. On one occasion, conveners planned marches for "Tuesday in the East End, Wednesday in the Hill District and Thursday in the North Side," where students would carry banners that displayed "all manners of advice concerning personal hygiene, home cleanliness and neighborhood improvement."[5] In April 1918, during what was apparently the ULP's first Negro Health Education Campaign, ministers of black churches added health care issues to their regular Sunday services and distributed more than 20,000 copies of public health literature provided by government agencies. During another early Negro Health Week celebration, physicians and dentists delivered an estimated fifty health lectures, including talks to schoolchildren on the importance of keeping "their faces clean; their bodies healthy; how to brush their teeth, etc."[6]

The ULP's health committee also established an "Inspection Day," whereby health workers and volunteers instructed families "how to keep their houses, yards, and cellars clean." The *Pittsburgh Courier* praised the agency for mobilizing adults and children alike and for giving the "districts in which colored people live . . . a cleaning up as [has] never been given before."[7] In the fall and winter of 1927–1928 the organization and its partners aimed to reinforce these efforts through a series of lectures on the diverse health challenges facing the city's black community. Topics included "A Chart Study of Negro Deaths by Various Ages in the City of Pittsburgh with Analysis and Interpretation," "The Relationship of the Negro Physician to the Negro Death Rate in the Community," "Is Tuberculosis Acquired or Is It Hereditary[?]," and "The Relationship of Prenatal Care to Infant Mortality."[8]

The ULP staged numerous Better Baby Contests to address the high infant mortality rate among blacks in Pittsburgh and western Pennsylvania. On one occasion, a Negro Health Week campaign adopted the slogan "Healthier Babies—Stronger Mothers." The contests appealed to black women's pride in their babies and created a public spectacle. However, as historian Carolyn Carson makes clear, the primary goal "was to provide health screenings" conducted by Jeanette Washington, the city's first black public health nurse. When Dr. Marie Kinner, a graduate of Howard University Medical School, opened a medical practice on the city's North Side during the 1920s, she helped "triple attendance" at the ULP's well-baby clinics. Kinner often handled cases referred from the Urban League "without charge."[9] In a meeting with executive director Alonzo Thayer, "young mothers" expressed gratitude "for the information they had received at the Better Baby Contest." The league also helped a group of black women set up an Infant Welfare Station to fight high infant mortality rates on the city's North Side.[10]

Closely connected with its health activities, the ULP created a food conservation, cooking, and nutritional program for black families. Key to this effort was home economics worker Margaret Mann. Supported by funds from the wartime US Council of National Defense, Mann organized a plethora of neighborhood groups and "instructed newly arrived women in the art of urban housekeeping," health, and nutrition. Under Mann's leadership, ULP officials visited more than 1,400 homes across the city. In February 1919 alone, the home economics secretary conducted a door-to-door campaign that reached more than eighty homes. In her 1925 report she described instructing newcomers and their families on "the use of gas, electricity, marketing of foods, how to purchase and prepare cheap cuts of meat," and how to repair clothing. In 1928 the home and community committee recommended that a weeklong "Food Show" be held in the Hill District. The committee urged cooperation with food stores and cooking utensil outlets to plan exhibits and demonstrations for housewives, housekeepers, and cooks on the most recent innovations in food preparation and nutrition, focusing on "preparing foods well and economically." Mann offered classes and hands-on instruction "in food conservation and cooking, cooperative buying, and 'making over' of old clothes." The home economics officer believed that, like other ULP programs that were tied closely to the recruitment of a black workforce, her work among the women helped "to steady and make their husbands more satisfied on their jobs."[11]

The ULP's health-related programs included not only public speeches, the distribution of literature, cleanup and food campaigns, and demonstrations of good health and dietary practices but also efforts to create a summer camp for black youth and open a public bathhouse and swimming pool in the Hill District to serve the city's black population. At its November 1926 meeting, the ULP executive board noted that no camping facilities in the Pittsburgh area accepted African Americans. The proposal to create a summer camp involved extensive discussion and debate over the need for suitable property and adequate funding and whether the league should control and run the facility or turn it over to another entity. Early in the process, the branch considered renting a hilly fifty-acre farm near the coal town of Harmarville in Allegheny County. The property was replete with fruit trees, berries, gardens, and a "running creek or spring" at the bottom of the hill. The buildings on the property, which used well water and would have required the installation of a pump to improve the water supply, were in fact "not worth much," but the farm itself was in "fine condition." The owner was offering free gas, light, and heat for the house in exchange for "the equivalent of the rent of a small house in return." At the November meeting, president May declared his support for a "Fresh Air Camp" or "Convalescent Home" to serve the needs of the African American community, but he was concerned about the cost of establishing and running such an institution and concluded that "the time was not ripe for starting such a project." Only during the 1930s would the league's Camp James Weldon Johnson for black youth (named after the Harlem Renaissance poet, novelist, and cultural historian) come to fruition on property in rural Beaver County.[12]

Over a period of two years, the ULP, the Pittsburgh Civic Club, and a variety of African American organizations—churches, women's clubs, and the press—urged the city to fund a public bath and swimming facility for black residents of the Hill District. In 1925 the City Council allotted $81,000 for the project, and the "Bath House and Comfort Station" opened in 1925 at the corner of Wylie and Crawford Streets. Under African American director James A. Dorsey, an employee of the city's Public Works Department, the bathhouse provided both recreational and bathing facilities. Less than five years later, the city announced plans to close the facility, citing declining use. The ULP quickly produced statistics to support the retention of the bathhouse and pool. Executive director Maurice Moss (Thayer's successor) showed that two-thirds of the housing units in the area "lacked bath facilities." Moreover, Moss noted that use of the facility had declined mainly because the heating unit was not working, one of many repairs needed after years of intensive use. The city reversed its position, and the bathhouse remained open; it even received a new allotment of funds for extending the hours of operation and making the necessary repairs.[13]

As suggested by the bathhouse campaign, the ULP placed increasing pressure on municipal officials to address racial disparities in the health field. On one occasion, the league forcefully alerted "official Pennsylvania to the shameful fact that there is not one bed in the state that can be used for a negro child during orthopedic convalescence."[14] Most important, the organization protested the exclusion of African American nurses from the ranks of the city's public health services. The ULP carefully documented discrimination against highly qualified black health professionals in Pittsburgh and western Pennsylvania. For instance, despite her stellar training at Philadelphia's Mercy-Douglas Hospital School of Nursing, the region's public- and private-sector hospitals steadfastly refused to hire Jeannette Washington. Similarly, Dr. Marie Kinner, who had a private practice on the North Side, encountered racial and gender discrimination in the city's medical profession. In 1922, after substantial pressure from the ULP and its allies, Pittsburgh's public health service relented and hired Washington. As the city's first black public health nurse, she advanced the ULP's widely regarded "Better Health Campaigns" and baby contests. But the employment of a lone black public health professional was inadequate to extend the full benefits of medical care to the city's black population, including access to state-of-the-art hospital facilities.[15]

As the fight for a black public health nurse was won, the push for an African American hospital picked up steam. In a 1922 letter to board member Francis Tyson, John T. Clark suggested that the ULP establish a hospital committee to help coordinate the efforts of two different movements to establish a black hospital in the city. Three years later, in November 1925, Payton Rose, a funeral director and chair of the ULP's committee on health, proposed the establishment of a "Negro Hospital to help obtain hospital facilities for Negro doctors and nurses" and improve convalescent care for black patients. Members of the committee included John T. Clark, Miss Finkelstein, Miss Hilma Satleroe, Mr. S. E. Elliott, and Dr. Roderick Brown. In 1930 the Livingston Memorial Association, a group chartered in 1917, purchased the old Montefiore Hospital at 3000 Centre Avenue in the Hill District to house a new hospital for blacks. The ULP's hospital committee approved a motion to ask the board to endorse but not operate the facility.[16] Although African American hospitals were established in a few major northern industrial cities during this period, the black hospital movement failed to gain traction in Pittsburgh.

Partly due to the ULP's health programs during the early years of the Great Migration, the city's African American death rate dropped between 1918 and 1923, even as the black population increased. According to Carson, the branch participated with a network of black physicians and nurses to replace southern black medical beliefs and practices that relied on "folk" remedies and "patent medicines" with greater confidence in and access to the licensed medical establishment. Health education and food programs also aimed to stamp out the vestiges of "superstitions" among southern black migrants, including their use of "spiritualists, crystal-gazers, or herb doctors." Urban Leaguers usually summarily dismissed newcomers' beliefs and practices as the product of racial inequality, slavery, sharecropping, and "ignorance" growing out of educational disparities between black and white people in the South. However, black migrants often resisted such assumptions and confirmed their commitment to the health practices of their southern parents and communities. After several years in Pittsburgh, one migrant recalled, "I didn't believe in doctors. I still don't, I'll be honest with you . . . I'll say right now . . . [my parents] were the best doctors I ever met."[17]

Thus, even as southern migrants sought treatment in mainstream health care facilities, they "continued to practice folk medicine, sometimes because they had neither the money nor the inclination to seek formal medical care." Even so, the ULP played an important role in African Americans' transition from dependence on midwives and other traditional practitioners to an increasing reliance on professional physicians.[18]

In his 1918 study of African Americans in Pittsburgh, Abraham Epstein provided data supporting the formation of educational programs for the city's black migrant population. According to Epstein, the African American school-age population had increased 40 to 60 percent during a ten-month period in the Hill District's public schools. Because these young migrants had attended school irregularly in the South, they were older on average than their northern-born peers at any given grade level. In his interviews with school principals, Epstein found that there was invariably a drop-off in African American achievement around the fourth grade. The principals advocated a vigorous system of "practical and industrial" rather than "purely academic" courses for both black and white students, but they emphasized that such education would "prove absolutely" beneficial to black children.[19]

Although the ULP regularly employed documentation from Epstein's study, it roundly refuted the idea of training blacks almost exclusively for industrial rather than professional and highly skilled jobs. The league repeatedly underscored its interest "in all phases of education affecting Negro children." It also consistently urged young blacks to train "for fields that were closed to them" and to work "steadily, patiently, [and] determinedly to advance into positions of responsibility that Negroes had never before occupied." Indeed, the ULP defined its social work fellowship program at the University of Pittsburgh as integral to its fight for equal education for black youth, including campaigns to raise money to provide college scholarships for "worthy students" from poor and working-class families. In 1922 the board sponsored a scholarship for Gertrude Clark to attend Carnegie Tech (later Carnegie Mellon University), where she received a BA degree in social science. The same year, the organization sponsored another scholarship for a black student at Carnegie Tech and a summer fellowship for the ULP's home and school visitor at the New York School of Social Work.[20]

To pave the way for the acceptance of blacks at previously all-white schools, the ULP announced plans to develop a "student interracial forum" to foster understanding, friendship, and cooperation among black and white students. Such forums, the league believed, would help diminish or even eliminate racial prejudice among young people and challenge the notion that the integration of blacks into previously all-white educational institutions, programs, and jobs would necessarily entail acrimonious and even violent conflict. In addition, the organization treated all its public meetings and general publicity as part of a larger campaign to highlight the needs of black children, especially their aspirations for higher education and training in the skilled trades. As early as 1922, the ULP not only encouraged the education of children across the board but also promoted young people's awareness of the Urban League movement through an essay contest on the league's work. Open to "every regularly enrolled Negro pupil" in the high schools of Pittsburgh and the surrounding area, the contest invited submissions on "The Value of the Urban League in Pittsburgh." First-, second-, and third-prize winners received $15, $10, and $5, respectively.[21]

Similar to its fight for health care, housing, and jobs, the ULP carefully documented the color line's deleterious impact on the education of black children. It vehemently argued that racial discrimination was the primary constraint on black children's ability to gain access to higher education and upward mobility in Pittsburgh and elsewhere in urban industrial America. In 1925 William Pickens, the NAACP's director of branches, visited the ULP's offices to consult with executive director John Clark.

He vividly recalled the moment when "a special caller from one of the public schools" asked the ULP director "the everlasting question": "what on earth to do with an 'unusually brilliant colored girl' who would graduate in a week or so and 'certainly ought to go on with her education.'"[22]

As part of its ongoing effort to encourage the education of black youth, the ULP held annual graduation parties for students completing the eighth grade and for high school graduates as well, although in some years these events did not materialize due to a lack of funds. In a letter to the board in 1926, the executive director sought approval to secure the $25 required to hold these parties through the contributions of "four or five prominent Negroes." The ULP believed that these efforts were partly responsible for the rising number of black students graduating from six grammar schools with sizable black student populations. In June 1921 seventy-five black students graduated from these schools, compared with fifty-eight the previous year. Still, migrants were sometimes so disappointed with their children's education in the urban North that they considered moving back to the South. In her report for March 1921, the league's home economics worker reported, "Mrs. Cook says she does not like the schools of the North, they do not teach much else but dancing and singing. Says her children do not learn anything here and she expects to send them back to Alabama in the Fall."[23]

Poverty and cycles of unemployment not only reinforced racial restrictions on African Americans' access to education but also fueled the ULP's campaign to remove the color line from the city's school-to-employment pipeline. In 1928, in a series of interviews with representatives of area firms, national and local branch officers apprised them that the growing number of capable young black women graduating from high school and college each year required new employment opportunities to keep pace with their "advancing educational status." On 3 December 1928 Grace Lowndes accompanied T. Arnold Hill and Cyrus T. Greene on a visit to W. W. Newmyer, superintendent at the Boggs and Buhl Company Department Store. Newmyer noted that black women had given "efficient service as sheetwriters" during the war but were no longer employed in that capacity, one of the few white-collar jobs open to black women.[24]

In an interview with W. E. Quimby, assistant to the vice president of the Bell Telephone Company, ULP members emphasized that Bell was a public utility and that blacks were major consumers of the firm's services; therefore, black women should be employed as telephone operators. Moreover, they noted, young black women had moved into these jobs in other cities. Quimby was not convinced, however, and argued that "the idea of mixing colored and white girls would not work out well," even though the company had made no effort to hire black operators in the Pittsburgh area. Indeed, Bell Telephone pursued a determined policy to restrict the employment of black men as well as women. At the same meeting, the ULP representatives identified several categories of work, including "drivers and repairers of trucks, men doing skilled electrical work in the setting up of new telephones and the collecting of coin from the boxes," that would not involve "race mixing," as these men "generally worked independently." Still, Quimby insisted that the company's labor policies would not permit such a move.[25]

As the ULP underscored the dearth of employment opportunities for black women who had graduated from high school and college, it also studied "what happens to Negro boy[s] in the trade schools of Pittsburgh." League officials met with Frank Leavitt of the Pittsburgh public schools to determine the experiences of trade school graduates. Leavitt claimed that contractors charged with employing graduates of the city's trade schools routinely rejected black youths for jobs in the skilled trades. One young man landed a job in the printing trade, but when his white coworkers "got their coats and threatened to leave," the firm swiftly fired the black youth. In the booming building and construction industry, restrictions on the employment of black men represented a major challenge for branch officers. As new technology and labor-saving machinery increasingly replaced men in the steel industry, the ULP intensified its push for "a reasonable share of work for Negroes" on the new buildings going up around the city.[26]

Integral to the struggle for higher education, skilled jobs, and the development of a black professional class was the fight to open up the Pittsburgh public schools to African American teachers. The branch strongly and regularly underscored the injustice of barring black teachers from jobs in the public schools. The city reported a payroll of $6 million for teachers, but "not a dollar goes to a Negro school teacher."[27] As early as 1921, the ULP urged the Pittsburgh public schools to hire black teach-

ers. It helped open the door for black students at the Henry Clay Frick
Training School for Teachers. Among the school's outstanding black
graduates was Georgine Pearce (Brown), the ULP's popular home and
school visitor.

Throughout the 1920s, ULP board member and newspaper editor
Robert Vann used the *Pittsburgh Courier* to demand changes in the Pittsburgh Board of Education's racially exclusionary policies. Vann repeatedly
declared his and the ULP's support for "Mixed Schools and Mixed Teachers." He implored every "man and woman to demand that this right
[to teaching posts in public, tax-supported institutions] be extended" to
qualified black teachers—graduates of such schools as the Cheney Training School for Teachers in the Philadelphia area and Pittsburgh's own
Frick Training School. But the school board resolutely refused to hire
black teachers until the 1930s. According to statements from ULP board
member Dr. A. W. Lewin and Daisy Lampkin, an Urban Leaguer and
head of the Negro Women's League of Allegheny County, the board of
education's "perennial excuse" for not employing black teachers was that
the "time was not ripe."[28]

Race Relations, the Law, Social Services, and Politics

The ULP's wartime and postwar "work plan" extended well beyond jobs,
housing, health, and education. It also included an agenda to address discrimination in public accommodations, racially biased news reporting,
police brutality and inequality before the law, and day-to-day interracial
conflicts in the city. In May 1919 the Urban League reported that "the
Second Avenue District has been much wrought up over the disturbances
of the police and the families are holding indignation meetings, protesting against the treatment." In 1925, when Mrs. Leona Carter moved into
a white neighborhood on the South Side, she was subjected to cross
burnings and harassment from white residents. When she took "a gun to
her harassers" after repeated attacks, she was arrested on firearms charges
and sentenced to thirty days in jail and fined $25 for defending her home.
ULP executive director John Clark wrote Carter a strong letter of support and offered the league's help. In November 1925 Clark sought Francis Stewart's help in securing members "for the large Hill District Protest

Committee" designed to address problems with the city's aggressive campaign aimed at "cleaning up vice" in the area. A year later, the league reported that police at the Jones and Laughlin plant had tried to enforce a curfew against black workers at gunpoint.[29]

The city created the Morals Court in 1918, and the ULP provided a social worker, Grace Lowndes, to help the court's staff address the needs of African Americans entangled with the law. Within a relatively short time, the magistrate courts were referring many cases involving African Americans to the Morals Court, and Lowndes reported that it was "swamped with work." Although volunteers from two churches pitched in to alleviate the burden on Lowndes, the ULP board acknowledged the need for regular follow-up assistance after cases had been handled in court. The executive board regularly searched for another better-financed social service organization to take over the work of the Morals Court and free the ULP to pursue other projects with its limited resources. Lowndes continued to perform her work until 1926, when the city dissolved the Morals Court and created the Women's Court and a Women's Bureau within the police department. Lowndes subsequently worked full time as the ULP's civic secretary until her retirement in 1944.[30]

The Pittsburgh Morals Court handled a variety of family issues, but it focused mainly on women embroiled in the sex trade. Police raids on prostitution resulted in the recurring arrests of a disproportionately large number of black women, who soon accounted for more than 20 percent of all Morals Court cases. Rather than imposing jail terms on all newcomers charged with indecent behavior, disturbing the peace, disorderly conduct, and the like, the court turned many of these cases over to Lowndes for "adjustment." Originally from South Carolina, Lowndes advocated for black women in the court and helped many return to the community and "find a fresh start in life." She also prevailed on the YMCA and the Morgan Memorial Community House to provide similar assistance to black men, who faced special forms of police harassment, including being arrested as vagrants and, in some cases, being forced back into what the local branch of the NAACP described as "the flames of the torturing South."[31]

To reduce the number of blacks, particularly female sex workers, appearing before the Morals Court, Lowndes organized numerous girls' clubs to address the educational, leisure-time, and other needs of young women. Between 1921 and 1923 alone, she spearheaded the formation of twelve clubs with a membership of 320 women and girls. In her report for 1921–1922, Lowndes reported "definite success along all lines of her work" with young girls, including two health lectures given to the Lawrenceville group and Girl Scout Troop 126. She also gave a talk to a group of mothers and daughters in the town of Jeanette, Pennsylvania. In one month, she reported "19 meetings" with "168 girls" in attendance. In addition, Lowndes secured access to facilities at the Girl Scout camp for forty of her girls during the summer and, through her contact with the director of the Soho Community Center, access to "the Swimming Pool of the Soho Bath House for the [colored] girls in that district."[32]

Near decade's end, the ULP added a girls' club department and hired Virginia Woodson to direct it. Woodson also served as a part-time stenographer. Under her leadership, the ULP soon formed a plethora of new girls' clubs and spearheaded the formation of the first "registered" Negro Girl Scout troop in the city. The league offered classes for young people in such diverse areas as "sewing" and "the rudiments of good character and better citizenship." In his report for October and November 1927, the executive director declared that Woodson was "over-worked, with her stenographic work and the clubs which she herself has developed."[33]

In the meantime, the ULP deepened its housing and health advocacy work. The board had been seeking to hire a much-needed health and housing secretary. As early as December 1920, the board set up a committee to explore the matter, and in 1924 it again announced the formation of a new "Health and Housing Committee" to explore "methods" for improving services in these areas of African American life. In keeping with its standing policy "to turn over any work developed to any Agency desiring it which was capable to properly continue the service," the ULP hoped to transfer some of its services to the Morgan Community House, which operated a well-regarded day nursery for working parents in the Hill District. However, the ULP worried that this move would only reinforce the fragmentation between the Lower Hill and the Upper Hill. The day-care service would be of greater value to black families in the Upper Hill, where many women took day work to earn a living, while poor and working-class women in the Lower Hill tended to stay at home and take in lodgers to help make ends meet.[34]

Closely intertwined with these efforts was the ULP's establishment of a variety of interconnected programs to help black youth deal with their encounters with the law. Such efforts, it argued, should involve close collaboration among the courts, probation officers, and the schools; Big Brother and Big Sister programs to connect youth to their older peers; and special programs for adults to assist "discharged and paroled prisoners to obtain a new start," set examples for young people, and reclaim their place in the family, the community, and the larger society.[35] The ULP's home and school visitor program was also part of this effort, and home and school visitor Georgine Pearce, a graduate of the city's Frick Training School for Teachers, was viewed as a vital connector between the home and the school in the absence of black teachers in the public school system. Established in 1923, the program focused considerable attention on work with the juvenile justice system.[36]

In June 1926 the ULP sponsored Pearce's attendance at a six-week training course on "school visiting and social problems" at the New York School of Social Work. The New York experience energized her work as head of the program and pushed her efforts into a variety of new directions, including helping the Homewood Civic Club establish its own home and school visiting program. In 1927 the ULP undertook a study of the need for a home and school visitor and concluded that rather than focusing on a selected school for many hours of the day, the visitor should spread her work over a broad range of schools serving sizable black student populations. ULP president E. C. May underscored the increasing volume and effectiveness of Pearce's work by noting that, in the previous year, the unit had taken on 101 new cases from the schools, reopened 14 old cases, and made 354 home visits. In addition, the home and school visitor program had made seventy-six contacts with diverse social service agencies to adjust specific cases, and Pearce had attended some thirty-nine meetings to promote the program's work.[37]

Even as the ULP carried out intensive one-on-one casework, it gradually shifted to a more systemic approach to meeting the social service needs of the black community. In 1928 the ULP's casework policy committee, chaired by Helen Glenn Tyson, urged the organization to curtail its "direct casework services," including its provision of black staff workers for a variety of specialized agencies. Instead, the committee implored the ULP to refer African Americans to the proper agencies serving the needs of all Pittsburgh citizens without regard to color.[38]

In its efforts to challenge the color line, the ULP took on Kennywood Amusement Park (particularly the swimming pool), local theaters, the white press, and the B&O Railroad. In a letter to Joseph P. Taggert, the B&O's assistant general passenger agent, the ULP urged the railroad to end "unfair treatment of Negro passengers." But in September 1924, when the ULP received a request from a community member "to go into the question of [racial] discrimination in all or most of the theatres in Pittsburgh," the board referred the matter to the local chapter of the NAACP. Despite the ULP's reliance on the NAACP and other social justice organizations for follow-up activities, this did not preclude its cooperation with the black nationalist movement of Marcus Garvey. In the interests of improving the lives of blacks in Pittsburgh and western Pennsylvania, the ULP invited Garvey to address the local branch in December 1921. Garvey kindly replied that his schedule was "tied up" until the late spring of 1922, but he would "be pleased to contribute my bit" at "any other time" thereafter. At the same time, the organization consented to join a massive, apparently Garvey-inspired Emancipation Day celebration and parade, although it hedged somewhat, agreeing to take part only "if it could possibly do so without losing the dignity of the League." One board member even offered the use of his "new truck to be decorated by the League."[39]

Although it often relied on the NAACP and other organizations to address racial injustice, the ULP regularly recorded and investigated evidence of day-to-day conflicts and assaults on black people. The minutes of its 20 September 1922 board meeting reported "a third degree assault on a young colored boy 17 years of age." The board did not follow up on this case, but it did agree to "keep a report of all such insults and report in a month or so as to the prevalence of such practice."[40]

In July 1927 the ULP investigated a *Pittsburgh Post* story headlined "Police with Riot Guns Patrol Hill after Race Clash." According to the article, a young Jewish cab driver named Jackie Werner had apparently assaulted a black youth. Werner, the report stated, "frequently courts trouble with the colored people in the community." It went on to explain that "the younger set of Jewish boys in the community do not work as hard and as often as the colored people [youth] in the community, and consequently have more time to pick fights. Colored women passing by on the street are molested by them with insulting invitations, at times they are even invited into taxi cabs with insulting remarks." Following the assault, the black youth reportedly went to the Soho District and recruited a group of ten to fifteen black men, and they returned to retaliate for the beating. In the meantime, Werner had evidently rallied a group of Italian boys, and the two groups fought. According to a Jewish policeman, however, "the colored boys were insulting the Jewish girls in the neighborhood and that would never do." At the police department, Werner filed a complaint àgainst two black youths for allegedly insulting and threatening to attack him. Police rounded up all the black youths who were "not able to give an account of themselves." Apparently, a white police officer also shot a black youth named Fred Boyce. The ULP's Thayer subsequently met with Sydney Teller of the Irene Kaufmann Settlement in the Hill District and reported that he had learned "the facts of the situation of the Jewish and Negro groups" in the district. He proposed a study of race relations in the area to address existing conflicts and misunderstandings.[41]

The ULP forged a strong relationship with board member Robert L. Vann and his nationally circulated black weekly the *Pittsburgh Courier*. Vann helped connect the league's social service agenda with the political and civil rights struggles of African Americans in the city, the region, the state, and the nation. Vann chaired a fund-raising campaign that generated $30,000 to build a new YMCA branch for blacks on Centre Avenue, across the street from the *Courier*'s offices in the Hill District. When the YMCA opened in 1923, it not only housed numerous ULP functions but also became the principal meeting place for African Americans seeking a voice and representation in municipal, county, state, and national politics. On these occasions, the Y's gymnasium was transformed into an auditorium to accommodate huge community-wide gatherings.[42]

Vann, the *Pittsburgh Courier*, and black political organizations such as the Colored Protective League of Allegheny County (formed before World War I) played major roles in the African American quest for political office. In 1919, when Robert H. Logan won election to the Board of Aldermen from the predominantly black Fifth Ward, Vann enthusiastically noted that this was "the highest elective office ever held by a black man in Pittsburgh," and he attributed Logan's win "to the solid bloc effort of black voters in the ward." Alongside and even more so than Vann and Logan, however, women like Daisy Lampkin shaped the African American quest for influence in electoral politics. When Lampkin joined the ULP board and its advisory council, she enhanced the organization's ties to local, state, and national politics. She forwarded her acceptance of the ULP's invitation to serve on the letterhead of the Lucy Stone League of Republican Women Voters of Allegheny County, of which she was the president. Lampkin later served on the board of directors of the *Pittsburgh Courier* and assisted Vann in his own bids for public office. When Vann announced his candidacy for the judgeship of the Allegheny County Court of Common Pleas in June 1921, he turned to Lampkin and the newly enfranchised black women voters. They helped Vann stump through Pittsburgh and Allegheny County, and he picked up 21,000 votes.[43]

Although Vann lost the election, his effort energized the African American pursuit of formal political power in Pittsburgh and western Pennsylvania. More important, it placed the Urban League of Pittsburgh not at the margins but very close to the center of the African American fight for empowerment in municipal, regional, and state affairs. In an October 1928 letter to Lampkin, Thayer described the shift of many blacks toward the Democratic Party of Alfred Smith in the upcoming presidential election. It is "not that they love the Democrats more," he wrote, "but that they love the Republicans less" for their increasing neglect of the interests of black people. Thayer described himself as a socialist, but he nonetheless wished Lampkin and the Republican Party "the best of luck and success and that Hoover will be our next president." Moreover, black residents encouraged the Urban League to pay close attention to the link between its quest for social services for the African American community and municipal politics. In a memo to ULP executive director Moss, one resident emphasized the close tie between the receipt of relief funds and support for the political machine. If a prospective recipient failed to present a poll tax certificate and proof that he or she had actually voted in the previous election, that individual would be denied relief benefits.[44]

Gender, Class, and Racial Bias within the ULP

Despite the ULP's strong challenge to racial and class discrimination in the socioeconomic, institutional, and political life of the city, it had a blind spot when it came to the treatment of poor and working-class residents and female employees and volunteers. African American women faced entrenched patterns of gender bias within the Urban League movement. The Pittsburgh branch was by no means blind to the gender biases that took a particularly high toll on black women. Perhaps partly due to the growing influence of black women like Daisy Lampkin in the ULP, in March 1922 Clark initiated a movement to eliminate the use of the term "Negress" to refer to black women in the Pittsburgh press. He not only urged Urban Leaguers to sign a letter of protest to the papers but also asked the women's clubs of the city to put their "strength and weight" behind the appeal.[45] Even so, historical accounts of the branch's founding offer little insight into the role of women in the early days of the organization. However, Mrs. Alice West, wife of the Reverend Thomas C. West, mother of twelve, and president of the Women's Auxiliary of the Pennsylvania Baptist State Convention, apparently played a key role in bringing the Urban League movement to Pittsburgh. Upon her death in 1929, the *Pittsburgh Courier* interviewed some of her contemporaries, who reported that West had been instrumental in urging Eugene Kinckle Jones to visit the city and formulate plans for "the splendid organization that now functions" as the Urban League of Pittsburgh. Some of the older residents went so far as to describe West as the "Mother of the Urban League of Pittsburgh."[46]

Christina Jeffries, affectionately called "Miz Jeff" by Urban Leaguers, was another influential woman in the Pittsburgh branch. A migrant from Gallipolis, Ohio, she served as assistant to the first five male executive directors of the ULP until her retirement in 1961. A college-educated teacher by training, Jeffries was the branch's first "in-take secretary" and later managed the organization's financial affairs and exercised considerable influence. Between November 1920 and February 1924, according to the *Pittsburgh Courier*, Jeffries was "furloughed from her position" because of a "lack of funds." Clark expressed regret and embarrassment at having "to put off paying the salaries" of people like Jeffries who were so central to the league's mission. In the case of Margaret Mann, he even sought to place her in a paid industrial job that would allow the ULP to reduce its financial obligations to the staff.[47]

No doubt these stringent cost-cutting measures helped explain the ULP's very optimistic financial statement of January 1922. The league's treasurer reported on finances for the previous two years and congratulated the agency for being "one of the few organizations who have come through the past year without a deficit." At the end of 1921, its bank balance was $1.65, and "all of the bills [had been] paid for the year." Two years after Jeffries returned, in 1926–1927, the ULP's board recognized her capabilities when it appointed her "acting executive director" following Clark's departure and before Thayer's arrival. The new executive director had been hired at an annual salary of $3,300, compared with $1,320 per year for Jeffries.[48]

Over her long career with the ULP, Jeffries recalled this temporary appointment as one of the great highlights of her life. During her tenure as acting executive director, Jeffries cogently laid out plans for the organization, including the quest for an industrial secretary and the launch of new research projects on black workers' experiences in the region's changing labor force. The league's University of Pittsburgh social work fellow was conducting a study of "the industrial situation here as it affects Negro men in the industries, from the point of common, semi-skilled, and skilled labor, working conditions in small plants and business houses, and general employment conditions, having in mind, the possibility of making new openings for Negro men," and Jeffries reported that she was "planning to make a similar study of conditions as they affect Negro women and girls." However, she delayed this work in order to complete a study of the "conditions and the causes which might bring so many Negro women and girls into this [Morals] Court."[49]

Along with evidence of gender discrimination and inequality within the Urban League movement, the ULP regularly revealed its class bias and sometimes disdainful attitude toward black migrants and their southern culture, ideas, and beliefs. The ULP's home economics worker described the Hill District's poorer sections as occupied mostly by newcomers from the South, while older Pittsburgh residents lived in somewhat "better houses and neighborhoods" within or near the Hill. In an interview with the *Pittsburgh Courier*, Margaret "Peg" Shaw, Clark's secretary during his tenure in Pittsburgh, recalled how old Pittsburghers resented the Urban League for developing programs on behalf of the newcomers. "They felt it was an intrusion because they were accustomed to taking care of their own. They did not like this organization giving hand-outs." According to Shaw, old Pittsburghers "had no experience with southern Blacks at all . . . with their gingham dresses and bonnets and were so polite." Shaw acknowledged "that she, too, resented the migrants." She recalled that when migrants passed her office door and greeted her in a friendly manner, she would not return the greeting until her mother sat her down and told her that she "had better speak to them" and be polite; "that she would not stand for me to ignore them." Only gradually, Shaw said, did both the community and Urban Leaguers become "accustomed to the migrants and stopped shunning and denouncing them."[50]

The ULP could sometimes be quite insensitive, describing its work among "the ignorant Negroes in the most neglected sections of the city" and "families of the lower type."[51] Presumably, the culture of these families was behind the league's widely distributed cards with the following specific injunctions regarding proper behavior in all walks of life:

1. Get a regular job and work every day.
2. Send for *your family* they need you.
3. Keep your home and person clean. Dirt breeds germs and disease.
4. Send your children to school clean and tidy.
5. Send for a doctor when sick, don't use patent medicines.
6. Join some church, attend regularly.
7. Open a bank account.
8. Don't buy on installment plan.
9. Be quiet on street cars, in the theatres and in crowds always appear clean and help *keep down prejudice.*
10. Do this and win the respect of your community and make the community better for Yourself Your Race and Your Country.[52]

Single young men were special targets of such advice. During the mid-1920s, an Urban League report criticized single migrant men "with money to spare" for encouraging the spread of prostitution among young black women in the city. ULP executive director Clark also focused attention on what he called the "irresponsible type," devoid of appropriate cultural values "for which to spend their money." Even as the ULP continued to help single men without families, particularly in the coalfields, it decried employers' reliance on such men. "New men employed at the mines are generally picked up. . . . The turnover among pickups is always great. Most pickups are floaters. Their social status and industrial record ought to be factors investigated before they are sent to the mines."[53]

Different shades of color also complicated the ULP's work within the African American community. In general, light-skinned blacks received the lion's share of skilled, professional, and clerical jobs available to African Americans. In her 1927 study of black women's employment, Grace Lowndes underscored white employers' insistence on drawing this internal color line among their black female employees. As she put it, "The attitude toward persons of light color or dark skin is peculiar—most of them preferring light color." This attitude made "the possession of light skin and smooth hair an economic asset." Rather than perceiving this as an unalloyed benefit for light-skinned black women, Lowndes observed that it proved "disastrous" for some women because it worked "strongly in favor of clandestine" and often destructive sexual relationships between black women and white men. At one popular cafeteria in the city, Lowndes learned that these women "make so many dates with the [white male] patrons of the place that they had no time left to work." One manager fired his black female employees and replaced them with white women, saying, "I did not wish to give up my 'beautiful colored girls,' but I got so many bad ones, that I was afraid the supply would run out on me suddenly, so I changed while it was safe." By contrast, Lowndes noted that dark-skinned black women were perceived as "untutored," "uninformed," "primitive," "less attractive," and "less graceful" than their lighter counterparts; although she was careful to counter that "much may be said to the contrary," she did not elaborate.[54]

The ULP's class and gender biases were partly a product of its abiding commitment to build and sustain a roster of allies among white professionals and elites. White men and women dominated the membership and leadership of the organization from its founding through the 1920s.

In 1922 the organization's ten-member board of directors included such influential white members and officers as Francis D. Tyson, president; Dr. Charles H. Carroll, vice president; Edwin C. May, treasurer; and Mary E. Bakewell, to name a few. Tyson, May, and Bakewell exercised considerable influence in the early development of the ULP. In late 1919 and early 1920, it was Bakewell who proposed a reorganization plan, partly to relieve the heavy workload of then-president May and executive director Clark. Bakewell's proposal, which was approved by the board, led to the creation of eight standing committees: industrial, education, health, housing, social service #1, membership, race relations, and social service #2. Chairs of the first five committees were appointed from among executive board members, and the other three chairs were appointed from among members of the community-wide Advisory Council. All committee chairs were expected to report to the executive committee, but the latter three committee chairs could not vote. Social service committee #1 took charge of travelers' aid work, while social service committee #2 took charge of the Morals Court and home economics program.[55]

Despite extraordinary interracial cooperation, there was ongoing tension between the executive director and certain members of the ULP board of directors. In January 1923, in an interview with the *Pittsburgh Courier*, past president of the board Walter A. May reiterated the necessity of and firm support for the ULP, "an organization that can speak with authority" for the black community. But he also hoped to rein in any impatience on the part of the executive director and the organization's staff. The league, he said, "in voicing the needs of the group, as well as its aspirations, . . . must offer sane advice and not merely protests." When Clark suggested the establishment of a committee made up of leading industrialists to address turnover among black workers, Tyson strongly opposed setting up an employment office with representatives of industry. He favored building closer working relations with the State Department of Labor and Industry. Moreover, he described Clark's proposal to "go into the employment game ourselves" as "quite a backward step."[56]

In a letter to the national office, Clark countered Tyson's position. "I suppose Tyson is in touch with you about doing a piece of educational work here. This no doubt is an excellent step, but I question the wisdom of taking this step without at least cooperating with the service which is supposed

to control the supply of labor to fill the openings which might be created."
Tyson had initially supported the creation of a new industrial relations
department to occupy the space vacated by the state, but he had also proposed eliminating the league's Morals Court work and reducing the activities of the home economics program. Less than a month later, he changed
his position and proposed dispensing with industrial work and moving to
a smaller headquarters. Furthermore, although black miners confronted
significant racial hostility from unionized white miners, Tyson sometimes
downplayed such conflicts, saying that they represented union "blundering
rather than discrimination . . . race prejudice did not enter in."[57]

The African American executive director worked hard to educate,
motivate, and activate white board members on behalf of the ULP's mission. Clark shared with board members newspaper clippings detailing inci-
dents of racial inequality and injustice, but these efforts were not always
appreciated. On one occasion, he sent board members a clipping titled
"Where the Fault Lies," reporting on a recent incident in Chicago, where
an Italian immigrant woman had gone into a public school and shot
a teacher for disciplining her sixteen-year-old son. The article pointed out
that no one had claimed that the woman's actions reflected the criminality
of all Italian people, and it suggested that, had the incident involved a black
woman and her son, there would have been an outpouring of popular sentiment that "the brute instinct" was more prevalent "in the dark than in the
light race." Board member Bayard Christy rebuked Clark for passing on an
article that "has the distinctly bad effect of stimulating and intensifying
feelings of grievance and resentment."[58]

Clark regularly appealed to individual board members, asking for their
help with fund-raising efforts as well as the day-to-day work of the organization. In a letter to board member Bakewell, Clark requested her assistance
in contacting corporate leaders to raise $5,000. Thus far, he said, only West-
inghouse Electric, Lockhart Iron and Steel, Carnegie Steel, Jones and
Laughlin, and Pittsburgh Plate Glass Company had made pledges ranging
from $100 to $600. In correspondence with board member and attorney
Christy, Clark complained that Edwin May and his wife would be away
from the city for "fully six months" and would be unavailable for consultation on league business. Another board member, Mrs. Scully, routinely
departed Pittsburgh for five-month periods to spend time on property she

owned in West Virginia. At about the same time, Bakewell announced her resignation from the board, as she planned to leave the city to care for an ill relative. Clark also took this opportunity to point out that ULP president Tyson was so consumed with his academic work at the University of Pittsburgh that he had little time for league programs. Thus, Clark pleaded with Christy to encourage "more of the white people of the city" to take an interest in the Urban League's work.[59]

Tension between Clark and the ULP board was not limited to its white members. In September 1924, in a stinging article titled "Urban League Said to Be in Dire Straits: Resignation of Women Employees Discloses Alleged Difficulties," the *Pittsburgh Courier* reported that the financial depression of the postwar years had pressed the ULP "to the wall of despair and defeat." In the wake of three months' work without pay, key employees Margaret Mann and Grace Lowndes had resigned from their posts. In its November 1922 report, the ULP board listed staff salaries as follows: executive director, $2,800; Morals Court worker, $1,200; home economics worker, $1,200; girls' worker and bookkeeper, $1,020; home and school visitor, $900; stenographer, $720. The *Courier* suggested that Clark had in fact raised his own salary while the women faced salary reductions. Accordingly, the paper suggested that the local branch stood "on the brink of failure." Moreover, one woman complained that Clark had promised to help her get a job with the city's Associated Charities, but instead, it was his wife who secured a position with the agency. The *Courier* also cited two other explanations for the ULP's "dire straits": the perception that its work was too narrowly focused on a "small circle" of concerns, and its failure to adequately educate the public about its mission and work.[60]

Clark quickly penned a sharply worded letter of disagreement with the *Courier*'s "dire straits" article. He pointedly argued that it offered a misleading picture of the branch's accomplishments and work on behalf of the city's poor and working-class black community. But Vann defended his newspaper's position, pointing out the article's emphasis on a variety of potential interpretations of the ULP's work under difficult social and economic conditions.[61]

In addition to pointing out deficits in the work of the ULP's white members, Clark concluded that "colored members have likewise given practically little support." He regularly pushed for more involvement from black members of the organization. Even so, he enlisted the help of Mrs. Scully (despite his disapproval of her long absences from Pittsburgh) to replace black board member S. R. Morsell, one of the branch's founders. Clark complained that Morsell's work had deteriorated and that the YMCA director no longer functioned on behalf of the ULP. Morsell, he said, "contributes nothing in the form of money, discussions or friends." Clark also lamented that the substantial inactivity among black and white supporters placed a heavy financial burden on the executive director and the league's small staff of low-paid and volunteer workers. "So you see," Clark wrote in one letter, "a good deal of financing the League has fallen upon my shoulders."[62]

Despite Clark's perception, the African American community provided significant financial support to the ULP's work. The league regularly conducted fund-raising drives within the black community. In the spring of 1921 the ULP board approved a membership drive focused specifically on the "Colored people." The plan entailed enlisting representatives from churches in the area and collecting pledges from the various congregations. In some cases, these drives pitted men against women in a contest to accumulate the most paid memberships. Invariably, the *Courier* reported, women took the lead in these membership drives, although men also contributed "unusually strong returns." As early as January 1922 the league's treasurer reported that "less than one white person out of five thousand in the city of Pittsburgh contributed toward" the work of the ULP, compared with "one out of every ninety-five Colored persons." The treasurer hoped to increase the percentage of black contributors to one out of every fifty. In his 16 February 1925 report, the treasurer stated that blacks had contributed 25 percent of the $10,138.66 received in a recent fund-raising effort. However, the ULP had a deficit of $1,442.59 from the previous year. On one occasion, board member Daisy Lampkin queried Edwin May about how much money the black community should contribute to support the organization, and he replied, "at least one-third," whereas the treasurer had suggested one-fourth. By the late 1920s, the ULP strategically divided the African American community into districts and mobilized increasing numbers of volunteers to solicit members for the organization. Somewhat similar to NAACP campaigns, it appealed to dedicated "race men and women" to contribute to the organization's growth and development. The ULP and the African American community also routinely supported annual citywide fund-raising efforts for the Welfare Fund of Pittsburgh.[63]

Building Bridges

Despite important class, gender, and financial constraints on the ULP's vision, it worked hard to bridge a variety of social divisions within the African American community. These activities included not only efforts to open up opportunities for African Americans in the economic, political, and social life of the city but also attempts to forge strong ties with NUL leaders such as T. Arnold Hill, L. Hollingsworth Wood, Oswald Garrison Villard, and others. Hill, for example, regularly visited Pittsburgh to encourage support for the local branch both inside and outside the black community. The NUL enhanced the prestige of the local group when it invited the ULP to host its annual conference in 1922. The board enthusiastically accepted the invitation but then engaged in a long discussion about the possible clash of national and local priorities and perspectives regarding the organization's work, particularly its posture toward organized labor. The ULP board concluded that the NUL was more or less "a federation of local autonomous groups" and that its national policies should not sway "the local organization if it was not agreeable to them."[64] At the 1922 conference, Justice Louis Brandeis addressed public attitudes toward interracial organizing, and Adam Clayton Powell Sr. spoke on the role of the church in social work among blacks.[65]

Most important, the ULP worked hard to alleviate fragmentation and conflict by advancing music, sports, history, and the arts as modes of cultural expression with profound cross-class, cross-generation, and cross-gender appeal. In early spring 1928 the branch launched its first annual art exhibit at Bethesda Presbyterian Church and Tabernacle Baptist Church. It also planned to sponsor an annual fashion show. At its yearly meetings, where it reviewed the organization's progress and projected a vision for the future, the ULP featured diverse forms of cultural expression for the enjoyment of attendees. In January 1929 sociologist Jesse J. Thomas, the NUL's southern field representative, visited Pittsburgh and was a guest speaker at the ULP's annual gathering. The program included a display of "the crafts and arts of the Pittsburgh Negro," the *Courier* reported, "such as perhaps has never been exhibited to the Pittsburgh public before." The creative works on display ranged from the "crayon drawings" of the youngest children to the pencil sketches, paintings, embroidery, and needlework of teenagers and adults. The Rankin Jubilee Quartet provided music for the occasion.[66]

In May 1925 the branch sponsored an amateur theater production titled *Vodvil and Revue* at the Pershing Theater under the direction of S. Nelson Arter. The show featured "vaudeville sketches, popular songs and fancy dances," as well as a "prologue" titled "School Days" featuring Ester Moore Reid as the teacher and several young people as students. The *Courier* described the show as "a simon pure amateur performance" with many "rough edges" but noted that it was "largely attended and appreciatively applauded." Two years later, in his keynote address at the ULP's annual meeting, Charles S. Johnson, director of the NUL's research department and editor of its *Opportunity* magazine, forcefully underscored how "expression in art, literature and music of the modern Negro" reflected "the general social conditions of the race." To illustrate his point, Johnson read selections from the poetry of Countee Cullen, Langston Hughes, Claude McKay, and others. Moreover, he accented the significance of history and historical knowledge in the African American struggle for freedom and upward mobility. Recounting key episodes in the black experience from enslavement through the early years of the Great Migration, Johnson concluded that black people were gradually gaining respect and admiration for their "contributions to American life."[67]

By the beginning of the Great Depression, the ULP was sponsoring free movies for the public. In March 1929, for instance, it planned movie viewings at the North Side Bidwell Presbyterian Church and the Metropolitan Baptist Church. Pastors of the churches served as masters of ceremonies for these movie screenings, and the ULP executive director took advantage of the opportunity to take the stage and report on the local branch's work. According to a *Courier* reporter, these film events provided the black community with much more than enjoyable leisure time with family and friends; the audience was able to acquire "some definite information on vital situations as they affect the Negroes" in Pittsburgh and across the nation. The ULP also regularly collaborated with YMCAs, settlement houses, and churches to advance the African American community's interest in sports, giving rise to the city's famous Negro League baseball teams the Pittsburgh Crawfords and the Homestead Grays. In his pioneering study of sports in black Pittsburgh, historian Rob Ruck concluded that it was during the early years of the Great Migration that sports started "to emerge as a source of cohesion for the community, transcending the divisions of class and place of birth"—and he might have added gender.[68]

By the onset of the Great Depression, the ULP had joined its civil rights efforts and its social service activities on behalf of the city's expanding black population. It collaborated with the Pittsburgh branch of the NAACP and a plethora of grassroots social justice organizations and advanced the fight against Jim Crow in all areas of life. Although the ULP's work was hampered by its own class and gender biases against poor and working-class blacks and women, it tried to bridge such differences and placed mounting pressure on the city's real estate developers, municipal officials, corporate leaders, and medical and social service providers to eliminate racial barriers. It worked to ensure that black people could work, live, educate their children, secure medical treatment, and utilize public accommodations on a nonsegregated and equal basis. Overall, according to ULP historians Edmunds and Bush, the early years of the Pittsburgh branch were the "bread and butter days" of the organization. "The priorities were . . . survival issues: finding shelter and jobs for those who had none, helping those who had jobs to hold on to them, teaching young mothers how to feed their families economically and nutritionally and how to keep their babies alive in what amounted to a foreign culture and environment."[69] Both the ULP and the community it served would confront even greater challenges to survival as the Great Depression took its toll.

Part II

The Depression and World War II

From the outset of its work in western Pennsylvania, the National Urban League invested considerable time and energy in the educational and vocational training of black youth. The Urban League of Pittsburgh hosted a one-day Youth Opportunity Conference in conjunction with the National Youth Administration. (Urban League of Pittsburgh, Manuscript Collection, ca. 1930–1940, Archives Service Center, University of Pittsburgh)

3

Surviving the Depression

The repercussions of the Great Depression, the New Deal, and World War II moved the Urban League's social service agenda from a preoccupation with industrial employers toward work with a variety of state agencies charged with helping ordinary working people make ends meet during a time of extraordinary economic suffering. Pittsburgh's shifting band of urban reformers joined and sometimes spearheaded broad-based community efforts to desegregate the city's social, civic, educational, medical, and economic institutions. In its fifteenth annual report, the branch boldly declared without much exaggeration that there was "hardly a single group or committee in the community dealing with a problem which effects Negroes on which some member of our staff is not a member, and is not actively participating."[1] By the end of World War II, the organization had hosted its second annual conference of the National Urban League, chaired a National Conference of Negro Organizations, and increased its influence on social policy and social justice movements beyond regional and even national boundaries. This chapter and the one that follows explore the influence of massive unemployment, government-sponsored welfare programs, and wartime exigencies on the transformation of the Urban League's social service ideas and practices.

The Depression Hits Pittsburgh

As it did elsewhere, the Great Depression affected Pittsburgh's African American community earlier than the city's white population and persisted longer. By February 1934, African Americans made up just 6 percent of Allegheny County's total population but accounted for 40 percent of its unemployed workers; 43 percent of blacks were on relief rolls, compared with 16 percent of whites. The city's black population had suffered recurring setbacks during the postwar recovery of the mid-1920s and experienced rising joblessness even before the crash of 1929. In his October and November 1927 report to the ULP's board of directors, Alonzo Thayer called attention to the impact of the "slackening of the iron and steel industries" on the fortunes of black workers, including "the fact that for every job now available there are 2.2 men seeking the same position." During the same period, Grace Lowndes, the ULP's civic and industrial secretary, reported that the Oliver Iron and Steel Company had "replaced all Negro women, not from any objection, but [from] a change in the economic situation."[2]

As the Depression took its toll on Pittsburgh's black community, the ULP's job placements dropped precipitously. In October 1930 the industrial secretary reported 114 job registrations (72 women and 42 men), but the league managed to place only 4 women and 3 men.[3] Lowndes reported a consensus that ULP units should help the families of unemployed workers bridge the gap between "the time which must elapse between an appeal [for aid] and the time an agency can arrange investigation and distribution" of relief.[4] Of the ten such cases received in the local office in October 1930, six were referred to the Family Welfare Association and two to the Association for the Improvement of the Poor; the Urban League's employment department handled the other two. Georgine Pearce recorded an intensive schedule of meetings with a variety of organizations to adjust a total of thirty-five cases during the month of October 1930 alone. These organizations included the Children's Service Bureau (ten cases), the Salvation Army (four), the Rosalia Maternity Hospital (two), and the Mother's Assistance Fund (one), to name a few.[5]

In December 1930 the ULP investigated rumors that the black elevator operators at Gimbel's Department Store would be replaced with white operators. Three years later, the executive board commented on the discharge of black elevator operators at Montefiore Hospital. Although management promised to "try" to rehire blacks as vacancies occurred, the industrial secretary revealed there had been "no progress" on the rehiring of black women elevator operators at the hospital.[6] At the same time, the agency reported "no progress" in the employment of black workers in the city's breweries, including the Pittsburgh Brewery, the Fort Pitt Brewing Company, and the Independent Brewery.[7] In addition, among Allegheny

County's 284 relief workers, only 15 were black, even though African Americans made up 20 percent of the relief rolls. Moreover, among the system's clerical employees, "there was not one Negro."[8]

As joblessness escalated during the Depression years, R. Maurice Moss succeeded Alonzo Thayer as executive director of the Urban League of Pittsburgh. A Virginian by birth, Moss attended public schools in Norfolk, Virginia, and Brooklyn, New York; he earned a BA from Columbia University in 1919 and later studied at the New York School of Social Work. Before moving to Pittsburgh, Moss served as director of the Baltimore Urban League. At about the same time, the ULP board hired Harold Lett, a statistician in the Michigan Department of Labor, as the new industrial secretary. Urban Leaguers later described Moss and Lett as a "dynamo duo" in the Urban League movement. Ruth Bowen, general secretary of the Social Service Bureau in Lansing, Michigan, described Lett as exceedingly capable but someone who "takes things a bit too seriously, undoubtedly a common fault of youth," whereas Moss, a gifted administrator, had "a lighter touch or sense humor." During his tenure as ULP head, Moss also served on the Pennsylvania Commission on the Urban Negro Population, the Allegheny County Board of Public Assistance, and the Interracial Committee of the Pennsylvania Department of Welfare; he was vice president of the Pennsylvania Social Welfare Conference and state director for the federal White Collar Study of 1936. During his time with the ULP, Lett also served as secretary of the Association of Negro Social Workers and secretary of the Committee on Courier Relief Benefit and was a member of the Federation of Social Agencies' committee on unemployment and its subcommittee on placement work.[9]

Under the leadership of Moss and Lett, the ULP made an "effort to participate in every worth-while program pointing to unemployment relief" in the city and county.[10] The league collaborated with many other organizations working on unemployment and relief issues, including the Community Council, the Committee on Homeless Men, the Welfare Conference at the Schenley Hotel, and the Joint Committee on Social Crisis.[11] Lett announced the branch's participation in the NUL's nationwide Vocational Opportunity Campaign, scheduled for the week of 20 April 1930. The ULP planned an "intensive publicity effort" focused on "the discrimination suffered by Negro labor in Pittsburgh and environs." Lett and Moss called for the creation of a "Citizens Committee" with representatives from all existing organizations concerned with the status of black workers. The ULP intended to make presentations before the Rotary, Kiwanis, and Hungry Clubs of Pittsburgh, which represented "the largest group of employers" in the city. Branch president R. Templeton Smith planned to deliver an address promoting the campaign on radio station KDKA and possibly on station WCAE as well.[12]

In early October 1930, when several industrial and commercial firms announced plans to relieve unemployment and suffering among the city's poor and working class, Lett met with their representatives to ensure that they included African Americans in any such projects. In addition to the A. M. Byers and Jones and Laughlin steel plants, he contacted McCann's stores in East Liberty and downtown Pittsburgh and Grant's Five and Ten Cent Store. Lett reported that McCann's downtown store employed fifteen black workers and added two more as a result of the ULP visit. A few blacks also gained employment at McCann's East Liberty store and at Grant's.[13]

Jones and Laughlin (J&L) intended to launch new building and construction projects at its Eliza and Soho plants and promised to employ roughly 17 percent black men on these projects, based on the percentage of blacks in the workforce at J&L's "chain of mills." For its part, A. M. Byers continued to operate its pipe and rolling mills, employing some 225 blacks (20 percent of the workforce of 1,100 men). In addition, about 20 percent of its skilled and semiskilled jobs were filled by black men. However, when Byers added a new division called the Ambridge plant, it hired an all-white workforce.[14]

The ULP's efforts extended into the Greater Pittsburgh metropolitan area. Executive director Moss helped organize and participated in conferences focused on the welfare of surrounding mill and mining towns. On one occasion, William Howell, secretary of welfare work, was "the moving spirit behind the conference." In this case, some seventy civic and religious organizations sponsored an "Activities Month Celebration" in eighteen coal towns operated by the Pittsburgh Coal Company. The series of events opened with a vocational conference at the Bethel African Methodist Episcopal Church in Monongahela, Pennsylvania. Discussion leaders included Antoinette Westmoreland, school visitor; Reginald Johnson, industrial secretary; and Marechal-Neil Ellison, education secretary.[15]

African Americans and the New Deal

From the outset of the New Deal, the ULP investigated discrimination in a variety of federally funded social welfare projects and reported mixed results for the African American community.[16] In his visit to a new agency called the Helping Hand Society for Homeless Men, Lett reported that blacks made up about 38 percent of the "guests" and were also well represented among staff. In short, Lett stated, "there was every evidence that Negroes were being given an equal 'break' here."[17] For its part, the Civilian Conservation Corps (CCC) accepted black applicants at a greater rate than whites, partly because whites applying for CCC support apparently had greater disabilities and even less education than black applicants. The CCC office rejected 20 percent of white applicants, compared with 17 percent of blacks, in October 1934. Lett reported that 30 black youths were among "the first Pittsburgh contingent" of 224 males sent to reforestation camps under the New Deal program.[18] According to the white recruiting officer, African Americans (he actually used the derogatory N-word) "are of a higher type than the whites. Most of the whites," he said, "are bums."[19]

Allegheny County sent 1,100 blacks to eight racially segregated CCC camps in the region. When queried about the camps' Jim Crow practices, the army sergeant in charge of recruiting declared, "Man we couldn't put them together; there would be a riot. We don't even put them on the train together." These men, selected from the county's relief rolls, made $30 a month and were required to send $20 of it home; their families were then removed from the relief rolls. The men's other necessities were furnished by the camps.[20]

In the fall of 1936, Moss underscored that the Works Progress Administration (WPA) had developed a remarkable reputation for employing blacks. It adopted a numerical goal for African American employment on projects funded by federal dollars.[21] The WPA's nondiscrimination policy opened the door to the gradual expansion of blacks in skilled occupations such as carpenters, brick masons, plasterers, and plumbing, heating, and electrical workers. In addition to employment as general laborers on maintenance and ground crews, black professionals slowly gained access to white-collar jobs in the tenant selection office and the relocation bureau and as managers and assistant managers on the projects themselves.[22] Lett reported that blacks had made significant progress in gaining access to Civil Works Administration (CWA) jobs compared to the early days of the project, when the white building trade unions had blocked blacks from skilled jobs. As Lett put it, the unions' "influence has been decidedly curtailed and the vast majority of projects . . . have been 'open-shop' jobs upon which Negroes have been placed." The State-Federal Employment Office estimated that blacks accounted for 10 to 12 percent of workers on CWA projects, including supervisory and professional positions.[23]

Nonetheless, in terms of serving the city's and county's needy African American population, the New Deal left a lot to be desired. The Allegheny County Transient Bureau and State Emergency Relief Board, funded by the Federal Emergency Relief Administration, provided little support for the city's black population. Designed to relocate homeless single men and women, the bureau operated a farm for men only, but few black men applied to work on the land four to six hours per day at $0.90 to $3 per week in exchange for shelter, food, and supplies.[24] At the same time, National Recovery Administration (NRA) codes covered most of the jobs occupied by blacks, but their concentration in the "unskilled" categories relegated them to the lowest minimum wages.[25] Moreover, "due to the adoption of the NRA codes [mandating higher minimum wages] and prejudice," the branch noted the displacement of black workers from higher-paying jobs at the Kroger Baking and Grocery Company and the Butler stores. The ULP also expressed keen interest in the potential impact of nascent urban renewal and public housing programs on the black community. Between 1934 and 1937, the city built just over 12,000 new houses but demolished some 20,000 low-income structures. As detailed later, the ULP expended considerable energy shaping the city's response to the housing needs of the African American community.[26]

In its evaluation of the impact of the CCC program on African Americans, the Pittsburgh branch complained that the CCC camps emphasized military regimentation rather than vocational training. Thus, they were "not genuinely for the benefit of the unemployed as human beings." The ULP likened the camps to "the care that is given to polo ponies, work horses and machines. These men are being prepared for 'service' in mine[s] and the army without much attention to vocational guidance, or aid to the individual to increase his individual powers."[27] Similarly, despite its benefits, the WPA failed to hire "several score of well educated young" black men and women who "lack[ed] training in any" particular specialty. When a government-sponsored survey that had employed large numbers of professional blacks came to a close, some forty young, educated black employees lost their jobs and found it "practically impossible" to secure WPA employment that matched their education and skills.[28]

Perhaps most discouraging, the ULP's industrial committee worked tirelessly but failed to secure funding for a federal theater project in the Hill District as a means of increasing African Americans' employment opportunities in the city. The struggle to broaden opportunities for blacks in the arts persisted into the war years. By June 1941, the ULP had created a fine arts department as one of its newest units. Moreover, the ULP found that the situation varied considerably from one government social service agency to another and over time.[29] Even so, as early as May 1934, Moss reported to the national office that blacks in Pittsburgh were, for the most part, "holding their own" and occupied "positions of significance and importance." African Americans served on the general committees of community councils regarding relief policies, and in the Hill District council, blacks were officers and committee chairs. Five blacks were employed in the local home loan office (two attorneys and three real estate agents), two in the federal reemployment office, three women at CWA headquarters, and two interviewers on the staff of the State-Federal Employment Office. Moreover, blacks in Pittsburgh served on a variety of planning and governing committees, including the subsistence homestead committee and the advisory committee of the State-Federal Employment Office; in addition, the ULP had been promised a paid staff person in the local compliance office of the NRA. Moss reported that "few if any" black public service employees were "handling only Negro cases." For his part, Moss had been appointed to the executive committee of the Pennsylvania Conference of Social Work and the League for Social Justice. He was also vice chair of the American Association of Social Workers' committee on personnel practices.[30]

The Urban League Carries On

When Harold Lett left Pittsburgh to head the Newark, New Jersey, Urban League in 1934, William E. Hill took over the job of industrial secretary with high recommendations from the national office. Hill came to Pittsburgh from Summit, New Jersey, where he had served as head of the city's "YMCA for Negroes." A graduate of Johnson C. Smith University in North Carolina, Hill also earned an MA from Columbia University. Under Hill's leadership as industrial secretary, the ULP intensified its push to secure services for African Americans. Integral to this effort was the league's ongoing commitment to empirical research and the training of professional black social workers as a means to bridge the color line, guide program development and policy recommendations, and transform race and class relations in the city.[31] In addition to well-conceptualized scholarly surveys (based on interviews and consultation with social service professionals and community organizers) to ascertain the scope of black Pittsburghers' social service needs, the ULP regularly gathered data through informal discussions with ordinary people, later described as "a kind of street corner" approach to the creation of knowledge.[32]

Despite the hardships of the Great Depression, the organization maintained its social work fellowships at the University of Pittsburgh. In 1932 the ULP reported that eleven of its twelve fellowship students had "finished their courses" and were "employed in social work, or an allied field." The one exception was a young woman who had married and left the profession after several years of productive social work in the city.[33] Two years later, the branch announced that ULP fellow Howard D. Gould had finished his work in June and accepted a position as industrial secretary at the Chicago Urban League, replacing former Pittsburgh executive director Alonzo Thayer. Thus, the ULP claimed in August 1934, "We maintain our record—fourteen fellowship students given training, fourteen employed."[34]

Funded through the University of Pittsburgh's tuition remission program and the contributions of both local Urban Leagues and the NUL, the fellowship program represented "12 unbroken years" of assistance to black students. The illustrious list of students earning master's degrees in social work included the first fellow, Myrtle Hull Elkins of Atlanta, Georgia. She went on to serve black children at the Cincinnati Children's Home. The second fellow, Gertrude Clark Morris from Pittsburgh, gained her MA in 1923 and secured a job with the Urban League of New York City before marrying and withdrawing from the field. Abram L. Harris earned his MA in 1924 and accepted a post as executive secretary in Minneapolis,

Minnesota. He later became a well-regarded professor of sociology at Howard University in Washington, DC, and coauthored, with economist Sterling Spero, the groundbreaking 1930 study *The Black Worker*. Ira deAugustine Reid, the ULP's fourth fellow, produced an important master's thesis, "A Study of 200 Negro Prisoners in Western Penitentiary," but he was best known as director of the "comprehensive and widely quoted survey of the social conditions" of black people in the city's Hill District. Financed by the Buhl Foundation, Reid's study was a stellar example of the impact the ULP's fellowship program had on scholarly research about the city's black community that transcended local and regional interest. Other ULP fellows included Dean Yarbrough, Gerald Edgar Allen, Floyd Covington, James H. Baker Jr., and Wylie A. Hall.[35]

Before the Depression, the ULP had invested the bulk of its energy cultivating the goodwill of industrial employers and the local philanthropic community. Massive unemployment increasingly shifted the ULP's center of gravity toward work with local, state, and federal agencies designed to address the fragmentation and suffering of families and communities. Closely intertwined with its shift in focus, the ULP moved into new quarters at 43 Fernando Street. The ULP occupied the second floor, the Homeless and Transient Bureau of the Allegheny County Emergency Relief Board took up the first floor, and the Hill District Community Council occupied the third floor. Also on the third floor was a 200-seat auditorium that the three groups shared. The ULP's new Fernando Street location placed it on what was popularly known as "Social Service Row," which included St. Ann Orphanage, the Salvation Army, and several Jewish organizations in what the *Courier* called the "Jewish philanthropies building."[36]

From its new base of operations, the ULP intensified its fight for better housing, jobs, and respect for workers' rights. It added the fight for public housing to its ongoing campaign to improve the living conditions of black workers. The Hill District Community Council (HDCC) emerged as the principal organizational vehicle for this effort. Representing a broad cross section of liberal synagogues and churches and a variety of social service organizations and settlement houses, the HDCC, under the chairmanship of ULP executive director Maurice Moss, pushed for religious and racial integration in the community. The HDCC also aimed to secure federal funds to "beautify" the city, remove "slums" or dilapidated buildings, and improve living conditions for black residents. In an interview with the Federal Works Projects agent, one resident stated succinctly: "Most houses and sidewalks need repairing. We need better garbage and rubbish service." Although the HDCC advocated the destruction of run-down homes in poor and working-class black neighborhoods, the ULP and its partners insisted on linking "slum clearance" to the creation of public housing and jobs for black workers and their communities.[37]

Following passage of the federal Wagner-Steagall Act in 1937, Pittsburgh claimed distinction as the first city in Pennsylvania to establish a local public housing authority, the Housing Authority of the City of Pittsburgh (HACP). The Hill District became the site of its first public housing project, Bedford Dwellings. Moss was instrumental in urging HACP head Bryn Hovde and councilman George E. Evans to support the Hill District site, and he pressed the Urban League's neighborhood councils into an active campaign to secure the project for the black community. Neighborhood groups attended numerous public forums and meetings designed to build support for public housing, with the ultimate aim of creating both jobs and housing for black Pittsburghers. Bedford Dwellings and a second site called Terrace Village soon opened for African American occupancy, resulting in not only greater access to public housing but also more paved streets and better sewer services.

The movement for public housing in the Hill District prevailed over the determined opposition of groups such as the Soho and Gazzam Owners and Tenants League under the leadership of Father Charles Rice, a Catholic priest. The Hill District Tenants Organization, an interracial group, counteracted the anti–public housing activities of the Soho and Gazzam League and pushed aggressively for public housing for blacks. It also demanded that private property owners repair existing buildings and charge lower and less predatory rents. As Catholic foes of public housing placed increasing heat on Hovde and the HACP, the ULP stood fully behind the public housing authority's efforts, despite what it described as "the protests of the few." During this period, as noted by historian Fidel Campet, the ULP and its partners envisioned public housing not only as a way to house poor and working-class people but also as a "method to uplift the race and eventually build a [black] middle class" through new and better job opportunities in the skilled crafts and the professions.[38]

As white competition for jobs previously reserved for blacks intensified, the ULP gave increasing attention to preserving these low-wage and "low-status" jobs for African Americans. Emphasis on efficiency and training took center stage in much of the league's strategic efforts to secure jobs for black workers. Lett conducted a training course for black waiters and presented the seventy-five men who completed the course with certificates of achievement. The *Pittsburgh Courier* listed the men by name in its article on the ceremonies that followed. In his report to the board, Moss described Lett's effort to establish a black waiters' organization as the "first step" toward organizing black workers in related occupational groups to increase their value and recognition in the city's economy.[39]

In October 1932 the ULP announced the creation of an institute for African American building maintenance workers, janitors, and porters employed in the downtown Pittsburgh corporate offices of Gulf, Koppers, Oliver, Carnegie, Frick, Union Trust, the Philadelphia Company, and the *Pittsburgh Press*, to name a few. Some 1,000 to 1,500 black men worked in these establishments, earning roughly $20,000 per week combined. The institute aimed to help these men hold on to their jobs in the wake of rising white competition. As the *Courier* reported, "The serious need of job-consciousness and of group solidarity in working out plans to protect this income is obvious." The institute presented a series of lectures by such leading figures as attorney Homer Brown, Francis Tyson, W. P. Young, and Frank M. Leavitt, associate superintendent of the Pittsburgh public schools with responsibility for vocational training. The goal was to strengthen the position of black workers in the face of increasing white competition for so-called menial jobs formerly "monopolized by colored workers." The institute held classes on Saturday, and they were open to the men free of charge.[40] The Pittsburgh branch reported the conclusion of training courses for elevator operators and bellmen conducted by the industrial relations department. Thirty-four participants received certificates of accomplishment after completing courses on "work attitudes and possibilities" for achievement in jobs otherwise considered "menial" or of "low" value. The recreation department also conducted courses on group leadership. At about the same time, the industrial relations department planned to hold a community-wide interracial roundtable to launch "a frontal attack" on the "deplorable conditions affecting young Negroes of Pittsburgh."[41]

Alongside efforts to protect the jobs of black janitors and porters, the ULP escalated its emphasis on training black women for household and domestic positions. In 1928 the industrial department of the YWCA spearheaded the formation of the National Committee on Employer-Employee Relationships at Home to professionalize the field of domestic service. In 1931 the organization changed its name to the National Council on Household Employment and intensified efforts to improve the lives of household workers. Some 100 training centers for household workers were established in nineteen states. When the WPA provided federal funds for household training demonstration projects, the ULP launched a campaign to open a training center in the Pittsburgh region.[42] At its September 1936 meeting, the industrial committee approved a proposal to develop a household training school for black workers and formed a subcommittee, chaired by ULP president Mrs. David Arter, to provide leadership on the issue; it also appointed Mrs. H. D. Stark, president of the Congress of Women's Clubs of Western Pennsylvania, to chair a planning committee for the center and Mrs. A. H. McCreary to head a committee on voluntary standards for household workers.[43] Employers, the report stated, "will be encouraged to accept voluntary agreements with their household employee[s], and household employees will be encouraged to take advantage of the training center in order that they may enjoy the benefits of a voluntary agreement." Similar to the professionalization of nursing, the ULP pushed for the setting of standards related to practices, pay, and respect for household labor.[44]

In its quest for a domestic service training school, the ULP collaborated with a variety of agencies, including the domestic service department of the State Employment Office, the industrial department of the YWCA of Pittsburgh, and the Congress of Women's Clubs. In her comments to the board, Arter reiterated that the aim of the school was to "professionalize" household work "so that it would be on the same level with nursing, secretarial work, etc." Supporters of the training school repeatedly noted that young black girls despised household labor "because of the stigma attached to it." Promoters of the training program regularly repeated the words of Selma Robinson, author of the *Reader's Digest* article "Maids in America." Household work, she wrote, "is an exacting profession—not something you just pick up." Acknowledgment of this fact, "the experts say . . . is the only way to remove the stigma which attaches to housework."

Robinson optimistically concluded, "We may never have a servant class in this country, but we may have something better—a class of household employees with pride and dignity in their profession."[45]

Adding to the urgency to address the needs of household workers in Pittsburgh, in 1936 the ULP's job-placement service received 429 calls for domestic help out of 668 applications for workers. It placed 247 women in domestic household positions out of 308 placements in total. Moreover, the ULP reported that black workers accounted for 23,000 of the city's 37,000 household employees, and these workers constituted about 43 percent of the gainfully employed black workforce.[46] The organization's committee on household employment prepared an agreement between employers and black household employees that explicitly laid out the obligations and duties of both. It specified hours of work, wage rates, time off, holidays, overtime, living conditions, and advance notice before quitting. In a radio address on KDKA, Arter accented the neglect of domestic employees, despite their immense contributions to the life of the city and the nation. "These are the workers who tend our children, prepare our meals, take care of our homes, and contribute so much to the general comfort of our households. When we think of how important they are to us it is surprising when we consider how little attention has been devoted to their vocational needs."[47]

The ULP vigorously campaigned to strengthen black workers' position in the organized labor movement. Following the historic break between the Congress of Industrial Organizations (CIO) and the highly discriminatory craft unions of the American Federation of Labor (AFL), the National Urban League escalated its nationwide support of the organized labor movement.[48] On 3 April 1934 T. Arnold Hill of the NUL informed branches of the dangers of the proposed Wagner labor relations bill if it were passed without an amendment prohibiting racial discrimination by labor unions. As drafted, the Wagner bill excluded strikebreakers from its benefits, a category of workers that included large numbers (and perhaps a majority) of blacks. Hill noted that blacks were often compelled to work as strikebreakers because of the racially exclusionary practices of labor unions, particularly the four railroad brotherhoods and several affiliates of the AFL. Thus, Hill emphasized that passage of this act without an antidiscrimination amendment would place "greater restrictions" on black workers and entrench discriminatory white labor practices. He suggested that when local branches wrote letters endorsing the amendment, they mention that blacks made up one-tenth of the nation's population and one-eighth of all workers—a group that was "large enough to seriously interfere with the successful operation of the bill, and important enough from the standpoint of their consuming power to make it imperative that they work under conditions that provide for their normal working and spending habits."[49]

In a letter to W. W. Clements, president of the Pennsylvania Railroad Company, the ULP supported the struggle of Local 4 of the Brotherhood of Railroad Station Porters. Formed in Chicago in 1937 by representatives of redcaps from around the country, the International Brotherhood of Red Caps fought for recognition as employees to guarantee its members a minimum wage, fair hours, and better working conditions. In 1938 the group appealed to the Interstate Commerce Commission (ICC) to end the railroad companies' practice of forcing station porters to rely exclusively on tips for their income and to treat them as "employees" of the company. In September 1938 the ICC ruled that redcaps or "hand-baggage porters" working in stations "in cities of over 100,000 population throughout the United States are employees." When this ruling went into effect on 24 October 1938, company policy required redcaps to report their daily tips, which became the property of the company; from those tips, the company paid recaps the $2 minimum wage required by the Fair Labor Standards Act. The public, believing that these men now received wages from the company, started to tip redcaps less or not at all.[50]

In April 1940 a "very good friend of the League" pledged $1,200 to pay union dues for black workers as part of a campaign to eliminate the color line in union membership. The "problem of money to pay the big joining fees" repeatedly came up, and in February 1940 the ULP's industrial relations department spearheaded the creation of an industrial loan fund to lend money "under very limited circumstances to individuals as a means of increasing employability." Applicants could use the loans to purchase tools and equipment, establish certain business ventures, and pay union dues or license or registration fees, along with other uses deemed appropriate by the committee. The committee hoped to secure approval from the board for the loan program.[51] In addition, Hill suggested an amendment to the state's Labor Relations Act outlawing racial discrimination by labor unions; it was introduced into the Pennsylvania legislature by assemblyman Homer Brown. Lester Granger of the national office requested a copy of the amendment to be used in a similar amendment for New York State. The ULP also advised black workers about qualifying for unemployment compensation under the new state law.[52]

The Urban League of Pittsburgh established a Workers' Council in 1933–1934. Some seventy-five skilled black workers took the lead in setting up the organization, adopting a constitution, electing officers, and initiating regular Monday night meetings at the branch's Fernando Street office.[53] In 1935 the agency reported 108 members, with individuals in the building trades leading the list, including plasterers, brick and stone masons, electricians, hoisting engineers, plumbers, and boilermen.[54] As Workers' Councils spread across urban America, the *Pittsburgh Courier* reported that "Pittsburgh is keeping pace with other sections of the country in its promotion of a Workers' Council and a Workers institute in line with the program of the National Urban League." The Pittsburgh chapter aimed to increase the proportion of skilled black workers on government emergency projects and to establish a workers' institute to hold forums, gather data, and set an agenda for future activities. The *Courier* encouraged skilled black union and nonunion workers to join the council.[55]

The ULP also cooperated in the development of a Workers School in western Pennsylvania. Founded in 1936, the Workers School offered education to officers and members of labor unions. In addition to mathematics, social science, health, social dance, and US and Russian history, the curriculum included a course on "The Negro Question in the United States." In its report for 1937–1938, the Workers School's administration thanked the ULP for its "very generous" help with "mimeographing necessary [teaching] materials" for classroom instruction.[56] The Pittsburgh Labor College also asked for the ULP's help in building a college that would transcend "any political philosophy or labor faction" and educate workers in "public speaking, current events, labor history and the law, and possibly dramatics."[57]

The local Urban League branch strengthened its ties to the labor movement when industrial secretary William E. Hill became chair of the local council of the National Negro Congress (NNC). Partly inspired by the American Communist Party, the NNC was founded in 1935 to unify a broad cross section of African American organizations involved in helping poor and working-class people. In 1936 the NNC's local chapter organized a planning conference in Pittsburgh. The NUL's T. Arnold Hill and local ULP officials took part in the event, underscoring the Urban League's increasing national and even transnational connections to the labor movement.[58]

A year later, in February 1937, steelworker organizer Ben Careathers convened a National Conference of Negro Organizations at Pittsburgh's Northside Elks Club, and the ULP's William Hill was chosen to chair the session. In a memorandum to local chapters, John P. Davis, secretary of the NNC, urged them to cooperate with the movement to organize black workers in the steel industry. Based partly on conversations with Hill and other local NNC officers, Davis outlined a comprehensive plan for assisting the Steel Workers Organizing Committee of the CIO to recruit black members through the black press, churches, fraternal orders, and other organizations.[59] While national leaders called on black steelworkers to commit their lives to the organized labor movement, the *Pittsburgh Courier* reported that "the steel workers themselves set the tone of worker aspiration and determination for all sessions." When a Russian labor organization invited Hill to travel to the Soviet Union under its sponsorship to observe social and labor conditions there and report back to US audiences, the ULP board of directors approved a leave of absence for Hill, "in recognition of his progressive activities in Pittsburgh."[60]

Even as the ULP intensified its efforts for relief, jobs, housing, and workers' rights, it conducted other day-to-day programs to address the leisure-time, social, and cultural needs of the African American population in the throes of the Depression. These programs extended well beyond the activities of the industrial, health, housing, and education committees. Several civic, youth, and recreational committees reinforced the changing social service agenda of the ULP. In January 1931, at a meeting held at the German Evangelical Lutheran Church, Moss reported a shift in the branch's emphasis from "curative" to "preventive" work. In particular, Grace Lowndes had been removed from the Morals Court and would now focus on "corrective measures in the neighborhoods" where young people lived and learned. Lowndes emphasized "forming and conducting neighborhood improvement groups" for young boys and girls. These ULP programs included leadership training for "Colored girls" in the Girl Scouts of America. Such efforts were intended to deflect young people from activities that might involve them in the criminal justice system. Understandably, when young people were incarcerated, they sometimes appealed to the ULP for assistance with their cases before the parole board in Harrisburg.[61]

In 1930 Virginia Woodson, head of the ULP's girls' club work, reported on six clubs with a total membership of 150; she cited a combined attendance of 501 at twenty-one different club meetings. The Fort Pitt School Play Group counted twenty-nine girls as members, the Lincoln Play Group had forty-six members, and the Lincoln Scout Troop No. 37 at the Warrington Recreation Center reported twenty-one members.[62] In 1932 the ULP's junior club worker reported nine active clubs with a total of 197 members. The groups held 290 meetings that brought some 4,885 young women together for a wide range of activities, including singing, storytelling, volleyball, basketball, dramatic productions, citizenship discussions, first aid, homemaking, and a Christmas jamboree where 265 parents and children enjoyed an evening of entertainment.[63] Under the direction of Edwin C. Berry, head of the recreation department, the ULP ran free programs for youths aged ten years and older; membership stood at about 1,600 youths participating in some twenty-four different groups or clubs. Volunteers from the National Youth Administration (NYA), WPA, and other groups helped run these programs. The ULP also organized its own basketball team and became a member of the citywide metropolitan basketball league. In addition to competing in the metropolitan league, the branch team played against other Urban League teams, including the one from Akron, Ohio.[64]

The Urban League's work on behalf of black youth took sharp focus in the movement to establish Camp James Weldon Johnson, and Edwin Berry played an important role in its development. *Courier* editor and owner Robert Vann initially agreed to finance the camp for black boys and girls, based on the *Life* magazine model of funding camps for white youth. Vann planned to invest his own funds and purchase property for the camp, which the ULP pledged to manage, including the recruitment of staff, selection of campers, and day-to-day programs for the children. But the project collapsed when Vann pulled out, reporting that the anticipated support of a wealthy white friend had not materialized and, regrettably, he could not honor his commitment. In the meantime, the ULP had secured vital support from the WPA and National Park Service to secure land in rural Beaver County. By decade's end, the ULP had opened Camp James Weldon Johnson for black youth in Pittsburgh and western Pennsylvania.[65]

For its part, the ULP's civic department, under the leadership of Mrs. Stewart, offered neighborhood services, children's welfare activities, sewing and other crafts, and budget and financial programs.[66] League-sponsored art exhibits, musicals, dramatic productions, and lectures also gained widespread attention. Nearly 300 people attended an exhibit of African American art during the ULP's annual meeting in 1932, held at the German Evangelical Lutheran Church on Smithfield Street. Under the leadership of William S. Fitts, the exhibit aimed to illuminate "the hidden talent of a people who are striving against discouragements of every nature, for self-expression."[67]

In March 1937 the organization reported enormous enthusiasm for an upcoming talk by Mary McLeod Bethune, director of Negro affairs for the NYA. The branch had organized the lecture by Bethune in the wake of her selection as "one of the fifty greatest living American women." Her promotional biography accented Bethune's rise from "the cotton fields of South Carolina" to the centers of power in the United States and around the globe. The ULP welcomed Bethune "at the height of her amazing career to lend her hand in inspiring local youth on the road to greater progress."[68] Radio station KDKA offered to broadcast her address to a wider interracial audience.

At about the same time, the ULP's industrial relations director Harold Lett delivered a lecture titled "What Is Happening to the American Negro," the first in KDKA's "Human Values" series.[69] In 1935 Howard University president Dr. Mordecai W. Johnson "electrified two large audiences" at the league's second annual religious service.[70] The branch had also scheduled Mary E. McDowell of the University of Chicago Settlement House to be the featured speaker at its annual meeting in 1931, but McDowell became ill and canceled her appearance.[71] Elmer Carter, editor of the NUL's *Opportunity*, was the principal speaker at a 1931 symposium sponsored by the ULP and the National Alliance of Postal

Employees. Carter's speech emphasized the destructive impact of racial discrimination in the workforce nationwide.[72]

Addressing tensions in black-white relations and striving to prevent the outbreak of racial violence were part of the ULP's ongoing agenda during the interwar years. Analysts would later describe the branch as "a voice screaming in the wilderness" and the "conscience" of Pittsburgh's social order.[73] The ULP also maintained regular contact with both black and white religious, philanthropic, and social service organizations interested in the socioeconomic plight of the city's poor and working-class black population. In 1932 alone, ULP staff members delivered some seventy-two presentations to black, white, and mixed-race audiences totaling more than 7,300 people.[74] In 1934 attorney Edward O. Tabor, chair of the Pittsburgh Interracial Commission and past member of the ULP executive board, delivered a talk at Trinity Cathedral on "Reducing Areas of Racial Friction."[75] The branch regularly urged white church leaders to support its program and to help expose the story of racism behind "mortality, health, morality and delinquency curves of the Negro element in the population."[76]

At the same time, the ULP facilitated interpulpit visits between black and white pastors to encourage interactions across the color line. Under the auspices of the Inter-Racial Commission of the Federal Council of Churches in America, 11 February 1934 was declared "Race Relations Day." The ULP's Moss collaborated with the Reverend C. A. Ward, pastor of the Central Baptist Church, to make this event possible. Participants in the exchange included Reverend Frenz of the Brushton Methodist Episcopal Church, the Reverend T. J. King of Ebenezer Baptist Church, the Reverend B. F. Crawford of the Perryville Avenue Presbyterian Church, the Reverend James S. Hatcher of the Bethel African Methodist Episcopal Church, the Reverend Richard M. Fowles of the Homewood Methodist Episcopal Church, and the Reverend H. R. Tolliver of the Grace Memorial Presbyterian Church.[77]

The Urban League's contributions to African American life and labor were not limited to Pittsburgh and western Pennsylvania. The influence of its research, social services, and professional social work training programs extended beyond local, regional, and even national boundaries. The ULP supported the vigorous nationwide movement to pass the Wagner-Costigan antilynching bill. It also hosted the National Urban League's annual conference in 1932, as well as meetings of the National Negro Congress during the late 1930s and early 1940s.[78]

The 1932 NUL convention attracted more than 1,000 participants, and at least 400 people served on various committees and programs for the event. NUL president Robert Lee Wilson declared the Pittsburgh meeting "the greatest in its history." At both the Central Branch of the YWCA (59 Chatham Street) and Ebenezer Baptist Church, more than 100 black and white social workers and other experts explored the best "way out" of the prevailing depression for blacks. The meeting featured talks by four executive officers from national headquarters; executive directors of branch offices in Chicago, Detroit, and Atlanta; the presidents of Howard University (Mordecai Johnson) and Florida A&M College (J. R. E. Lee); and Mrs. Clara Burrill Bruce, assistant manager of the Paul Lawrence Dunbar Apartments in New York City. Robert Vann presided over the sole community-wide meeting open to the public, and the *Courier* reported that the "interest in social work and intellectual circles ran high as so many nationally known men and women came to the city for the meeting."[79]

Similarly, meetings of the NNC brought a number of national figures to Pittsburgh, including Philip Murray, head of the CIO's Steel Workers Organizing Committee; T. Arnold Hill, national secretary of industrial relations for the NUL; and John P. Davis, secretary of the national body of the NNC.[80] Hill asked for Moss's help in organizing a local movement to support the liberation of Ethiopia from Italian tyranny. Hill's request involved fund-raising for the Ethiopian cause: "You understand that Lij Zaphiro [first secretary of the Imperial Ethiopian Legation in London] is interested in securing financial support for the Ethiopian government, which of course, needs hospital supplies and material assistance of various sorts." It is not clear how Moss responded.[81]

Along with hosting national meetings, the Pittsburgh branch contributed to the Urban League movement through its research projects, its innovative monthly newsletter the *Informer*, and even local amateur dramatic productions. Following the completion of one socioeconomic survey of poor and working-class life in Pittsburgh initiated by Harold Lett and completed by William Hill, the organization received inquiries from the federal government as well as Urban League branches in Newark,

Kansas City, Allentown, Chicago, and Tampa.[82] The agency printed about 700 copies of the *Informer* each month, distributing 400 by mail and dropping off another 300 at various locations around the city. The publication gained special recognition at the May 1931 National Conference of Social Work in Philadelphia. A representative of the Russell Sage Foundation described the *Informer* as one of the "seven best mimeographed house organs in the country."[83] Two years later, five Urban League affiliates requested permission to stage *Scrap*, a local play sponsored by the Urban League of Pittsburgh.[84] Even more important, in her popular textbook *How to Interpret Social Work*, published by the Russell Sage Foundation in 1937, Mary Swain Routzahn praised the ULP's innovative "series of board and staff dinner meetings as a means of stimulating active interest on the part of board members, and improving board and staff relations. Before the first of these gatherings, each department head was asked to 'dream of what you would do if you somehow found that you had ten thousand dollars for your department for the next year.' These dreams, as reported, served as discussion points for setting goals."[85]

Whereas working directly with industrial employers took the lion's share of the ULP's energy and resources during the 1920s, the nation's expanding welfare state took center stage in the programs of the Urban League movement during the tumultuous years of the Great Depression. The ULP's increasing engagement with state-supported social service agencies gradually produced results and helped transform the nature of its social service work. The move from its overcrowded Wylie Avenue location to Fernando Street symbolized the creation of a new social service agenda. From its new base of operations on "Social Service Row," the ULP amplified its fight for public housing, domestic service training classes, and workers' rights. As discussed in chapter 4, these diverse but overlapping efforts reinforced grassroots challenges to the pillars of Pittsburgh's Jim Crow order.

Although men took the lion's share of top administrative and professional jobs in the Urban League of Pittsburgh, women employees and volunteers carried out most of the organization's day-to-day social service and political work. Emblematic of these women was Christina Jeffries, shown here at a banquet to broaden opportunities for African American business and professional people. Jeffries served the organization for thirty-five years, including a brief stint as "acting executive director" during the late 1920s. (Charles "Teenie" Harris Photo Archive, Carnegie Museum of Art, Pittsburgh)

4

Establishing a New Social Service Regime

The Urban League's fight for workers' rights and low-income public housing deepened its ties with grassroots social movements and the larger civil rights agenda of the African American community. The Pittsburgh branch not only facilitated the emergence of the city's "Don't Buy Where You Can't Work" campaign, spearheaded by black women, but also advanced movements to demolish the color line in Pittsburgh's medical, educational, and defense programs. The Urban League's energetic engagement in these diverse but overlapping movements broadened its contributions to the development of the African American community and the transformation of black politics. Boycotts of discriminatory grocery chains, demands for the hiring of black teachers in the public schools, and the struggle to gain equal access to wartime jobs in industries with government contracts foreshadowed the rise of the modern black freedom movement in Pittsburgh and elsewhere in twentieth-century America.

The Housewives Cooperative League

Pittsburgh's "Don't Buy Where You Can't Work" movement started at the outset of the Depression. The branch's civic secretary Grace Lowndes and industrial secretary Harold Lett led the early black consumer boycott movement in Pittsburgh.[1] This movement reached the city in 1933, when African Americans launched a "selective buying campaign" to protest the discriminatory employment practices of the Atlantic and Pacific (A&P) and Butler grocery store chains. These firms responded to the boycott by hiring black workers but then swiftly let them go as the economy worsened and white workers sought jobs available to black workers.[2] In 1936, however, Urban League officials William Hill and Roy Garvin renewed the boycott movement. They spearheaded the formation of the House-wives Cooperative League and reinforced Pittsburgh's participation in the national "Don't Buy Where You Can't Work" campaign.[3] Although men initiated the movement in Pittsburgh, black women organized and imple-mented the effort on the ground. Activists Daisy Lampkin, Alma Illery, and Frances Stewart, among others, diligently worked to "open up new avenues of employment" for blacks in skilled and white-collar jobs, par-ticularly as "clerks," and to abolish "Jim Crowism" and the "discourte-ous" treatment of blacks in a major segment of the consumer economy.[4] The NUL conducted a study of consumer pressure groups in a variety of cities (Chicago, New York, Atlanta, Cleveland, Columbus, Pittsburgh, and Washington, DC) to establish what it described as "Consumer Pres-sure as an Employment Program for Urban Negroes."[5]

The Housewives League clearly outlined its four major goals and pri-orities: to boost the *Pittsburgh Courier* as the principal advertising medium for the African American community; to support every African American–owned and –operated business; to educate the community on the benefits of patronizing the black press; and, most important, "to 'spend our money where we can work.'" The organization reported that African Americans in Allegheny County spent $16 million each year on food alone. The women worked to harness this buying power and impose an economic boycott of businesses that excluded blacks from their workforces. They targeted key products—milk, gas, bread, and coal.

At a second meeting of the Housewives League, Garvin delivered a speech outlining the rationale for a consumers' group. According to Garvin, Allegheny County's 83,000 black residents spent $63 million a year—close to 28 percent of that on food. Garvin declared, "If the housewives banded together, they would do a constructive job for Pittsburgh." The women responded enthusiastically, and the organization soon reported a rise in white advertisers in the *Courier* as well as the employment of blacks by local companies, including the Haller Baking Company and Bieck's Milk Company. At the same time, the organization initiated a boycott of the Meadow Gold Company, refusing to buy its milk because it had rejected calls for the employment of African American deliverymen. The organiza-tion also pushed for the appointment of an African American municipal food inspector in Pittsburgh.[6] *Courier* editor Robert Vann emphasized the spending power of the Greater Pittsburgh Housewives League and its ability to "move mountains when properly applied." The organization built on the work of activists in other cities, and in September 1932 it invited Fannie B. Peck of Detroit to serve as the principal speaker at its mass meeting. According to the *Pittsburgh Courier,* Peck had helped the Detroit Housewives League enlist 8,000 black consumers as members.[7]

Health and Education

The struggle for better health care and education and equal access to public services of all kinds reinforced the fight for better jobs, entrepreneurial opportunities, consumer and labor rights, and respect. When activists launched the Pittsburgh chapter of the National Negro Congress, they by no means limited its agenda to labor unions and workplace issues.[8] From its inception, the local NNC set up two committees: one to deal with the exclusion of black teachers from the Pittsburgh public schools, and the other to address discrimination against blacks at the Tuberculosis League's hospital in the city. For its part, the ULP health committee regularly described Pittsburgh's African American community as the "cynosure of all our large urban centers, both as to morbidity and mortality," as well as the site of "obsolete physical equipment, archaic scientific appliances and poorly qualified leadership." In 1934, at the ULP's annual meeting held at the German Evangelical Lutheran Church at 620 Smithfield Street, the principal speaker was Dr. C. Howard Marcy, medical director of the Tuberculosis League, located on Bedford Avenue. Marcy had directed the Tuberculosis League's recent health survey, and his talk, titled "Unrecognized Health Hazards," promised to "arouse Pittsburgh to the dire necessity of concerted action in combatting the many menacing conditions affecting the health of Negroes of the Hill District and other congested areas" in the city.[9]

Among its priorities during the Depression, the Urban League's health committee investigated the growing demand for a hospital to serve the escalating health care needs of the city's black population. Although African Americans had launched the all-black Booker T. Washington Hospital and Nurse Training School in 1912, this facility apparently faded out just before the onset of the Great Migration during and after World War I. Throughout the 1920s, the ULP had established committees to study the feasibility of setting up a black hospital, but this movement failed to gain traction. During the 1930s, however, some proponents of better health care for black residents justified the call for an African American hospital on the premise that other cities with large black populations had taken this step, including Chicago, Philadelphia, New York, Los Angeles, Atlanta, and Washington, DC. Moreover, an estimated 95 percent of Pittsburgh's black community consulted black rather than white physicians. Yet some 83,000 blacks in Allegheny County were "without adequate hospital facilities as compared with other groups." The committee chair identified "a Negro controlled hospital as the most urgent need of our people in Pittsburgh." Although board members believed it would be "more democratic having the Negro placed" in existing hospitals, they "doubted" that this could or would be done. Thus, the board approved a motion to establish a committee "to study the most practical adoption of a hospital for Negroes for both training and other purposes."[10]

Because blacks accounted for 85 percent of patients at the city's Passavant Hospital, some proposed transforming this facility into an all-black hospital employing black doctors and nurses. Proponents of this idea argued that white Pittsburgh was already "over hospitalized," while African Americans were extremely underserved by area hospitals.[11] By the beginning of World War II, according to the ULP's education secretary, the number of trained African American nurses had increased to twenty-five, but only fourteen of them reported "regular" employment. Furthermore, despite black nursing students' admission to training programs, the medical establishment continued to bar graduates from viable employment in the city's hospitals and clinics.[12] Although the movement to establish black hospitals succeeded in other cities, it failed in Pittsburgh, and Urban League officials repeatedly expressed fear of the long-term impact of setting up a "Jim Crow" hospital facility in the city.[13]

Perhaps most important, Moss impressed on board members the significant differences between Pittsburgh and other cities with large black communities, such as New York's Harlem, which had two black hospitals —Harlem Hospital (Municipal for Colored) and Lincoln Hospital (Private Colored Training School). Moss emphasized that Pittsburgh's African

American community was geographically dispersed and, unlike Harlem, lacked a large central concentration of people and resources. Thus, the ULP's emphasis on integrating blacks into the predominantly white social service organizations that already existed seemed better suited to the needs of Pittsburgh's black community than a variety of parallel institutions. Thus, only with the escalation of the modern black freedom movement during and after World War II would African Americans gain greater access to established medical institutions as patients, students, physicians, and nurses in Pittsburgh and western Pennsylvania.

Tom Barton, the league's former industrial secretary, returned to the Urban League after earning a law degree from the University of Pittsburgh. Following employment with the region's Unemployment Board of Review, he was appointed the assistant city solicitor in 1938 and later became president of the Urban League board (serving from 1942 to 1952). At a March 1941 meeting of the board, shortly before he assumed duties as president, Barton reported for the health committee that the city of Pittsburgh (later corrected to read a subcommittee of the City Council) had approved $10,000 to repair the old municipal hospital building to be used as a health clinic for the Hill District (presumably for blacks). The plan would provide clinical training for black physicians under the supervision of University of Pittsburgh doctors. When asked "if this did not mean that ultimately we would have a segregated hospital," board member Dr. Carroll said, "The ultimate objective of the Hospital Association was, first, the gradual integration of Negro doctors into the hospitals as they now exist, and, second, an Inter-racial hospital manned by Negroes under the supervision of white physicians." Barton added that the groundswell of popular support for the facility among young black doctors precluded any objection to the plan. As he put it, "We have waited too long to protest, that young Negro physicians have gone to [the City] Council and asked for this clinic." He then suggested that the ULP "get these young Negro physicians together who have been most vitally interested and try to sell them on our point of view"—that is, opposition to a racially segregated black hospital. The board then approved a motion to set up a subcommittee to meet with the young black physicians, "to the end that the danger of an ultimately segregated set-up is avoided."[14]

The ULP's April 1941 report offers a detailed discussion of the black hospital movement and the league's determination to block the development of an all-black hospital. Nevertheless, the city transferred white patients out of the old facility and made plans to transform the old building into a health clinic for blacks in the Hill District. The local press described the proposed facility as one for "Negro patients and a place where Negro physicians could be trained." But the ULP was determined to block the "creation of a Jim Crow institution supported by tax funds." Both the Urban League and NAACP noted that although no racial language appeared in the ordinance creating the health clinic in the Hill District, no blacks were employed in the city's new (white) facility. Thus, both organizations predicted that a racially segregated hospital would result. Opponents of the plan requested and were granted a public hearing on the matter by the City Council (scheduled for 9 April 1941). The ULP and the NAACP lamented plans for a Jim Crow facility "at the very time we are seeking to end discrimination in those . . . which already exist."[15] Following the public hearing on the hospital issue, the City Council moved forward with its plans. For its part, the ULP reiterated its policy of nondiscrimination and its opposition to the use of tax dollars to support racially segregated institutions. The league also approved a resolution to launch an education campaign to deepen public support for desegregation of the city's medical establishment.[16]

A somewhat similar but more successful story emerged in the fight for equal access to public education in the city of Pittsburgh. In his annual report for 1933, issued during the celebration of the ULP's fifteenth anniversary, Moss emphasized the agency's shift toward organizing for greater and equal access to education. As he described it, the ULP took part in developing "a community-wide approach to the question of the relation of the Negro to the public educational system of the city. As an outgrowth of the Urban League's roundtable in December of 1931 has grown the Citizens' Committee on Public Education composed of the representatives of every live organization among Negroes in the city."[17] He was referring to a December 1931 meeting in the offices of the Chamber of Commerce to discuss African American grievances with the Pittsburgh public schools. That gathering enabled African Americans to voice their dissatisfaction with a broad range of educational issues, including the routine placement of black students in a narrow range of vocational or trade courses rather than a college preparatory or highly skilled "practical arts" curriculum, the exclusion of black women from nursing and medical schools, and a long-standing ban on the employment of black teachers in the public schools. Following that meeting, the Citizens' Committee on Public Education was created, a thirty-five-member body comprising men and women "from every walk of life in the Negro community—civic, fraternal, professional, and church." Over the next several months, the committee utilized graduate students from the University of Pittsburgh and Duquesne University to conduct studies of various phases of African American education in the city, organized public debates on the integration of black teachers into the public schools, compiled lists of professional men and women prepared to serve as vocational counselors to black students, and pledged to devote even more time and energy to eradicating "inequities" in the city's educational system.[18] Moss announced the formation of a "steering committee" to formulate a plan for desegregating the Pittsburgh public schools and hiring black teachers and counselors. He aimed to select committee members "representing a cross section of the thought of the community" and touching "all phases of our fraternal, civic and social life," including long-time property owners as well as new residents and parents of black school-children. Committee members included attorney Richard F. Jones, the Reverend B. F. Glasco of the Presbyterian church, and labor activist and writer Ernest Rice McKinney.[19]

In the summer of 1930 the branch contacted the Tuskegee and Hampton Institutes to secure the names of potential black vocational schoolteachers for the Pittsburgh school system. Dr. Leavitt, associate superintendent of schools, promised to cooperate with the effort to integrate black students into the public schools' vocational training classes. Members of the ULP met with representatives from the state employment office and YMCA to coordinate job-placement efforts; they created a standard registration form and centralized applicant and placement lists. The industrial relations secretary also convened a meeting of "industrial field workers" in the city, including representatives of the YWCA, the state employment service, and the ULP, and produced an agreement to adopt a common reporting form and to meet biweekly to discuss the results of their work.

The industrial department held a joint meeting with the education committee to address the issue of vocational training for black youth. Lett interviewed Leavitt and Dr. Anthony Goldberg of the University of Pittsburgh and visited the Arsenal, Bellefield, and Connelly Trade Schools to advance movement on vocational training for black youth. Lett also reported on job-placement efforts, including three orders that were not filled "because of the ridiculously low wages offered" and one client who "wanted white help."[20] At about the same time, under the general leadership of education secretary Marechal-Neil Ellison Young, the scholarship committee launched a variety of fund-raising drives to benefit the education of black children. In addition, the interracial committee, which had more than 100 members and was headed by Winnifred Moss, wife of the executive director, was committed "to increas[ing] opportunity of Negro youth for higher training." The committee had contributed about $350 over the past year to promising students. On one occasion, the scholarship committee, chaired by John B. Coyne, sponsored an elite concert at the Stephen Foster Memorial Hall on Forbes Avenue.[21]

Both the Urban League and the NAACP lined up behind newly elected black state representative Homer Brown to fight for equal access to education. As historian Adam Cilli notes, Brown "turned first and often to the ULP industrial secretary William Hill" for advice on employment policies affecting African Americans. Working closely with Brown, the local branch office and the NAACP secured the establishment of a special legislative committee charged with investigating racial discrimination and injustice in the Pittsburgh public schools. Based on the committee's findings, the state ordered the Pittsburgh public schools to desegregate its workforce and hire black teachers.[22]

The movement to desegregate Pittsburgh's public schools gained national interracial support through the endorsement of the National Education Association (NEA). In 1936 the NEA approved a resolution entitled "Democracy in the Profession" that stated: "Teachers of equivalent training and experience doing the same kind of work should receive equal pay regardless of sex. Teachers should not be discriminated against because of race, color, belief, residence, or economic or marital status." In March 1937 the ULP's education committee enthusiastically reported the employment of "two Negro teachers" in the Pittsburgh public schools. The NEA's support, the league believed, helped produce "an entire change of attitude on the part of the School Board towards appointment of Negro teachers." The employment of black teachers paved the way for the ULP to focus on the search for "properly qualified applicants, who can make the first grade in the necessary examinations," and to identify "especially qualified High School students" and urge them "to prepare themselves for teacher work."[23] In the late 1920s and early 1930s the ULP's home and school visitor program emphasized work with the juvenile justice system. During the 1930s, however, this program's emphasis shifted from "investigating truancy and its causes to motivating" young people "to aspire to a wide range of career options" after graduating from high school. At a February 1931 meeting, the board moved to replace Georgine Pearce as visiting teacher, a post she had held for eight years. The committee recommended Virginia Pangburn, former head of "Colored Work" at the McKeesport YWCA, to replace Pearce. Under the leadership of education secretary Marechal-Neil Young, a graduate of the University of Pennsylvania with a degree in sociology and social sciences, the home and school visitor program emphasized raising money for college scholarships for African American students from poor and working-class families.[24]

A year after the hiring of the city's first black teachers, at the ULP's request the Pittsburgh Board of Education convened a meeting of all the city's high school guidance counselors "to consider the problem of counseling among Negro pupils." In 1931 Daisy Lampkin had chaired a roundtable discussion at which Robert Vann had called for black counselors in the schools and a revised curriculum that was sensitive to black history and culture "because the colored students in the local high schools are taught along the educational lines adapted to the white students only."[25] Following the appointment of black teachers, the twin projects of hiring black counselors and expanding opportunities to study African American history proceeded apace. In the fall of 1933 Urban League fellow Howard G. Gould offered the league's first community-based class, "Negro History and Achievement," at the Larimer School in the city's East End. The course attracted some twenty-two students, lasted fourteen weeks, and explored the black experience from African roots to recent times. As such, the course claimed to survey the "entire known history of the Negro race."[26]

In collaboration with the Pittsburgh Board of Education, the Urban League organized a conference of personnel administrators from the major industries and vocational guidance counselors to discuss how to close the gap between promising black high school graduates and access to jobs in the changing urban economy of the Depression years.[27] As it did for most of its groundbreaking social service programs, the organization secured the promise of a visit from the national leadership, but landing T. Arnold Hill for this event proved especially challenging. Hill canceled his scheduled attendance at this historic meeting at the eleventh hour, claiming that an unforeseen conference in Washington, DC, took precedence over the Pittsburgh visit. Moss pointedly disagreed and apparently prevailed on Hill to reconsider and make an appearance in Pittsburgh to advance the goals of the local and national offices and avoid "a most unfortunate and embarrassing situation if forced to cancel this program."[28] The education department opened a vocational guidance program for "out-of-school" black youth that combined the ULP's counseling services with those of the Herron Hill Community Center under the direction of George Culberson. Together, these entities helped students with testing, books, supplies, course selection, college applications, and training opportunities.[29] As World War II got under way, the ULP reported the first use of black speakers in the city's Vocational Opportunity Campaign.[30]

Wartime Programs

As World War II loomed, the Urban League of Pittsburgh took a hand in shaping the March on Washington movement (MOWM). It enhanced the struggle for equal employment opportunities for African Americans and tied the league's agenda even more closely to governmental labor, social welfare, and even military projects. Under the leadership of A. Philip Randolph and the Brotherhood of Sleeping Car Porters, local chapters of the MOWM had emerged in Pittsburgh and other major cities by June 1941. In Pittsburgh and elsewhere, local branches of the Urban League joined forces with the NAACP, churches, fraternal orders, and other organizations to give substance to the threat of a massive march on the nation's capital if President Franklin Delano Roosevelt failed to end racial discrimination in the defense industries. When Roosevelt relented and issued Executive Order 8802, outlawing racial discrimination by firms with government contracts, and set up the Fair Employment Practices Commission (FEPC) to carry out its mandate, the ULP intensified its quest for employment, housing, and other opportunities for the city's black population.[31] Urban League secretaries from forty-six cities convened in Pittsburgh in the fall of 1942 and declared "positively that they wanted the Negro to play his full part in the entire war effort—that they wanted all types of discrimination based on race or color lifted." In a reference to World War I, they asserted that "the Negro must not become the post-war beggar again."[32] Under the leadership of industrial secretary Reginald Johnson, the branch worked with the NUL in a nationwide movement to register "every unemployed Negro worker in the country, including the unskilled, professional, and clerical." Johnson had joined the Urban League staff following the departure of William Hill in 1937. T. Arnold Hill of the NUL had offered a ringing endorsement of Johnson, noting that he had followed Johnson's career for nearly ten years, through Johnson's tenure as an assistant with the Minneapolis Urban League, industrial secretary at the St. Louis Urban League, and executive secretary of the Atlanta Urban League. Johnson also served as the NUL's representative at National Recovery Administration hearings, including preparing "a brief on Negro labor" for use at these hearings.[33]

With Johnson at the helm of the industrial relations office, the Urban League urged unemployed black workers in Pittsburgh to register at any state employment office. This registration effort was part of the ULP's ninth annual Vocational Opportunity Campaign, lasting from 15 March to 15 April 1941. The state employment offices would be in charge of referring workers to defense industry jobs as some 600,000 men answered the call to military duty after 1 July. Nondefense work would also be handled by the state employment offices. The campaign included the vocational guidance film *Your Future,* featuring African Americans.[34]

Under the leadership of industrial secretary George E. DeMar (Reginald Johnson's successor), the branch helped black workers challenge the color line in Pittsburgh's labor market. In preparation for their expanding role in the nation's defense program, Moss announced the upcoming visit of economist and New Deal administrator Robert Weaver to the city. Also discussed was the recent formation of the East Boro Negro Council to address the needs of blacks employed in the defense industries. At an October 1940 meeting at Grace Memorial Church, called by the NAACP and the ULP, attorney Homer Brown opened the discussion by stressing the need for accurate information about the defense plans of the city, county, state, and nation. Moss became part of the interim committee to devise a plan of work.[35]

"The National Defense Program," the ULP's June 1941 report stated, "has increased the activity of this division. Its function is to place Negroes in jobs." But the defense program also emphasized a commitment "to eliminate prejudice toward the Negro in defense, building and other projects." Thus, the ULP moved swiftly to document cases of racial discrimination and exclusion and helped black workers file complaints regarding unfair employment practices. Working closely with DeMar, black men and women filed numerous affidavits with the FEPC.[36] Harold Parker testified to the FEPC that the American Bridge Company would not allow blacks to fill out applications for available jobs. Parker was permitted to submit an application only after he complained, but the interviewer commented, "It will do you no good."[37] In her affidavit, F. Marie Thompson declared, "The very name 'Dravo' and 'American Bridge' spell discrimination to me . . . and a colored man know better than ask for a job of the lowest type at *either firm*." She reported trouble gaining access to training as a welder, with the common excuse that "they did not have lockers, etc. for the [colored] women." Thompson protested, "We are supposed to sweep and mop and buy *war bonds,* etc. and work at night, while the white women get daytime shifts. Our boys are getting killed in the *day* as well as at *night*."[38]

Along with advocacy for black men, the ULP pushed to place black women in skilled wartime jobs, arguing that "Negro women are American workers too." League officials applauded black male workers' support for the movement to hire black women at the American Bridge Company. The men delivered a signed petition to the company, calling for the training and employment of black women in skilled jobs at the firm, concluding that "Negro women . . . can do other jobs besides clean lavatories. They should be in production, too."[39]

In a letter to Lawrence Cramer of the FEPC and the War Manpower Commission, DeMar complained of discrimination against black women at the Pennsylvania Railroad, Carnegie-Illinois Steel Corporation, and H. J. Heinz Company. Carnegie-Illinois policy called for new black and white employees to perform the arduous job of "jamb-cutters," with the understanding that they would shortly be moved to other less strenuous labor; however, the company forced black women to work long term in this capacity. Several black women were fired when they protested such treatment. For its part, Heinz refused to accept skilled black workers trained at the government's National Youth Administration (NYA) schools. In a letter to Heinz, Moss expressed profound dismay that "competent trained individuals should be refused placement under present conditions because of the source of their training." Although the president of Heinz declared that the company was "not averse to employing graduates of the NYA schools," he insisted that its employees needed special training and certification by the Pittsburgh Board of Education. Thus, Heinz bluntly informed Moss, "we must insist that they follow the procedures outlined" for employment at the company.[40]

In addition to documenting widespread patterns of discrimination against black men and women in the defense industries, DeMar gathered data on wartime firms that employed black workers with satisfactory results. T. A. Reynolds, superintendent of McConway and Tarley Company, reported that "Negroes are good workers and quite as satisfactory as the white. Some now employed in the plant have seen twenty years of service." At Hubbard and Company, paymaster J. R. Mullen described black workers as "very good especially since the loosening of the labor market." C. A. Peterson, employment supervisor at the American Steel and Wire Company, said, "The average Negro at the plant is faithful, reliable and is highly skilled as is the average white and his wage is quite high. . . . The Negroes at the plant are mostly skilled men, probably the best of the whole force and are respected workers who stick to their jobs." Although some managers limited their praise to certain kinds of labor, most of the comments accented blacks' ability to perform well in a variety of jobs across several occupational categories and types of businesses, including grocers, hotels, and bus and rail lines.[41]

The wartime ULP also continued its efforts to organize black workers into labor unions to fight the persistence of discrimination. As noted earlier, in line with a National Urban League initiative, the branch had already established a local Workers' Council. In 1940 the organization conducted a survey of council members regarding years of service in their trades and their experiences with white union officials and rank-and-file workers. Most of the men reported more than twenty years' residence in Pittsburgh, and some reported working in their trades even longer, having entered their specialties before arriving in Pittsburgh. Nearly all the men surveyed supported unionization, and with only one exception, they had never served as strikebreakers. However, the men uniformly justified strikebreaking as a means of securing employment in the face of the discriminatory policies of organized white labor. The group included carpenters, painters, cement finishers, plasterers, brick masons, and plumbers. Some of these men had paid union dues and carried union cards either in the Pittsburgh region or elsewhere, including Ohio and West Virginia.[42]

In February 1942 the ULP held a meeting, chaired by the industrial secretary, to revitalize interest in the Pittsburgh Workers' Council. It was attended by eight workers in the building trades. The ULP noted the "difficulties the council had faced in the past two years in coordinating their activities toward breaking down prejudice of AFL unions and of building contractors." To stimulate greater interest in its work, the ULP suggested the formation of local clubs along craft lines—particularly carpenters, painters, and bricklayers.[43]

The wartime Urban League also pushed for better housing for African Americans in general and for war workers in particular. In February 1943 the local office demonstrated that all war workers, black and white, confronted challenges in finding suitable housing for themselves and their families. However, it underlined blacks' struggle to find housing that met their needs under the heading "The Negro Worker's Housing Worry." Although vacancies had increased in some parts of the city to accommodate the growing number of white war workers, blacks continued to face a housing shortage. In November 1942 the local Homes Registration Office terminated its work filling vacancies in the private housing market and focused exclusively on serving the needs of war workers under the new federal Housing Center of the National Housing Agency. It submitted a list of fifty-nine families—all of them black—whose applications for housing had not been filled. As the Pittsburgh Housing Association (PHA) put it, there seemed to be "only a grim [housing] outlook for the Negro worker."[44]

In May 1944, at a dinner meeting of the industrial relations committee, Wilson S. Borland, executive director of the PHA, reported that blacks occupied 15,000 homes in the city; 56 percent of those homes were designated "substandard facilities," and 23 percent required major repairs. In a survey of the most dilapidated housing, Borland noted that about 75 percent of the dwellings occupied by blacks were deemed unfit for human habitation. Moss repeatedly underscored the persistence of discriminatory housing practices, despite the wartime emergency and the drive to construct housing at government expense. "Some agencies refuse to rent to Negro people," he noted. He related the story of "a house on Sachem Way [that] recently caught fire. . . . Three years [earlier] . . . the house was purchased by an individual who in turn split the house into apartments and rented these to some eight or nine families." Over that three-year period, the owner collected more in rents than he had paid for the building. Moss underscored the city's failure to enforce safety and health codes and to inform black tenants of their rights under municipal building and housing laws.[45]

Following the outbreak of large-scale racial violence in Detroit and other cities in 1943, the ULP intensified its efforts to prevent violence and build peaceful race relations in Pittsburgh. Addressing black-white tensions had been part of the agency's ongoing agenda during the inter-war years, and these efforts accelerated during World War II. Partly due to the influence of the Pittsburgh branch and other African American and interracial organizations, the Pittsburgh Chamber of Commerce spear-headed the formation of the Allegheny County Race Relations Commit-tee. As the war came to a close in 1945, the committee issued a report underscoring the combustible state of social relations in Pittsburgh "on account of race, color, creed, and birth." It also advanced a comprehen-sive set of recommendations designed to end racial discrimination in employment, housing, health, education, and other social services that foreshadowed the goals of the city's postwar black freedom movement.[46]

Turnover and Discrimination within the Urban League

The Pittsburgh branch made immense contributions to social service and social justice reform in western Pennsylvania against the backdrop of bud-get cuts and regular changes in its own roster of professional employees. In relatively rapid succession, the branch hired new industrial relations secretaries—Lett, Hill, and Johnson. Then in 1941 Reginald Johnson requested a sixty-day leave of absence to take a job with the NYA. In March 1945 Edwin C. Berry, the ULP's community organization secretary, announced plans to leave Pittsburgh to become executive secretary of the new Portland, Oregon, branch of the Urban League. Berry had joined the ULP in 1935 and shortly thereafter became its recreation secretary and later community organization secretary. During his stay in Pittsburgh, Berry played a pivotal role in the creation and development of Camp James Weldon Johnson. More than 700 black children took part in activities at the camp in 1938 alone. Under Berry's leadership, instructors trained at the camp were later employed in eleven "mix[ed] and Negro camps" in the region. The *Courier* also credited Berry's work on the ULP's Vocational Opportunity Campaign. Based on his work for the league, Berry was appointed to the mayor's Advisory Committee on Recreation. He was also a member of the Association of Negro Social Workers, American Camping Association, and Hill District Community Council. At the time of Berry's departure, the ULP's industrial secretary, Charles W. Washington, and community organization secretary, Edgar Wright Flood, had been with the league for less than a year.[47]

Influential black women staffers also left Pittsburgh for other cities. Gertrude Tanneyhill, assistant industrial relations secretary, took a position with the Brooklyn, New York, Urban League. Tanneyhill, the *Courier* reported, "was quite prominent in the fight for employment of Negro operators by Pittsburgh Railways Company, the battle for an FE[P]C with enforcement powers, the use of Negro women in Pittsburgh war industries, and the defense of Ralph Johnson," a black man facing extradition to the South on criminal charges, even though a Pennsylvania court had exonerated him. As able black leaders left the ULP, however, other capable blacks moved to Pittsburgh and replaced them. When Tanneyhill departed for Brooklyn, Leroy Kirkland Irvis replaced her as assistant industrial relations secretary. Originally from Albany, New York, Irvis had most recently been head of war production training for the Baltimore branch of the Urban League. He quickly moved up to assume the job of public relations secretary. In the meantime, the ULP appointed Louis Mason, who had a degree in biology and was considered a "blueprint and industrial plant operations expert," to the post of assistant industrial relations secretary. Mason came to Pittsburgh from the Urban League of

St. Paul, Minnesota, where he had gained "the confidence of both AFL and CIO" union leaders.[48]

Despite the organization's tremendous achievements during depression and war, internal disagreements and gender discrimination within the Urban League movement did not disappear. For instance, the ULP took a position against a local fair employment law, believing that pursuit of a local law would divert efforts from state and national movements for fair employment laws. The ULP cited the views of attorney Thomas Barton, who based his position on the opinion of a group of lawyers, including African American attorney Homer S. Brown, convened by the American Civil Liberties Union.[49]

Within the ULP, black women staffers and volunteers were the backbone of the organization's fund-raising efforts and provided the bulk of its day-to-day social services, yet they faced entrenched patterns of gender bias. In her column in the *Pittsburgh Courier,* Julia B. Jones commented on the career of Grace Lowndes upon her retirement, lamenting that Lowndes had not received the public recognition she deserved for her contributions to hundreds of black families in the city. Jones concluded that Lowndes represented the genesis of the Urban League in Pittsburgh. "Her famous civic units . . . Pittsburgh's first food and fashion show. . . the dynamic Women's Auxiliary . . . Grace discovered the problems, worked them out, and after a solution she would pass them on to other groups to continue." Lowndes "lived a beautiful life in this community."[50]

Following the NUL's annual conference in 1938, Moss solicited input about gender discrimination from all ULP attendees at the gathering at Green Pastures in rural Michigan. Christina Jeffries noted that the gender gap was a nationwide problem, not just a local Pittsburgh issue. She declared that the 1938 meeting was "the first time" the NUL had given "the clerical workers an opportunity to lift their voices and say what they thought they were entitled to and what they thought of the executives, etc." Jeffries noted that among the ten cities represented at the conference, only nineteen clerical workers were present. During a closed session of clerical workers, she discovered that "some of them were not permitted to have contact with their Board members and in some instances they were barred from Staff meetings." Jeffries stated that, compared with many of her counterparts in other cities, Pittsburgh clerks were "not discriminated against" and were "well paid." The clerical workers also discussed whether to join unions and concluded that they had "the right to join if we so desired," although, Jeffries said, "we did not advocate it."[51] Even so, the ULP's black women staffers were paid significantly lower salaries than their male counterparts. During the 1930s, the top male staffers earned annual salaries of $2,700 to $3,600, while the highest paid woman received 1,000 less.[52] Notably, Jeffries had a BS in business education and an MA in sociology and had done substantial course work toward a PhD in social work at the University of Pittsburgh. She managed the financial affairs of the organization and once served as interim executive director of the Pittsburgh branch. Yet, despite her extraordinary capabilities, education, training, and long years of experience, racial and gender barriers blocked her access to leadership positions, such as department head or executive director, of the organization.[53]

Community Building and Conflict

The Urban League of Pittsburgh sometimes helped reinforce class divisions within the African American community. Despite its commitment to equal opportunity for African Americans on government construction projects, the ULP supported a strict, class-based tenant selection process for residence in Pittsburgh's public housing communities. The selection process of the Housing Authority of the City of Pittsburgh (HACP) mandated that all tenants, but especially blacks, meet certain prevailing sociological conceptions of "normal" family structures and "social mores." Accordingly, the HACP limited access to public housing to conventional "double-headed, man, wife, and children" families or other approximate "family groups." This policy excluded single-headed households from consideration. The tenant selection criteria also included proof of income and citizenship status, as well as an assessment of applicants' current housing conditions, which involved visits to prospective residents' homes. In addition, a series of detailed questions was designed to ascertain the so-called moral character of applicants. In other words, the HACP diligently worked to exclude families with a "record of immorality or crime."[54] Moreover, under the HACP's guidelines, only 20 percent of occupants could be receiving government relief, which denied access to some of the neediest members of poor and working-class communities.[55]

Despite ongoing social, political, and cultural conflict, the Urban League of Pittsburgh forged programs designed to bridge differences within the African American community as well as the chasm between blacks and whites. One of the organization's signature community-building events was its Community Sing, sponsored by the *Pittsburgh Courier* and the civic department of the Urban League. It featured a 1,000-voice choir, "allied church choirs," and "a massed orchestra of 200 pieces." Staged at Greenlee Field, owned by Negro League entrepreneur Gus Greenlee, this event also brought together Pittsburgh's staid black elite and the underground world of black numbers runners, gamblers, and sex workers. The *Courier* described Greenlee Field as "an ideal setting for the cultural expression of the group," where "thousands of participants and observers" will witness "the novel spectacle of a giant choir and massive orchestra responding in unison, as if by magic, to the weavings of the thin baton of the talented musical director, S. Nelson Arter." Moreover, the *Courier* reported, no registration or admission fees would be charged for participation in the Community Sing. "The gates of Greenlee Field will swing wide for all who wish to come. This has been made possible by the courtesy and interest of William A. Greenlee for whom the field is named."[56]

During the Depression and war years, the ULP intensified its synthesis of civil rights, political rights, and social service work on behalf of the city's black population. In collaboration with a variety of interracial and African American civil rights and political organizations, the Urban League helped secure passage of pivotal labor, housing, health, and education legislation and policies designed to desegregate Pittsburgh's social service system. The ULP's fair employment, fair housing, and school desegregation projects gradually opened the door to better jobs, better neighborhoods, and better public education for Pittsburgh's African American community. They also influenced the Urban League movement nationwide and helped fuel the rise of a new social service agenda focused on the resources of the nation's expanding welfare state. Most important, Pittsburgh's branch helped lay the groundwork for the emergence of the postwar modern black freedom movement, which increasingly challenged the city's racially segregated social order.[57]

Part III

The Modern Black Freedom Movement and Beyond

Artist Carlos F. Peterson depicts the violent uprooting of Pittsburgh's Lower Hill District in this photograph. The Urban League's programs both resisted and reinforced the spread of urban renewal projects in post–World War II Pittsburgh. (Courtesy of Carlos F. Peterson)

5

Combating Inequality in the Postwar City

Despite significant achievements during the interwar years, the Pittsburgh branch of the Urban League encountered the persistence and even intensification of racial inequality in the postwar urban political economy. Deindustrialization, urban renewal, neighborhood depopulation, and global economic restructuring reinforced the color line in mid-twentieth-century Pittsburgh. The Urban League emerged at the center of early efforts to offset the destructive impact of these local, national, and transnational developments on the city's African American community. The agency pressed employers and public officials to increase opportunities for African Americans in a broad range of skilled, clerical, and professional occupations and stimulated the growth of the black middle class. It also urged the organized white labor movement to actively recruit African American workers into unions and apprenticeship training programs on a nondiscriminatory basis. The struggle for jobs unfolded in tandem with the Urban League's fight for equal access to housing, health care, and education for the city's black community. The league's social service agenda increasingly converged with the massive grassroots civil rights movement and black power assaults on all facets of Pittsburgh's Jim Crow order. As such, the ULP would play a key role in the simultaneous expansion of the city's African American middle class and the fall of Jim Crow.

Fighting for Equal Employment Opportunities

A survey of race relations in Allegheny County in 1947 revealed an increase in the industrial employment of African Americans during World War II, but most firms employed "no Negroes in skilled capacities." Nearly 50 percent of the firms that did employ blacks "offered no training facilities" to upgrade their positions, and no blacks occupied supervisory, foreman, or office and personnel staff positions.[1] At about the same time, a governor's commission study reinforced the findings of the Allegheny County survey. "Job discrimination," the state study concluded, "increases progressively, being lowest at the unskilled level, rising for semi-skilled and skilled levels, and reaching a peak for office, engineering and sales occupations." The state study also concluded that "discriminatory employment practices were highest in Southwest Pennsylvania, 98% of the firms were found to discriminate."[2]

As the Cold War got under way, young black men increasingly turned to the military for training in the skilled trades, but they faced a chilly reception from employers upon their return to the civilian labor market. David E. Ellis encountered racial barriers despite being honorably discharged after four years of military training in computer technology.[3] After George Bolden graduated from the University of Pittsburgh in 1950 with a degree in mechanical engineering, he took a job at RCA in Camden, New Jersey, because no company in the Pittsburgh area would hire him.[4] In 1951 the ULP gave US Steel the "lowest grade" among employers because of its lack of "promotion of black workers into plant, office, and technical positions."[5] The Urban League also pinpointed destructive discriminatory practices among labor unions in the booming construction trades. Some black workers, the league reported, took jobs as "sub-employees" or "independent contractors" to circumvent racial restrictions imposed by white organized labor.[6]

Determined to combat the spread of economic inequality into the postwar years, the ULP increased pressure on employers, labor unions, and the state to employ and upgrade black workers in the changing global economy. In 1950, when executive director Alexander (Joe) Allen took charge of the ULP, it made the transition from a comprehensive social service agency "through which all social work for Negroes must be channeled" to one that employed the "skills, techniques, and philosophy of social work" to remove systemic racial barriers from all aspects of the urban political economy—particularly jobs, housing, education, and health services. The league's shift away from intensive casework methods had started on the eve of the Great Depression and accelerated through the 1930s and 1940s. It strove to improve the general employment climate so that "all workers" could "find jobs without the fear of discrimination because of race." In the health care field, the league moved away from "baby clinics" for black parents and worked with a variety of established health care agencies to ensure that black families were afforded equal access to all the services available to their white counterparts. The ULP prioritized "erasing the Negro's second-class citizenship" in all areas of life. It prodded a broad range of institutions "to provide the services they were in business to provide to all regardless of color."[7]

Influenced partly by the Urban League movement and ongoing social justice struggles, the 1947 Allegheny County survey of race relations strongly recommended "accelerated vocational training" for blacks in all skilled trades, corporate recognition of the "economic loss" resulting from the exclusion of black workers from the skilled trades and supervisory positions, and the active recruitment of blacks into unions on a "non-discriminatory basis."[8] After publication of the results of this survey, the ULP launched a variety of programs in relatively rapid succession designed to open doors for black professional, clerical, and business people. It also aimed to break the job ceiling and facilitate the movement of poor and working-class blacks into the skilled crafts and supervisory positions in the manufacturing sector. These efforts included the launch of the Pilot Placement Project in 1948, the Defense Manpower Project in 1951, and the Management Council in 1958.[9]

The Pilot Placement Project became the center of the ULP's employment-related efforts during this period. Previously, the league had focused on placing poor and working-class blacks in a variety of jobs in the manufacturing and corporate sectors and gradually moving them up the ladder into more highly skilled technical and professional posts. The Pilot Placement Project, based on an idea suggested by Charles S. Johnson of Fisk University, acknowledged the failure of this earlier strategy. In the past, the ULP had urged well-educated and highly trained African Americans to take jobs for which they were overqualified and demonstrate through persistence and excellence that they deserved to be promoted into positions that were commensurate with their experience and expertise. In reality, however, these skilled and knowledgeable African Americans languished in lower-echelon posts for years—and sometimes for their entire working lives—without upward movement. In a talk before a Homewood-Brushton audience, the ULP's assistant director of industrial relations, Irving Finley, underscored this point: "We have information in our office of men who have been employed for eighteen or more years on the same job in various local industries. We also have information [on] . . . job lines which are in effect in a number of local industries. These jobs lines are designed so that Negro workers can progress but so far, regardless of their ability or 'years of employment.'"[10]

Accordingly, the Pilot Placement Project encouraged employers to hire skilled and professional blacks in appropriate positions from the start, but mainly as an experiment to determine how well they performed. Assuming that their performance proved satisfactory, their presence would operate as a wedge, opening the door for the hiring of other highly educated and trained blacks. As historians Guichard Parris and Lester Brooks explain: "Each of the placements was to be followed and noted, case-study fashion, to record the effects on (a) white workers associated for the first time with a black colleague; (b) the employer and his hiring practices; (c) the black 'pilot's' progress up the job ladder; (d) the black worker himself—the entering wedge for additional black placements."[11] Moreover, as an adviser to President Harry S. Truman's Committee on Government Contract Compliance, industrial relations secretary Richard Dowdy reinforced efforts to expand the corporate recruitment of "educated and technically trained" blacks for engineering and other occupations that had previously been filled almost exclusively by whites. Truman's executive order establishing the committee mandated an end to racial discrimination in employment by any firm conducting business under a federal government contract.[12]

Committed to its new strategy of job creation and upgrade for black workers, the ULP developed an extensive and diverse body of promotional literature and research on African American life and labor in the Pittsburgh metropolitan area. Designed to explain the league's mission, recruit allies for its programs advocating racial equity, and improve race relations, these materials included a special "labor and industry" issue of the *Pittsburgh Courier;* a *Business Week* essay on the work of the National Urban League; the publication of ULP data on black workers, prepared for the Ninth Annual Institute on Human Relations; and a powerful "Message to American Businessmen" penned by the Reverend Samuel M. Shoemaker, minister of Pittsburgh's Calvary Episcopal Church, calling for changes in racial policies and practices. In addition to mounds of written materials, correspondence via US mail, special luncheon meetings, and telephone contacts with area firms, the league maintained a full schedule of face-to-face meetings to improve employment opportunities for black workers. Emblematic of the group's energetic efforts to spread its message of equal opportunity, in 1955 representatives of the ULP met with "the major basic steel producers and fabricators; the five major department stores and other selected retail merchandizing outfits; two of the local operations of the airline industry; three food processors; the major petroleum, chemical and electrical machinery and equipment manufacturers; the various public utilities and the area's major atomic power research centers."[13]

In 1954 the ULP's industrial relations department organized a "management luncheon" featuring a talk by Julius A. Thomas, the NUL's industrial relations director and the individual with primary responsibility for the Pilot Placement Project. When Thomas arrived in Pittsburgh, he was exceedingly optimistic about the future of the pilot program. He had managed to convince General Electric to send recruiters to historically black colleges and universities (Howard University among them) and discover for themselves the enormous potential there. Other corporations soon followed suit, and the NUL's "Career Conferences" became a principal vehicle for recruiting African Americans for these new pilot projects. In his speech in Pittsburgh, Thomas described how the "nation's leading corporations" were "tapping the skilled and technical abilities of nonwhite workers," and he strongly encouraged closer NUL-ULP cooperation in "furthering this trend" in the Pittsburgh region. Some thirty personnel managers from the region's industrial and commercial businesses attended the event. That same year, the ULP launched a "skills registration month" campaign to expand its roster of "trained persons available" for its Pilot Placement Project. In 1955 alone, the agency provided more than 200 firms with current statistics on the economic status of blacks in Pittsburgh and the nation. The ULP also offered job counseling to nearly 300 individuals "seeking employment or upgrading opportunities."[14]

The fight for equal employment opportunities intensified following the passage of new state and local fair employment legislation in the mid to late 1950s. After the expiration of the federal FEPC in 1945, the ULP, NAACP,

United Steelworkers of America, and a variety of Jewish and Catholic agencies pushed for passage of a Pennsylvania fair employment law, proposed by African American state legislator Homer Brown.[15] In his opening statement introducing the bill, Brown quoted from the report that had led to a similar law in New York State: "Discrimination in opportunity for employment is the most injurious and un-American of all the forms of discrimination. To deprive any person of the chance to make a living is to violate one of the most fundamental of human rights." Pennsylvania governor Edward Martin and conservative Republican lawmakers roundly opposed the Brown measure. Martin and his colleagues argued that government should not and could not enact and enforce laws designed to create equal opportunity for black workers. As they put it, "You can't make equality by legislation." Instead, they claimed, "You can by education and other means, create a better feeling among the different races, religions and nationality groups."[16]

Urban League executive director Maurice Moss not only firmly endorsed the Brown bill but also supported the idea of some 2,000 supporters marching on the state capitol in Harrisburg to urge its passage. Over the next decade, the branch repeatedly argued that such legislation represented "an important legal and educational tool in the effort to eliminate racial barriers in employment."[17] New York enacted the first state fair employment law in 1945, but it took another ten years of struggle for Pennsylvania to follow suit. After enactment of the Pennsylvania law in 1955, the ULP recalled that it and "many other agencies and organizations" had supported the measure by attending scores of meetings in western Pennsylvania and in Harrisburg. Over a ten-year period, these efforts helped "interpret the importance of such legislation" to the larger community and facilitated its passage.[18]

The city of Pittsburgh enacted a municipal fair employment law in 1953, two years ahead of the state legislation. Although the ULP played a key role in the movement for a state-level fair employment law, executive director Moss and state legislator Brown opposed the movement for a Pittsburgh law. They strongly believed that such a local movement would undermine the statewide campaign. In its news bulletin *Facts*, attorney and president of the Urban League board Thomas E. Barton reinforced Moss's position. "Pressure for Federal and State legislation should not be diverted to work for a city ordinance," Barton said. Moreover, he concluded that local laws were "of very doubtful legality and, even if passed, would affect so limited an area."[19] Pittsburgh Housewives Guild president Alma Illery and labor activist Ben Careathers were not persuaded. They both forcefully argued that a municipal law would reinforce rather than detract from state and national movements for fair employment legislation.[20] Illery reported that she and all her "women supporters" would stand "behind any effort to secure local, State and Federal FEPC legislation." Careathers made the same point, declaring, "I favor the local law, absolutely, because I think . . . that it would lend strength to the fight to secure State and Federal FEPC legislation." A resolution passed by the Pittsburgh branch of the American Civil Liberties Union also called for the city to enact a law barring racial discrimination in employment.[21]

Passed in 1953 and 1955, respectively, city and state fair employment legislation banned employment discrimination based on "race, color, religion, creed, ancestry, age or national origin." The ULP increasingly pushed businesses to address economic inequality along the color line as a matter of law and justice rather than merely a question of conscience. In a report for the Commission on Manpower Utilization of the National Association of Intergroup Relations Officials, for example, the branch underscored its determination to use the new laws to strengthen its position in negotiations with employers and labor unions on issues of racial inequality. League publications, including its newsletter the *Informer,* also sought to influence the culture of corporate Pittsburgh by building relations with business schools in the area. In one issue, the *Informer* enthusiastically reported that the Carnegie Institute of Technology's School of Industrial Administration used Urban League research data on racial inequality in its courses for industrial executives.[22]

One by one, African Americans obtained production, skilled, clerical, and professional positions at Bell Telephone, the Pittsburgh Cracker Bakery (part of the National Biscuit Company), Steiner Manufacturing Company, and Jones and Laughlin Steel before the 1950s ended.[23] The ULP also celebrated the employment of a black engineer at Westinghouse, a black research chemist at US Steel's Monroeville research center, and a full-time black reporter at the *Pittsburgh Post-Gazette*. Regis Bobonis, the first African American to gain employment with the newspaper, later praised the league for opening the door to his employment and thanked the league "for all of the men selected for interviews, for its interest and . . . activities which helped to make" his appointment possible.[24]

As the 1960s got under way, the Pilot Placement Project played a key role in opening up clerical positions for black women in government and corporate offices outside the African American community. The ULP helped pave the way not only by hiring black secretaries in its own offices but also by offering secretarial training classes for black women.[25] The league took pride in placing black women in secretarial posts that had previously been off-limits to African Americans. In 1960 one of Arthur Edmunds's first acts as executive director was to place an accomplished young black woman—winner of the *Courier*–Urban League Guild's Best Potential Secretary Award—in a pilot placement job at Westinghouse Electric Company.[26] The national office lauded the ULP not only as an outstanding exemplar of the Urban League movement but also as a major influence on twentieth-century African American and American life and history. Hugh Price notes that the history of the Pittsburgh branch "reveals a portrait of a black community and its white allies" coming together to address the challenges of industrialization, urbanization, and "pervasive discrimination and *de facto* segregation in the North that, for so long, denied Black America access to the middle class."[27]

While the Urban League of Pittsburgh invested an extraordinary amount of energy into building strong corporate support for its programs, it also urged organized white labor to actively recruit black workers into unions on a nondiscriminatory basis. The organization pressured the Civil Rights Committee of the Allegheny County Labor Council and its constituent unions to open their doors to black painters, bricklayers, and electricians, to name just a few trades.[28] In 1950 the ULP documented discrimination against black workers in a variety of skilled construction trades and pledged to continue efforts to change these policies.[29] A year later, the ULP's industrial relations department applauded "three colored youth[s]" who completed apprenticeships in "meatcutting, tailoring, and upholstery."[30] The same year, the branch helped black taxi drivers process union grievances with the Yellow Cab Company, but the men filed a lawsuit before the union could resolve the issue. In 1954 the ULP's industrial relations director applauded Harold T. Calloway's acceptance into Local 458 of the Painters, Decorators, and Paper Hangers of America. Calloway's membership represented the first time the union had granted full, "unrestricted" membership to an African American. The ULP had worked closely with *Courier* columnist Harold Keith and Clarence Rogers, the manager of Belmar Gardens, a federally supported cooperative housing development on the city's East Side, to secure Calloway's admission, and it was working with other African American candidates for union membership in the building trades. At the same time, the ULP joined other intergroup agencies and worked with management and labor during "a crippling department store strike" to prevent practices "considered harmful" to black workers.[31] The following year, the ULP reported the admission of another fifteen black workers to the painters' union, and union representatives sought the league's help in reaching "other Negro painters employed by municipal and state agencies."[32]

Branch officials worked closely with African American company and union representatives to improve the position of black workers. Executive director Allen and industrial relations secretary Dowdy regularly collected black workers' grievances and passed them on to W. P. Young, a welfare worker at the Lockhart Iron and Steel Company in McKees Rocks and later Pennsylvania's secretary of labor and industry, and Boyd Wilson, member of both the ULP board and the international board of the United Steelworkers of America.[33] As noted earlier, Dowdy was also involved with Truman's Committee on Government Contract Compliance, charged with carrying out the federal mandate to end racial discrimination by companies and unions benefiting from government contracts. Dowdy regularly met with union officials as well as the director of education and training for US Steel and other firms and pushed for the admission of more African Americans to apprenticeship programs.[34] Even as it chipped away at the brick wall separating black and white labor, the ULP repeatedly urged blacks to join labor unions and become active participants in the labor movement. In his Homewood-Brushton talk, Finley urged blacks to deepen their participation in labor unions and use "grievance machinery" to further their own interests. By engaging in union activities and challenging inequality from within the house of labor, he suggested, black workers could overcome barriers to their progress up the job ladder and break the entrenched pattern of racial injustice, reinforced by discriminatory union and employer policies and practices.[35]

Expanding Access to Housing, Health Care, and Education

In the years after World War II, the ULP forged a new housing agenda designed to erase the color line in the metropolitan housing market. Efforts to combat the potentially destructive impact of urban renewal projects loomed large in the branch's postwar housing programs. These issues had engaged the league's attention even before Maurice Moss left the city in 1949 and moved to New York to serve as associate executive secretary of the National Urban League. Before his departure, Moss kept a close eye on urban renewal projects and the potential threat to African Americans. In a letter to his successor dated 9 March 1950, Moss confided that he believed Pittsburgh's economic and political elites were preparing to demolish the Lower Hill's poor and working-class black neighborhood through a calculated process of property acquisition and demolition, forcing African Americans out of the area. Writing to Allen "in the deepest of confidence," Moss urged him to discuss his ideas with Percival Prattis, the Urban League's representative on the Civic Unity Council's Standing Committee on Housing, "because he, of all the folks in Pittsburgh, would have an awareness about this sort of thing." Specifically, Moss wrote:

> As briefly as I can put it, here is my theorem: The Allegheny County Committee on Community Development is financed largely by Mellon and department store money. It desires to take over all of the planning for the future of Pittsburgh. The one planning body which it did not control was the Federation of Social Agencies. Certain of the Committee's leaders, a couple of years ago, announced a plan for clearing away the property between Fifth Avenue and Bigelow Boulevard and Sixth Avenue and Fullerton Street and rehabilitating it by erecting of a civic auditorium, parking facilities, etc. This would have been developed with private capital, with some governmental assistance through re-development program.
>
> The Mellon interests now own most of the land up to the Sixth Avenue boundaries. Above that line, the district is inhabited

by Negroes, Italians, Jews, Greeks, and Syrians. If they were to be displaced, other living quarters would have to be provided, and there just aren't any available spaces that convenient to the Golden Triangle.

Now who might be expected to protest such a displacement? The Urban League, because of the Negroes involved; the American Service Institute, because of other racial groups; the Community Councils and the Pittsburgh Housing Authority, for obvious reasons; and the Public Charities Association, because it has favored and promoted legislation in this area of human relations.

If my theory is correct then you have not heard the last of this with the compromise reached on last Wednesday, for these interests will not bide their time until a more auspicious period.[36]

Despite this sensitivity to the potential downside of urban renewal, the ULP increasingly viewed federally supported "slum clearance" as a vehicle for improving housing and job opportunities for the African American community. The 1954 Housing Act urged municipalities to develop work plans that incorporated citizen participation. Both the NAACP and the NUL urged local affiliates to use new legislation to empower their communities and advance their demands for equality on local projects. The ULP joined the local chapter of the NAACP, the *Pittsburgh Courier*, and other organizations in supporting the city's urban renewal plans, seeing this as an opportunity to demand new and better housing for black residents. State representative Homer Brown played a major role in securing passage of the program's enabling legislation. Pittsburgh's urban renewal program displaced some 5,400 families from the city's historic Lower Hill District, but it spurred the growth of African American neighborhoods in other parts of the city, most notably the East Side communities of Homewood-Brushton, East Liberty, and Larimer and others on the lower North Side.[37]

Similar to the fight for jobs, the ULP's housing efforts unfolded on the basis of new research on the status of postwar African Americans. In 1954 the league encouraged the city's leading newspaper, the *Pittsburgh Post-Gazette*, to publish an article on the "untapped housing market" among African American residents. Staff writer Albert W. Bloom underscored African Americans' growing economic capacity to purchase homes in the private housing market. To advance this goal, the report highlighted Mellon National Bank's interest in funding "a pilot project in cooperation with local builders." The ULP's housing committee, chaired by W. P. Young of the Lockhart Iron and Steel Company, conceptualized and proposed the project, collected and supplied the research data on minority housing issues, and "arranged for the family interview" featured in the *Post-Gazette* article. Despite the report's optimistic portrayal of African American income growth and home-ownership potential, the Urban League sadly concluded that there had been no major change in the "practice of restricting Negro home purchases to housing in neighborhoods where Negroes already live." The rapid growth of the city's black population made this restriction increasingly intolerable, the league reported, and the practice had already forced the creation of new sites of black residence outside city limits. Hence, in its quest for suitable housing for African Americans in the larger Pittsburgh metropolitan region, the ULP organized field trips for landowners, builders, and representatives of the Federal Housing Administration (FHA) to underscore the dire housing challenges confronting the city's black residents.[38]

At about the same time, the Urban League collaborated with the Pittsburgh Housing Association (PHA) and persuaded the Federal Housing Administration to study the precise "size and nature of the unmet housing need" among blacks living in Pittsburgh and Allegheny County. In consultation with the league's housing committee, economist Frank R. Mucha of the PHA directed the study. Mucha's study, the league reported, represented "the most valuable piece of current research on population and housing trends" among the city's black residents.[39] In 1957 a ULP study reiterated the role of racial barriers in limiting blacks' movement into better housing. An African American "seeking to buy a home or rent a dwelling in neighborhoods other than the traditionally 'Negro' areas is almost always met with resistance. Often this comes from white neighbors. More often it is evident in the fact that real estate brokers will not rent or sell a building to Negroes other than in the known 'Negro' or transitional areas." In October 1957, in testimony before the Joint Congressional Committee to Investigate Housing, Moss deplored racial discrimination in Pittsburgh's housing market and described its results as "criminally dangerous overcrowding in the scant housing available," creating "a vicious and threatening pattern of high rents (taken from low income), excessive disease rates, social maladjustments and crime."[40] Based on an assessment of 1960 data on housing in Pittsburgh, another study concluded that African American home owners and prospective home owners encountered what amounted to a racially discriminatory "color tax" in the city's real estate market.[41]

Building on the insights gained from this new research, the Urban League assaulted the discriminatory housing policies of banks, the real estate industry, and federal home financing agencies. The ULP also joined and often led the push for fair housing legislation, corporate and government support for new interracial housing construction projects, and shifts in the racial policies governing the city's public housing projects. Following the FHA study, the ULP invited housing pioneer Morris Milgram, builder of an interracial private housing community in suburban Philadelphia, to consult with home builders and civic organizations interested in creating a similar housing development in Pittsburgh. At the same time, the organization gave its support to a group of tenants seeking to build interracial housing cooperatives designed to improve both race relations and housing options for the city's black population.[42] As early as 1954, the branch had spearheaded the opening of Crestas Terrace in North Versailles, using FHA funding to build new private homes for blacks outside the central city.[43]

In the struggle to break down color barriers in the private housing market, the ULP joined the campaign for fair housing legislation. Until the city enacted its fair housing law in 1958, the league strengthened its network of influential white allies in the housing struggle, heightened its negotiations with the Pittsburgh Board of Realtors, and intensified day-to-day efforts to erase the color line one case at a time.[44] As director of the ULP's housing department, Leon Haley wrote a column for the *Pittsburgh Courier* calling attention to the housing needs of the African American community. Haley steered a middle path between arguments for "integrated" and "segregated" housing, emphasizing the quality of housing but accenting the limits on improvement in all-black areas.[45]

The ULP escalated its efforts to establish black middle-class neighborhoods where black home owners could maintain the residential character of their communities and prevent their inundation by the growing number of displaced renters and publicly subsidized housing projects for the poor. The branch turned to the neighborhood unit to support and reinforce the proliferation of black home owners and community groups, including those in Herron Hill and Schenley Heights, the East Liberty–Homewood League for Civic Improvement, and the Greater Pittsburgh Improvement League. Specifically, in 1955 the ULP facilitated the formation of the Homewood Civic Improvement Association, a group of African American home owners seeking to save their working- and middle-class neighborhood from a "depreciation of property values" caused by migration into the community from the Hill District and elsewhere. The branch joined the NAACP in supporting a variety of interracial housing developments, including two cooperative ownership projects in West Mifflin and North Braddock and others in Spring Hills and East Hills. In particular, it supported housing developments initiated by ACTION-Housing under the 1954 Housing Act and the FHA loan program, geared toward residents who did not qualify for public housing but could not afford to buy homes in the private housing market. The ULP also supported the Citizens Committee for Integrated Housing, an interracial alliance that pressed for an open housing law, which was passed in 1958. Shortly thereafter, a proliferation of "associations on racial equality" culminated in the Greater Pittsburgh Fair Housing Movement in 1966 and a revision of the city's fair housing law in 1967.[46]

Pittsburgh's real estate industry adamantly resisted efforts to place black home owners in previously all-white neighborhoods. In 1963 a developer denied black physician Oswald J. Nickens access to home ownership, in violation of the city's open housing law. Only by taking his case to court was Nickens able to occupy his home in an all-white area of the city. The ULP submitted a brief in defense of Nickens, joining a long list of organizations affiliated with the Pennsylvania Equal Rights League and the Allegheny County Council on Civil Rights. This document also contained an affidavit of support from attorney Wendell G. Freeland, a black Republican activist and former senior vice president of the NUL board of trustees and branch president. Similarly, William Russell Robinson, a former league employee, supported Nickens's case against the Stanton Land Company. The Allegheny Common Pleas Court ruled in Nickens's favor and ordered the developer to sell him a lot in the Stanton Heights development.[47] Similarly, the

ULP, the NAACP, and an interracial coalition of allies supported black realtor Robert R. Lavelle's case against the racially exclusionary polices of the Greater Pittsburgh Multilist, which barred African American membership and denied access to its property listings on the basis of race. The Western Pennsylvania Federal District Court ordered the Multilist to drop its racial bar and admit black realtors on an equal basis.[48] Thus, African American home-ownership rates gradually increased, but it was a slow and tedious process. The branch soon reported the first black home owner, a dentist, in Squirrel Hill and another in the all-white Stanton Avenue community. Although this case-by-case approach resembled the labor market pilot program, it was not discussed in these terms, partly because it came up hard against the despised practice of "blockbusting," which became a convenient mode of resisting African American access to the housing market.[49]

Beginning during the interwar years, the Pittsburgh branch of the Urban League increasingly emphasized the expansion of public housing projects to meet the needs of poor and working-class blacks. After World War II, this effort persisted and even intensified alongside the struggle for equal access to the private housing market. Through the 1950s, the ULP continued its work to obtain public housing for African Americans on an "open occupancy" and integrated basis. This work now included new projects built after the war: St. Clair Village on the South Side, Clairton Annex, Hayes Village in McKees Rocks, and Sharpe Terrace in Sharpsburg.[50] In 1950 the ULP, represented by P. L. Prattis, played an important role in the Civic Unity Council, which produced Bryn J. Hovde's study of changing migration and housing patterns in early postwar Pittsburgh. Hovde credited the ULP and other African American organizations for bringing the needs of poor and working-class blacks to his attention as he thought about the future of social services in the city. Hovde stated:

> The more I think of it, the more sure I am that a really professional job of research ought to be done on: 1) the subject suggested by Messrs. Prattis and Richard Jones, i.e., the effect of ghetto life on the Negro Spirit of Enterprise (in business, education, etc.). Some foundation should be willing to underwrite it. 2) An effort to determine at what proportion of Negro population do the manifestations of Ghettoization begin to dominate neigh-

borhood life. 3) A new "rental map" of the city by census tracts as soon as the full 1950 census reports are available. 4) A discreet, but thorough, investigation of the sources of opposition and aid to the opposition to public housing projects on the North and South Sides. The anatomy of the opposition must be known if combinations are to be prevented. 5) Maintenance of a running inventory of the Negro Housing Market. In this connection, nothing is more important than to follow the facts on discrimination against the Negro in employment.[51]

At about the same time, William P. Young chaired a special housing committee for the ULP and "persuaded" the Housing Authority of the City of Pittsburgh (HACP) and Allegheny County to desegregate public housing.[52] Under Young's leadership, the league's housing committee also emphasized strengthening contacts with Pittsburgh public housing authorities, urban redevelopment officials, and the Pittsburgh Human Relations Commission to shape "proposed urban redevelopment and urban renewal" plans for the city and county in the interest of the city's black community.[53]

Building on its interwar work, the ULP intensified its push for the full and equitable integration of blacks into the city's public housing projects. It moved against the earlier so-called checkerboard approach to integration, whereby African Americans and whites occupied homes in the same project but in racially segregated buildings. Under HACP director Hovde, African Americans gained access to public housing at a ratio that matched their proportion in the surrounding neighborhood. They also advocated for and received staff positions within the administrative and occupational hierarchy of the housing projects themselves. First Homer Brown and later Richard Jones served on the PHA board. As the need for public housing among blacks far outpaced the need among poor and working-class whites, the ULP produced a report advocating the termination of racial quotas so that blacks could occupy white housing units, where vacancies were nearly two times higher than in black units. Under housing director Al Tronzo, the city permitted more housing units to become predominantly black, despite the ULP's original hope to integrate them.[54]

The postwar fight for better housing was closely intertwined with the struggle for equal access to the city's health care system. In 1950 the branch transformed its community organization department into the health and welfare department and charged it with developing programs in health, education, recreation, and housing.[55] As it did for other aspects of postwar African American life, the agency pushed for up-to-date documentation of the status of blacks in the city's medical institutions. Postwar health surveys reinforced the league's vigorous push to erase the color line from the health field. In 1954, for example, under the leadership of David W. Kuhn, the ULP conducted its second comprehensive study of employment and training practices in hospitals in the Pittsburgh region. Somewhat in contrast to the employment and housing situations, the branch reported "a substantial trend toward broader opportunities in the four year period." Covering eighteen hospitals in 1950 and twenty-six in 1954, the study found an across-the-board increase in the number of African American registered nurses (from ten to nineteen), nurses' aides or practical nurses (from seven to eighteen), orderlies (from six to thirteen), staff physicians (from three to six), and resident physicians (from zero to one).[56] The 1954 report underscored the intensification of the ULP's work with the Hospital Council of Western Pennsylvania and its members to address racial disparities in "accommodations" for African American patients and "admission practices."[57] In the meantime, the league continued to press area hospitals to hire more African American doctors and nurses and improve access for African American patients. Gaines T. Bradford, director of the league's community services, also directed the league's health program during the 1950s. The health committee reported substantial cooperation from the medical establishment. In 1955 it optimistically reported, "In most instances, the influence of the committee, exerted through recognized and respected members of the medical profession, was sufficient to achieve the changes sought."[58]

Nonetheless, the ULP reported an uphill climb when it came to broadening African American access to the medical establishment. It was a long and arduous process. In fall of 1949, partly under pressure from the Pittsburgh branch "in cooperation with other agencies," one of the city's major hospitals "accepted its first Negro nursing student who was screened and referred by the Urban League." The report noted that this accomplishment "was one more step in an effort initiated more than three years ago by a special committee of the Urban League."[59] In 1950 the Civic Unity Council reported, "In truth, institutional care facilities for Negroes is lacking in all categories. There are no private institutions where Negro convalescents may go and only two for the Negro aged. Generally, they have to depend on public institutions of the Allegheny County Institution District."[60]

Into the early 1960s, the ULP documented the persistence of discrimination against the city's black physicians, clients, and potential medical school students. University of Pittsburgh professor and ULP board member Eric Springer declared that black doctors could quietly practice among black clients in their own neighborhoods, but efforts to access the "predominantly white hospital" provoked substantial resistance.[61] In July 1963, under the leadership of Dr. Earl R. Smith, the ULP health committee reported that "Pittsburgh still has a long way to go in wiping out discrimination in medicine." The league's health study praised the Veterans Administration hospital for its "total racial integration of patients in all facilities," while expressing great "regret that private hospitals have not followed suit." Even though the city had moved toward the integration of black patients in private facilities, discrimination persisted, particularly in room assignments. Hospital staff routinely asked whites, "Do you object to being housed with a Negro citizen?" Furthermore, although most hospitals had hired at least one black staff physician, Columbia, Pittsburgh, Mercy, and Shadyside Hospitals had no black doctors. The study also called attention to the segregation of black and white patients among white physicians' private practices. "Some white physicians . . . restrict or segregate Negro patients to certain days or hours of the day. Others will not accept Negro patients in their practice." Of the 400 students at the University of Pittsburgh School of Medicine, only two were black. Consequently, the report recommended a three-point program for change in the medical field: (1) encourage black students to enter the medical profession, (2) increase African American enrollment in local medical schools, and (3) create opportunities for African American "participation in advanced medical training."[62]

As the Pittsburgh branch advanced the fight against inequality in the city's employment, housing, and health care systems, it also redoubled its push for equal access to education for black youth. In 1954, the year the US Supreme Court handed down its historic decision mandating the desegregation of public schools across the nation, the annual meeting of the National Urban League convened in Pittsburgh. The convention, held at the Fort Pitt Hotel, included five days of workshops and sessions "on all aspects of American race relations and agency programs." The meeting represented a model of interracial cooperation as more than 100 Pittsburgh and Allegheny County organizations welcomed the NUL to town. Local residents served on a variety of planning committees for the event. The Pittsburgh Railway Company set aside a car for Urban League conventioneers, the US Steel Company offered a tour of its Homestead works, Howard Heinz Endowments underwrote a majority of the expenses connected with the event, and the *Pittsburgh Courier* devoted its entire city edition to NUL conference sessions. Close to 900 people registered for the conference, and participation in all proceedings exceeded 1,200 people. Branch officers reported that the 1954 convention represented "an all time high for these gatherings, not only in attendance but in efficiency of operations, value of program content and participation of local community personalities and groups."[63]

A year later, in 1955, the National Urban League met in Kansas City to "resurvey the League's goals and procedures" in light of rapidly changing social, economic, and political conditions. Described by the league as a momentous "policy meeting" and the "first of its kind" in the group's forty-five-year history, this gathering brought together a broad range of nationally and internationally known scholars and researchers on race relations and African American life, including Eli Ginzberg of Columbia University, Charles S. Johnson of Fisk University, and Ira Reid, former NUL director of research, to name a few. While the new bylaws adopted by the gathering retained the Urban League's "basic character" as a "planning and counseling agency," the conference also sought to deepen the organization's "base of public support" and develop "more skillful interpretations of its work" as a social service organization with a broad civic mission in this new era of social change. To sum up, the Kansas City conference produced a policy statement that reiterated the organization's commitment to "use its full resources to eliminate racial discrimination in public or private employment, housing, education, health and welfare services, and to lend its full support to those agencies and institutions whose purposes are consistent with these aims."[64]

Meanwhile, ahead of the Supreme Court's historic *Brown* decision, the ULP's education committee had already developed an agenda for expanding vocational opportunities for black youth, dismantling the city's racially segregated schools, and fully integrating black teachers into the workforce of the Pittsburgh public schools. Following the initial opening of the public schools to black teachers in 1937, the hiring of black teachers had stagnated. But the league's popular and robust vocational education campaigns persisted into the postwar years. In 1949 the annual Vocational Opportunity Campaign focused on "training for jobs." Between 1 November and 15 December, the project involved some 600 participants, more than thirty organizations, thirty-seven speaking engagements, and the distribution of 1,000 pieces of promotional literature.[65] The community organization department continued to address such racially charged issues as interracial swimming pools, school proms, and senior class plays; career counseling; and curriculum development.[66]

Under the chairmanship of attorney Wendell Freeland, the ULP's education committee delivered a report to the board showing a dearth of black teachers in the Pittsburgh public schools. However, it underscored that the goal was neither segregation nor integration but rather "equal" educational opportunities for black children. As the league pressed for desegregation and the hiring of black teachers, it also pushed for scholarship funds to enable high school graduates to attend college. Under the direction of guidance counselor Goldia Dargan, the league established the Negro Education Emergency Drive (NEED), a grassroots-funded college grant program for black students.[67] A product of the segregated school system of South Carolina, Dargan held a BA from Rockford College in Illinois and an MA from Ohio State University.

Following World War II, the ULP's social work fellowships persisted. By 1956, a total of twenty-eight fellows had received professional training under the program. During the 1950s, these social work fellowships were supplemented by a variety of new scholarship programs. Whether these new scholarships were under the direct auspices of the ULP or its partners, the league played a key role in their development and administration. The ULP provided staff services for the "Barr-Brown, Avery, Robert L. Vann, Iota Phi Lambda, and certain general senatorial scholarships," and it cooperated with the scholarship committee of Elks Lodge #115.[68] In 1954 the ULP's community services department dispensed scholarship information to eighty students and assisted the Barr scholarship awards committee at the University of Pittsburgh.[69]

Movements to desegregate Pittsburgh's urban political economy were an uphill battle. The fight for equal access to jobs, health care, education, and housing persisted well into the 1960s. By the mid-1960s, however, the Urban League movement increasingly converged with a new and more militant phase of the modern black freedom movement. Mirroring developments nationwide, a growing number of black activists embraced more aggressive responses to the city's entrenched system of segregation, including defensive if not preemptive violence as a form of political struggle. Although the ULP would not openly support the most militant wing of Pittsburgh's civil rights and black power movements, it collaborated with young militants and their organizations to demolish the city's segregationist order.

Although the National Urban League is often portrayed as a conservative force that seldom questioned the status quo, the history of the Pittsburgh branch challenges this notion. This headline from the *Pittsburgh Courier* captures efforts to desegregate the city's public swimming pools, years ahead of the landmark Montgomery bus boycott of 1955. (*Pittsburgh Courier*, 30 June 1951)

6

Navigating Civil Rights and Black Power Struggles

By the mid-1960s, the Urban League of Pittsburgh appeared to be a largely conservative force in the evolving African American freedom movement. The political and social terrain on which the Urban League worked had changed dramatically. The Pittsburgh-born children of southern black migrants had come of age and were pushing hard against the color line in the city's economy, politics, and institutions. National headquarters and local branches across the country worried about the black nationalist turn in African American politics. But the ULP had helped establish the postwar groundwork and even models for the militance of Pittsburgh's civil rights and black power struggles of the 1960s and early 1970s. The league's contributions to the rise of the city's grassroots social movements included, most notably, the early fight for jobs in downtown department stores and equal access to the city's public swimming pools.

"The Civil Service of the Civil Rights Movement"

In 1946, under the leadership of executive director Maurice Moss and publicity director K. Leroy Irvis, the Pittsburgh branch joined the city's Interracial Action Council, a broad-based coalition of civil rights, civic, social welfare, and labor organizations that included the NAACP, AFL, CIO, and Committee against Discrimination in Pittsburgh Department Stores. The Interracial Action Council launched a direct-action campaign to end employment discrimination in the large downtown retail outlets. Protesters distributed postcards and handbills underscoring the contradiction between the city's claim to support citizenship and democracy for all and the reality of the color line in Pittsburgh's central business district. "PITTSBURGH is a progressive vital AMERICAN" city, they claimed, but "THIS FREEDOM IS NOT THEIRS!"[1] The group "took the fight right to the people." Young black women were key supporters of this movement, particularly the Young Women's Committee for Fair Employment in Pittsburgh. Moss reported that women had "flooded" his office, looking "for more postcards to have signed. Out of 3,000 given the girls, over 2,500 have been returned, signed and ready for mailing." Moss stated, "It is encouraging to note that these girls, all of whom are qualified to work in the department stores, have aided in the program. They are willing to assist in any way possible."[2]

As picketers prepared to march in front of the offending stores, Mayor David Lawrence convened a meeting with protest leaders and implored them to call off the demonstration for the sake of the city's reputation. "We must not . . . give our city a black eye. Pittsburgh has just had an unfortunate series of labor disturbances . . . I implore you to cancel this 'poster-walk' for the good of the city and of all concerned." Moss quickly replied, "Mr. Mayor, we feel that the department stores have something to do with preserving the good name of the city, and we don't believe that we should be held entirely responsible for what is about to happen." Moreover, Moss explained that the ULP and other coalition leaders had spent more than two years trying to obtain "even an audience, even an answer to our letters, or an answer to our telephone calls," with no success. Troubled by the impact of the protests on the business district, store owners gave in and hired black clerks. According to the *Pittsburgh Courier*, Urban League branches in Los Angeles, Boston, Chicago, and Philadelphia used Pittsburgh as a model in launching their own postwar protests against the color line in downtown department stores.[3]

In 1961, ahead of the more militant events in the city's black freedom struggle, the ULP joined a coalition of civil rights organizations—including the NAACP, the Negro American Labor Council, and the Greater Pittsburgh Improvement League—to demand jobs for blacks at the new downtown Civic Arena. Initiated in the wake of Pittsburgh's urban renewal program of the 1950s and the destruction of the African American community in the Lower Hill District, the Civic Arena construction project had promised to provide equal employment opportunities for area residents. When these jobs failed to materialize, the ULP and the civil rights coalition pledged "to take positive action" unless the Auditorium Authority and the director of the Civic Arena project made "some move to equalize the employment picture at the arena."[4] Following escalating protests, including a massive march around the arena, city officials relented and took steps to hire African Americans.[5]

The local branch not only established a model of militant leadership in the struggle for jobs but also pioneered the movement to desegregate Pittsburgh's public swimming pools. In June 1951 ULP executive director Alexander "Joe" Allen (Moss's successor) and Gaines Bradford, the ULP's director of community organizations, defied the color ban at the city's seg-regated Highland Park pool. When Allen dove into the water, "a gang of a hundred white teenagers" ejected him from the pool while hurling racial epithets at him and Bradford. When police arrived at the scene, they confirmed that blacks had a right to use the pool but insisted that they could not protect black swimmers against mob violence. Allen and Brad-ford rejected the Pittsburgh police force's abrogation of its responsibility to protect citizens lawfully exercising their civil rights. They demanded police protection and a meeting with the mayor to enforce their claim to unrestricted access to the public pool. In the mayor's absence, they met with acting mayor Howard R. Stewart and presented him with a copy of the ULP's multifaceted program for peacefully desegregating the city's swimming pools. Specifically, the league urged the city to post public notices of the desegregation policy in a prominent place, transfer or fire employees who failed to comply with the policy, organize interracial swim-ming events at the pool, hire African American lifeguards, develop classes on intergroup relations for the staff, and close the poorly maintained all-black pool on Washington Boulevard to signal the city's determination to open all city pools to all residents. Violent white resistance to black bathers persisted until the NAACP filed a lawsuit against the city in the Common Pleas Court. Once black police officers were posted at the pool, the vio-lence dissipated, and the NAACP suspended protests as blacks regularly gained access to the city's pools.[6]

Although the Urban League was prominent in the early postwar eco-nomic justice movements, new and more militant grassroots organizations emerged during the 1960s, transforming the league's role in the escalating civil rights and black power struggles. These organizations included, most notably, the United Negro Protest Committee (UNPC), an arm of the local branch of the NAACP; the Black United Movement for Progress; Operation Dig; and the Black Construction Coalition. While these groups addressed a wide range of economic, social, and institutional issues, other influential grassroots organizations were more narrowly focused on housing, education, and poverty. Specialized organizations included Citizens against Slum Housing (CASH), Forever Action Together (FAT), the Metropolitan Tenants Organization (MTO), and local branches of the federal War on Poverty Community Action Programs (CAPs), designed to ensure the "maximum feasible participation" of poor citizens in municipal decision making.[7]

The modern black freedom movement both ruptured and strengthened the Urban League's agenda for equal employment opportunities, housing, and education. It increasingly challenged the National Urban League's definition of itself as a "social service" rather than a "civil rights" organization. The Pittsburgh branch never fit neatly into this categorical definition of the Urban League's mission. Nonetheless, the local branch found itself on the defensive with large numbers of its constituents by the mid-1960s. As historian Ralph Proctor put it, "The League had a reputation as a middle class group that did not work with poor people. It was considered, by many Black folks, as being too tied to the establishment. They said that the League could not speak out against injustice because they depended upon those who committed the injustice to give the League money."[8]

The Pittsburgh branch carefully navigated the civil rights and black power campaigns of the 1960s and early 1970s. Detroit native Arthur Edmunds, executive director of the ULP between 1960 and 1985, later vividly recalled his arrival in Pittsburgh in 1960. "Employment for Blacks was bleak," he said. The city reported that 20 percent of its employees were black, but "99 percent of those were employed as garbage men." Moreover, Edmunds observed, "You could stand downtown and watch the people leave as the offices closed and you would see almost no blacks. This was despite the fact that the city had already passed fair employment laws."[9] In 1963 the ULP estimated that "24,600 additional Negroes would have to be employed, as of now, to give them an equal share of white collar jobs." The *Pittsburgh Press* countered that even if such jobs were available, "there would not be 24,600 qualified Negroes to fill them." Thus, the paper underscored the importance of education and training to broaden the potential for "Negro employment" in the city.[10]

To address the growing political divide within the African American struggle for equality, the ULP collaborated with a variety of new organizations. As the grassroots black freedom movement pressured the city, the school board, and diverse employers to hire blacks, the ULP served as the key mediator between militant black activists and the city's political and economic elites.[11] According to Edmunds, "We were considered the good guys because we were not participants in the demonstrations. Companies would run to us for help, so that they wouldn't have to deal with the trouble makers. What these companies did not realize was that we were very much involved in the strategy. We knew who was going to be targeted, so we just sat back and waited for the 'militants' to scare the companies in our direction. Even some Black folks did not understand and accused the Urban League of being too docile." Edmunds provided vital information to activists regarding corporate responses to efforts to increase job opportunities for black people. When an official at Equitable Gas Company "lied to the UNPC and said that they had tried to get qualified Blacks from the Urban League," the ULP "was able to tell Jim McCoy [head of the UNPC] that the man was lying."[12] In an interview for the Remembering Africanamerican Pittsburgh oral history project, Edmunds reiterated the same point: "We used to try to supply to them the research, the information on which they could base their activities . . . we wanted to support them the best that we could . . . we all had a kind of role to play and we tried to fulfill ours as they tried to fulfill theirs."[13] Proctor concurred. Under Edmunds's leadership, the branch walked "a tightrope between young, militant Black people and conservative corporate leaders who always seemed poised to take away their financial support should the Urban League become too 'militant.'" More important:

> When the other groups were "kicking down the door" and generally raising very vocal issues relating to equality, the League was quietly waiting for the inevitable phone calls from the companies that had been feeling the heat of demonstrations. . . . They turned to Edmunds without understanding that he was often in on the strategy used against companies that later called him for help.

Companies felt safe going to the League because of its conservative reputation. When the companies needed warm bodies to hire, they turned to Edmunds, who always had a ready supply of educated, trained Black folks ready to step in.[14]

In an interview with Jared N. Day, David Epperson, former chair of the ULP board, recalled that civil rights attorney Wendell Freeland described the Urban League's changing mode of work as "the Civil Service of the Civil Rights Movement." Freeland, a former Tuskegee airman, became the major "strategist" for challenges to the city's old Jim Crow order. As Epperson explained, "If you're looking for someone to carry it through, then it is the Urban League."[15] Much of this good fortune emerged under the influence of what ULP president Esther Bush later described as "the hammer of affirmative action." She said, "People knew you were putting them on the line. People knew they might get a call from the Feds."[16]

In June 1969 the UNPC's James McCoy requested a meeting with County Commission chairman Leonard C. Staisey and Arthur Edmunds to discuss racial discrimination in "county government employment, contracting agencies used by county government, and concessionaires." At the meeting, the county commissioners argued that 151 blacks had been hired since the new commissioners had taken their seats in January 1968, accounting for 25 percent of all new hires. The activists countered that the vast majority of these hires were in the sanitation department and general laborer positions, not professional or clerical jobs. Grassroots organizers like McCoy and others declared that they were "damned tired of seeing Negroes come to meetings like this and beg."[17] Informally aided and supported by the Urban League, they determined to exercise real influence on the power structure. Accordingly, Operation Dig picketed the Three Rivers Stadium building site in August 1969 to challenge racial discrimination by the Master Builders Association and the Building Trades Council.[18]

Three months later, in November, the NAACP and the United Black (formerly Negro) Protest Committee (UBPC) prepared to march on the Sears department store in East Liberty to force the employment of African Americans and "heighten the selective buying campaign" against seven Sears stores in the Pittsburgh area. McCoy declared, "If Sears continues to shirk its responsibilities in making its announced policy of 'fair employment' a living reality; if it continues to contribute to poverty and humiliation of a very important segment of the total populace—the Black community, who are spending millions of dollars with this company annually, then it can be assured that there will not only be 'Black Mondays,' but [Black] Tuesdays, and every day it chooses to open its doors to the public."[19] As the Sears boycott continued into the winter and early spring, the NAACP-UBPC called for statewide agreements on jobs and positions for blacks, the purchase of products from black manufacturers, advertising in black media outlets, sensitivity programs on race, and the modification of policies that disadvantaged the poor, including "investigatory practices" related to the employment and credit histories of prospective employees. In March 1970 the Sears Company entered into an agreement with civil rights groups to set hiring goals for African Americans at 30 percent in its Pittsburgh stores and 15 percent in the surrounding suburbs. McCoy also reported a plan to use the Sears model to negotiate agreements with Kaufmann's, Gimbel's, Joseph Horne, and other stores in the city and region.[20] The ULP remained behind the scenes in the Sears protests, but it was very much involved in strategic efforts to increase job opportunities for black people throughout the urban economy.

The grassroots black freedom struggle also affected the league's fight to desegregate the public schools, housing, and other social services. In the field of education, for example, the civil rights coalition pushed simultaneously to desegregate the public schools, decentralize authority and provide greater community control over education policies, and reform the curriculum, with an accent on African Americans' contributions to the city's and the nation's history and culture. As early as 1963, branch officials had warned of an impending racial "crisis" in the city's public education system.[21]

By the mid-1960s, the Pittsburgh Board of Education expressed a growing awareness of racial disparities in public education but continued to obstruct the creation and implementation of new and more equitable policies. In the meantime, the ULP pioneered the development of "alternative" high schools before the Pittsburgh public school system was prepared to embrace them. These included, most notably, the Street Academy on the North Side and the Educational Medical Program (known as the

Ed-Med School) for pregnant teenagers. The Board of Education only slowly incorporated these alternative programs into the established curriculum. These innovative educational programs foreshadowed the ULP's later use of funds provided by the Office of Economic Opportunity to establish a program to help pregnant girls continue their high school education. Supported by access to prenatal care at the city's Magee-Women's Hospital, this War on Poverty program was lauded as the "first of its kind in the United States." It "combined a full academic curriculum with regular health care and training in child development."[22]

In the spring of 1966, despite the Urban League's creative efforts to address racial disparities without significant public funding, African American activists had reached their limit of tolerance and staged mass protests at the Board of Education's Oakland offices. African Americans vehemently rejected the board's decision to open a loophole permitting white parents to transfer their children to schools with low black-to-white student ratios. NAACP spokesman Reverend LeRoy Patrick concluded that superintendent of schools Sidney Marland "talks . . . a good line" but pursues practices that "show that the Negro child is not getting quality [equal] education."[23] Activists pressed the board to institute citywide "compulsory busing" to achieve balanced black-white student populations in the public schools. The ULP supported this effort, but it also endorsed Marland's "Great Schools" integration plan, which advocated integration from the high school level down rather than from the elementary school level up. At the same time, the league criticized the board for failing to involve the local community in its decisions and warned that the city had taken only a small step forward. "What we need now, though, is a giant step to help the thousands of students still in segregated conditions." Only a plan that aimed to integrate both the high schools and the elementary schools would constitute a "giant step."[24]

As it pushed to desegregate the public schools, the ULP also demanded and secured the employment of black teachers. Freeland and McCoy later underscored their role in moving the Pittsburgh Board of Education toward a policy of the "conscious preferment" of African American teachers in the public schools, based on "past inequities." After quietly applying this policy for nearly two years, school board president Robert I. Sperber declared the board's resolve to continue it "as a moral necessity" to rectify past practices. According to Freeland, this program reinforced both the ULP and the NUL in "urging the entire nation to make a special effort to, in regard to the Negro, make up for the centuries of deprivation. We have called for a Marshall Plan, or a crash program, and we feel that it is only with such a crash program can the Negro enter the mainstream of American life. The alternative for the rest of America is to deny the Negro this opportunity to enter the mainstream of American life, thereby, perpetuate second-class citizenship, and make the Negro dependent and an outcast." McCoy reinforced Freeland's point: "The school board is taking the leap towards the ultimate goal of equality in employment for all people. I hope that America will follow in the same task. . . . To me, this is a bold step forward, and I see no reason why anyone who is an American citizen, be he black or white, can find any grounds for criticism."[25]

The employment of black teachers reinforced the push for employment equality in the Pittsburgh public schools. Once they were hired, black teachers mobilized and made additional demands on the system, vying for positions as vice principal, principal, counselor, and other administrative posts previously off-limits to black educators. In short, as Proctor notes, by "persistent pressure on their supervisors and other administrators," black teachers "opened the doors for Blacks to positions previously held only by whites."[26]

The Urban League of Pittsburgh vigorously pushed for the decentralization of the Board of Education and greater local control over education policies. Picketing at the offices of the Board of Education and protests at school board meetings eventually forced a reorientation of administrative procedures from a fundamentally top-down model to more open and democratic proceedings. Urban League president Ronald R. Davenport urged "the election of district superintendents by concerned parents" to "bring about the community involvement needed to help save the public school system." Specifically, Davenport argued that "the racial hostility and financial structure" of public education placed it "on the brink of destruction." Movement and community leaders agreed with Davenport when he said, "there is still time, but I don't know how much," to remedy the situation. Massive grassroots protests at board meetings broke the logjam. In February 1970 the Pittsburgh Board of Education rolled out its new operating plan. Although officials proudly proclaimed that the new plan would "bring the administration of the schools closer to the community," it did not go far enough for most grassroots activists. In the new administrative structure, the board retained control over the budget and staff, but new area superintendents and directors of education reported directly to the superintendent of schools. Despite its shortcomings, this plan represented a breakthrough for activists as well as the ULP. John Brewer, assistant superintendent of school-community affairs, declared in no uncertain terms that African American access to top administrative posts increased significantly with the new structure. In addition, residents could now meet with authorities close to their homes and schools and carry on face-to-face conversations with area superintendents, who had "exclusive jurisdiction over a network of schools" in their locales. As such, Brewer concluded, there had been "a significant change in and a retreat from the status-quo method of problem solving."[27]

In the wake of Martin Luther King's assassination and the outbreak of violence in black neighborhoods, the Pittsburgh branch encountered increasing resistance to the desegregation movement. At a May 1968 dinner, NAACP president Byrd Brown decried what he called the distortion of African American life and history in the Pittsburgh public schools. "We can no longer allow a Black child to feel shamed and humiliated because of his race. . . . A superintendent of schools with his old guard staff and a Board of Education which permits these racist lies to poison our children must be removed or forced to resign." Brown's speech impressed on his Pittsburgh audience the importance of curriculum reform.[28] Similarly, at a community forum in the Hill District, Mrs. Franklin Pace of the Mayor's Commission on Race Relations pointedly questioned the one-way desegregation of the schools. "Why is it that we [black people] always have to be bused? . . . Why can't they put something fine in our neighborhood and bus other people in here."[29] Pace's query underscored the growing dissatisfaction with the busing strategy of liberal civil rights organizations. When the school board released plans to open the Columbus School as a middle school facility "with a more healthy racial balance" of black and white students, widespread community opposition quickly emerged. This led the ULP to criticize the board for failing to involve the local community in the decision, although the league expressed support for superintendent Marland's desegregation plan as an important step forward.[30]

The fight for better housing escalated alongside the struggle for better jobs and education. During the late 1960s the Urban League created a new housing department that, under the energetic leadership of James T. G. Frazier, strengthened and expanded grassroots organizations in the housing field. For example, Citizens against Slum Housing (CASH) emerged on the city's North Side in 1965 under the leadership of activist Dorothy Ann Richardson, a church leader and part-time domestic worker. The *Courier* described Richardson as a "self-termed 'grassroots' citizen" who was "bitter in a matter of fact way about the middle class Negro." In her words, "They aren't concerned with us grassroots people. . . . They act like . . . if they don't look, we might go away. . . . How are the people to know what we want in a neighborhood unless we tell them." CASH aimed to abolish the exploitative rent-gouging practices of local landlords. Although the organization emerged from the day-to-day lives and activities of North Siders, the ULP and other interracial organizations facilitated its growth and influence. CASH gained a leg up in the movement when the ULP and NAACP organized a conference under the auspices of the Greater Pittsburgh Housing Association. This conference on the city's housing problems gave CASH an opportunity to present its mission to a broader audience of activists. Richardson made the case for a new state law that would withhold rent from landlords until they made improvements in their rental properties. Similarly, the Citizen Clergy Coordinating Committee, an interracial alliance led by Father Donald McIlvane (a white priest), protested the unfair practices of landlords and demonstrated outside the homes of the most egregious offenders. Again, the Urban League reinforced and facilitated these protests. Housing director Leon Haley chaired the Greater Pittsburgh Fair Housing Movement, an interracial alliance that included CASH and the NAACP. The group held protests aimed at exposing the unscrupulous real estate practices of the president of the Pittsburgh Board of Realtors and owners of neglected "slum" property.[31]

In 1967 the Pittsburgh branch received funding from the NUL's Operation Equality. Financed by the Ford Foundation and local matching funds, Operation Equality pursued a two-pronged objective: help residents find housing "outside the ghetto," and "improve and upgrade" housing in existing communities where the agency's satellite offices were located. Operation Equality's director was Carl Ware, a graduate of the

University of Pittsburgh's master's program in public and international affairs; he worked at Pittsburgh's ACTION-Housing agency before taking the Operation Equality post. James Frazier, another University of Pittsburgh graduate, served as the program's housing specialist. Dorothy Graves, a graduate of Carnegie Mellon University and a former employee of the Pittsburgh Association for the Improvement of the Poor, took the job of information specialist. Operation Equality planned to open offices in the Hill District, North Side, Homewood-Brushton, and East Liberty. These efforts to open satellite offices also reflected the growing activism of blacks in neighborhoods outside the Hill District. In 1964, for example, the citizens of Homewood-Brushton approached the mayor of Pittsburgh and asked that "a Planner [be] assigned to our neighborhood to help us make a comprehensive plan."[32]

Buoyed by Ford Foundation funding, the agency opened new branch offices in the North Side, Homewood-Brushton, and East Liberty–Larimer. The black population had increased in these areas following the demolition of the Lower Hill community, and the ULP used its resources to ignite a variety of new housing development projects. According to Frazier, the Urban League did not want to be encumbered with the tasks of collecting rents and maintaining the properties, so it encouraged the creation of independent housing entities to serve low-income African American communities. These new organizations included the Greater Allegheny and Monongahela Housing Corporation (later the Allegheny Housing and Rehabilitation Corporation), Neighborhood Rehabilitation, and the Mini Corporation, to name a few.

Established in early 1968, the Allegheny Housing and Rehabilitation Corporation (AHRCO) soon produced nearly 200 homes on the North Side and launched plans for another 1,300 units. AHRCO was emblematic of the ULP's commitment to provide jobs as well as professional and entrepreneurial opportunities for African Americans. It provided a road map for the employment of skilled black craftsmen and stimulated African American entrepreneurship through the use of black subcontractors. According to Milton Washington, an early employee and later president and owner of the firm, AHRCO aimed first and foremost "to build and rehabilitate primarily inner city properties, and make them available primarily through governmental programs for low, moderate income families" in the city of

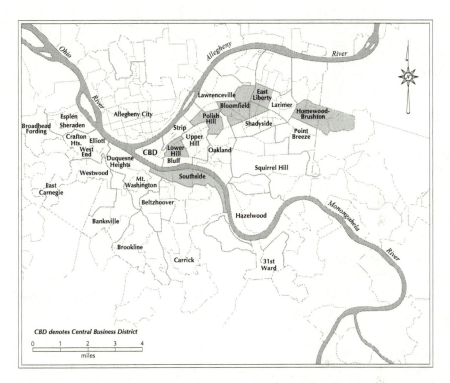

Pittsburgh's twentieth-century African American communities. (Map by Dick Gilbreath; reproduced from Joe William Trotter Jr. and Jared Day, *Race and Renaissance: African Americans in Pittsburgh since World War II* [Pittsburgh: University of Pittsburgh Press, 2010], 3, courtesy of University of Pittsburgh Press)

Pittsburgh and in some of the nearby mill towns. It ultimately built more than 2,000 houses and continued in business through the twentieth century. According to Washington, results "were mixed but they were good." One black electrician employed by AHRCO stated that he always knew he "was capable . . . but this has been the only time I've had a chance to find out." The company pledged to pay prevailing union wages, even though workers may not have belonged to a union or collective bargaining unit. In 1969–1970 AHRCO employed nearly 800 workers from the predominantly black areas where it rehabilitated buildings. An estimated 70 percent of its workforce was African American. AHRCO also stimulated the employment of black construction workers by forming the Beacon Construction

Company as another component of its quest to provide affordable housing to black residents. Similarly, the for-profit Neighborhood Rehabilitation firm contracted with United Steel Craft, an organization of skilled black tradesmen, on its housing projects.[33]

The city enacted a new ordinance defining the powers of the Pittsburgh Commission on Human Relations in 1967. The 1958 law had exempted owners of fewer than five housing units from compliance, but the new ordinance made the owners of "all housing located within the territorial limits of the City of Pittsburgh" subject to prosecution for discrimination on the basis of race, religion, nationality, or place of birth. The new ordinance also outlawed the practice known as "blockbusting"—using scare tactics to force residents to sell their houses cheaply because of the threat that African Americans or some other presumably undesirable neighbors would be moving into the area. As a result of these changes, Pittsburgh was credited with enacting "the strongest fair housing ordinance of any city in the nation, with the most complete coverage." ULP executive director Arthur Edmunds was one of a long list of individuals and organizations testifying before the City Council on behalf of the new ordinance. Other supporters included Dr. LeRoy Patrick of the NAACP; John B. McDowell, auxiliary bishop of the Catholic Diocese of Pittsburgh; John Flanigan, chairman of the Greater Pittsburgh Fair Housing Movement; and Rabbi Walter Jacob of Rodef Shalom Congregation. In the wake of this stronger antiracist housing legislation, the ULP intensified its campaign against the racially fragmented private housing market.[34]

Declining demand for public housing among white residents created numerous vacancies. Meanwhile, because of the racial quota system, African Americans languished on long waiting lists of prospective tenants, even as "white" units remained empty. In 1962 the ULP called on the Housing Authority of the City of Pittsburgh (HACP) to change its policy of "controlled occupancy" and allow blacks on waiting lists to fill vacancies in existing housing projects. ULP board members David T. Epperson and Oswald J. Nickens insisted on retaining racial quotas in public housing in the interest of maintaining integrated units, but Edmunds and others moved steadily toward abolition of the quota system. They placed a priority on meeting the day-to-day housing needs of poor residents. By opposing the continuation of the quota system in public housing, the Urban League broadened its support for the poorest segments of the black working class and eased its expectation that public housing could serve as an immediate springboard for ascension into the middle class and home ownership. The NAACP and its militant new arm, the United Negro Protest Committee, reinforced this movement. Rather than screening out families with a history of so-called dysfunctional behaviors—including arrest records, frequent joblessness, and physical and mental disabilities—the new policy targeted these families as a priority for assistance because current policies had "denied civil rights to many" and perpetuated a poor standard of living that the Urban League and the larger African American community could no longer tolerate. In November 1967 the agency also supported the movement to build new "scattered site" public housing units in previously all-white neighborhoods of Sheraden as a way to prevent the segregation and confinement of blacks and low-income families to "certain areas." The ULP challenged the persistent arguments of white home owners and realtors that African American occupancy led to declining property values and "neighborhood deterioration." The league urged the HACP and other housing agencies to produce and publish "a comprehensive master plan" for housing low-income residents throughout the city without regard to the existing racial or ethnic makeup of an area. Blacks accounted for 47.5 percent of all Pittsburgh public housing tenants in 1949; this proportion increased to 76.2 percent in 1970.[35]

The War on Poverty, the Search for Resources, and Internal Conflict

Under the influence of the community action provision of the federal War on Poverty program, the Urban League of Pittsburgh embraced an expanded role for poor residents in the social service structure of the community. A 1965 report recommended that the new Community Action Program (CAP) become the "central agency responsible for the development of appropriate social services connected with urban renewal in the city of Pittsburgh." The CAP, a nonprofit organization created by the municipality of Pittsburgh, operated under a board of directors that represented a cross section of governmental, educational, business, social service, and "minority" groups. Arthur Edmunds later recalled that one of the major accomplishments of the poverty program was "to encourage individuals to become assertive and gain confidence." He opined, "To some extent it enabled them to get the wherewithal to get additional education. Some of it was through the [ULP's] inservice training programs and some through actual tuition money. . . . That's the reason why, in my opinion, there is a higher level of participation at grass roots level now than there was before."[36]

Before the advent of the federal poverty programs of the mid-1960s, the ULP operated neighborhood units, organized at the block level, that put it in touch with the grass roots. While the initial block clubs emphasized "clean up, paint up," and "fix up," they gradually broadened the scope of their services to address a host of other issues, including the spread of neighborhood bars and the rise in juvenile delinquency and certain adult crimes. The poverty program soon took over much of this work through the establishment of neighborhood councils with "as many as five staff members in the Hill District neighborhood alone"; previously, all the neighborhood units had been served by only two staff persons, Ella Jackson and James Bradford. According to Edmunds, "That's why the Urban League got out of that business because we could not justify it. We could never compete with them and we wanted to support them all that we could. We tried to get our neighborhood units to work with them." NAACP president Byrd Brown reinforced Edmunds's assessment of the poverty program, arguing that it "accomplished a lot more than people think it did . . . many of the proposals that originated in the neighborhoods accomplished what they were set out to do."[37]

Philadelphian Ronald Davenport, a professor (and later dean) at the Duquesne University School of Law, succeeded Wendell Freeland as president of the ULP's board of directors in 1967. With colleague Matt Holden, Davenport spearheaded the formation of an ad hoc committee comprising Byrd Brown, K. Leroy Irvis, and others that monitored and largely controlled the flow of funds from the federal War on Poverty program during the 1960s. The ad hoc committee selected first Dave Hill and later David Epperson to head the city's poverty program. Davenport later recalled that the ad hoc committee "controlled millions of dollars and made certain that the monies got to the *people!* We made certain that average and poor people were on the Board and made decisions rather than having pawns of the politicians control the program. I do not believe that there was any other program in any other city that involved so many Black people and gave them so much control."[38] The Pittsburgh branch also helped form the Program to Aid Citizen Enterprise (PACE). A predominantly African American social service organization, PACE aimed to broaden the scope of social services by funding grassroots efforts to address the economic, health, and social service needs of the black community.[39] Assessments of the War on Poverty in Pittsburgh by Edmunds, Brown, and Davenport were crucial, given the scholarly treatment of this issue by historian Kenneth J. Heineman, who argues that the poverty program in Pittsburgh was ultimately "largely irrelevant" and "left in tatters," having been "shaken to its core" by deindustrialization and the demise of the manufacturing economy.[40]

An expanding budget, fueled by a combination of federal contracts and private philanthropic grants, underlay the proliferation of new and more effective Urban League programs and services. The branch finally left what league officials described as the era of the low-budget "tin cup" and entered an era of substantial financial solvency. At one point during his tenure as head of the organization, Edmunds noted that it "had maybe three or four hundred staff people and a budget of six or seven million dollars, but we had a whole lotta contracts." One contract with the state allowed the ULP "to run twenty-something daycare centers and each daycare center . . . would have six or eight staff people." Based on expanding access to federal government contracts and grants from philanthropic organizations, the budget rose from less than $50,000 in 1953 to $60,000 in 1960 and to well over $4 million in 1970.[41]

The ULP's improving financial fortunes were not solely thanks to the War on Poverty programs and the Ford Foundation–funded Operation Equality. They were also a product of the financial contributions of African Americans themselves. Civil rights–era fund-raising efforts relied heavily on both volunteers and paid staff members such as Christina Jeffries.[42] In the years following World War II, Jeffries continued her stellar service to the ULP. Her influence extended far beyond Pittsburgh and western Pennsylvania. She became the principal organizer and first president of the NUL's Administrative and Clerical Council. Under her leadership, the NUL provided in-service training for the organization's clerical personnel across the country. Women also spearheaded the work of the NUL guilds, formed in 1941 under the initial impetus of the national office. The Urban League guilds emerged as a major fund-raising source, a vehicle for building bridges between the league and the larger community, and a mechanism for expanding the pool of volunteers available for league projects. The guilds had local chapters in twenty cities by the mid-1950s. In December 1954 Mollie Moon, founder of the national guild, visited Pittsburgh to help launch its chapter under the leadership of Mrs. Toki Schalk Johnson. The Urban League guilds raised thousands of dollars through theater parties, dances, dinners, luncheons, and fashion shows. Guild members also provided summer camps for youth, special programs for teen mothers, and elder-care programs, including assistance for the historic Lemington Home for elderly African Americans, founded in the late nineteenth century. Perhaps most important, the guilds helped host the 1954 meeting of the National Urban League in Pittsburgh and later supported the 1963 March on Washington, an effort cochaired locally by ULP executive director Arthur Edmunds and the NAACP's Herbert Wilkerson.[43]

The Urban League's accomplishments did not come without conflict and turmoil. Following K. Leroy Irvis's early postwar activism to desegregate the city's department stores, executive director Maurice Moss fired him as director of public relations. Although Irvis appealed the decision and won reinstatement, he immediately resigned and went on to have a distinguished career in state and local politics. Moss had supposedly fired Irvis for "incompetence," but the underlying reason was that powerful white opponents of his tactics, including Mayor David Lawrence and downtown businessmen, had called for his removal. Irvis maintained his regard for the Urban League's work and for Moss. He later recalled that Moss was "honest about what he wanted to get done, and I was a young firebird who was upsetting things around the nest. I had offended the white man downtown." Furthermore, when the department stores hired their first black female salesclerks, it was a somewhat bittersweet victory for Irvis. One young woman worked in "toys" and the other "jewelry," but the color factor figured prominently in their hiring. Levi Sanders, vice president of Local 29 of the Building Service Employees Union, reported, "No one could tell whether these girls were white or colored."[44]

In his powerful personal account of Pittsburgh's civil rights and black power struggles, historian Ralph Proctor, a former ULP director of public information and research, reveals that, like Irvis, he too left the branch office following clashes over the organization's relationship to the modern black freedom movement. Early in his tenure with the ULP (sometime around 1967), Proctor traveled to the NUL's New York City headquarters for "mandatory training." He vividly recalls that Whitney Young, executive director of the NUL, underscored that the league's mission was social work. The organization's job was to provide "training programs" designed "to prepare Blacks for entering the mainstream" of American life and culture. When he was told that Urban League staffers "could not picket, demonstrate, boycott or engage in any other direct action," Proctor quietly muttered, "That's a damn shame! They *ought* to be side by side with the rest of us 'radicals.'" When Young asked him to repeat himself, he did so without hesitation, and word soon got back to the local office that its upstart young director of public information and research might be trouble. Unlike Irvis, though, Proctor was not fired. Nonetheless, his ideas about the Urban League movement mirrored the growing perception among poor and working-class blacks that the league had lost touch with their needs and with the needs of the larger black community.[45]

William Robinson worked at the Pittsburgh branch of the Urban League at the same time as Proctor. Both were dedicated to including "poor folks" in the league's programs and making "sure they were represented at the League." Born in Pittsburgh to a maid and a porter, Robinson was a graduate of Ohio State University. When his growing militance and embrace of the emerging black power movement put him at odds with the top leadership of the ULP, Robinson was fired. He later recalled interrupting a board meeting and urging greater involvement in the lives of poor and working-class blacks. "The administration said that I was the ring leader of a group of Urban League troublemakers, and I was summarily dismissed. I am not sorry about what I did, because much of what the Urban League does today can be traced back to my demonstration in the board room."[46]

Tensions between the city's grassroots movements and the ULP intensified during the outbreak of street violence following the assassination of Martin Luther King in 1968. Edmunds received "threats that the rioters were going to burn down my house. A friend was on my roof with a rifle, ready to protect us. That was frightening but it did not happen." Epperson recalled that because Freeland was light-skinned—he was "very fair, very fair, very fair indeed, as fair as you [the white interviewer]"—his friends warned him, "Hey man, you better get out of the neighborhood because people may not know how to address you." While taking steps to protect themselves and their families, league officials played an important role in efforts to curtail the racial violence in the aftermath of King's assassination. Edmunds later praised Mayor Joe Barr and his staff for embracing some of the advice they received from the ULP, NAACP, and other civil rights and black power organizations.[47]

The ULP's ongoing efforts to build interracial alliances reinforced its financial solvency and the impact of its social service programs. The league cultivated and maintained the support of influential white residents, including Orleans Ricco, Peg Albert, Moe Coleman, Father Donald McIlvane, and Marguerite Hofer, to name a few. Albert not only supported the league's wide-ranging programs but also played a key role in researching and writing the ULP's most comprehensive published history, *Daybreakers*. Edmunds wrote in the preface to the first edition: "To the League's Public Information Director, Peg Albert, who initiated the idea for this book, who coordinated the efforts of the research team, who conducted the interviews, and who translated substance into form, my special thanks." Hofer took a leading role in the ULP's efforts to desegregate the city's housing market and swimming pools. As she remembered, "We learned to swim on our backs . . . so we could see the rocks before they hit us." Originally from rural New York, Hofer worked part-time for the Pittsburgh Presbyterian Church's Council on Industrial Interracial Relations. She also served as a "tester" for the housing desegregation movement in Pittsburgh, visited public housing sites and interviewed residents about desegregation of the units, and helped construct Pittsburgh's first interracial housing development, Calumet City, in the East Hills section of the city.[48]

In the years after World War II, the Urban League of Pittsburgh intensified its fight for equal employment opportunities for the city's African American community. In addition to pressing employers and labor unions to eradicate the color line in skilled crafts and supervisory jobs, the organization pushed even more aggressively to expand access to education, to business, and to professional jobs previously closed to black people. As this struggle increasingly converged with massive grassroots social movements for economic equality and social justice, the segregationist system gradually gave way to a new era of equal opportunity as federal, state, and local governments moved to stop racial discrimination in employment. But the organization's role in dismantling the old Jim Crow order was not limited to the job market. It was also an integral part of the larger fight for open housing, school desegregation, and equal treatment before the law. Before African Americans could fully reap the benefits of the city's new and expanding equal opportunity programs, the confluence of several global socioeconomic and political developments unraveled the industrial economy and signaled the demise of the material foundation for social change. But the Urban League movement adjusted its sights and forged a new roster of services designed to address the challenges of the emerging postindustrial age.

ULP leaders (left to right) Arthur J. Edmunds, executive director (1960–1985); Leon Haley, president and CEO (1985–1994); and Wendell G. Freeland, board president (1962–1967). (*Pittsburgh Courier,* 23 July 2003)

Esther L. Bush, ULP president and CEO (1994–present). (Courtesy of Urban League of Greater Pittsburgh)

7

Confronting Decline and Facilitating Renaissance

As elsewhere in late industrial America, the collapse of the Jim Crow system in Pittsburgh coincided with the fall of its industrial economy and a sharp conservative turn against the equal opportunity regime. During the late twentieth century, as the city transitioned from a predominantly manufacturing base to a new economy driven by high-technology medical, educational, financial, and marketing institutions, African Americans suffered disproportionately higher unemployment, disease, poverty, and incarceration rates than their white counterparts. They also experienced a resurgence of segregation in the public schools and persistent racial discrimination in the housing market. Near century's end, the Urban League of Pittsburgh's CEO, Esther Bush, described the triumphant downtown "Golden Triangle" as less a symbol of the city's reinvention than a new manifestation of racial, class, and gender inequality. "For many working African Americans," she said, "the notion of obtaining a living wage is nothing but a dream deferred."[1]

Entering the Postindustrial Era

During the last two decades of the twentieth century, Pittsburgh's historic manufacturing sector evaporated. In rapid succession, US Steel closed blast furnaces and mill complexes across western Pennsylvania. At the same time, Westinghouse dismissed 15,000 workers from its East Pittsburgh plant and soon terminated the production of air brakes and electric generators altogether. By century's end, less than 15 percent of the region's workforce was employed in the manufacturing sector. In the meantime, US Steel purchased two large energy companies and changed its business name to USX. This signaled the end of the industrial era and the rise of a service-oriented economy focused on computer technology, innovative research universities, and a thriving health care and medical industry. The city's Urban Redevelopment Authority proudly articulated its abiding commitment to "Pittsburgh's evolution from a town founded on heavy industry to a city on the cutting edge of innovative research and technology."[2]

Pittsburgh's postindustrial transformation took a toll on the African American community. As the manufacturing sector declined, African American unemployment steadily increased, reaching 37 percent by 1990, compared with 13 percent for white workers. For the first time since the onset of the Great Migration, the city's black population also declined—from 105,000 in 1970 to about 90,000 in 2010.[3] At the same time, African Americans confronted escalating assaults on the gains achieved by the modern black freedom movement. Legislators increasingly trimmed social services for single-parent families, unemployment relief, and access to better jobs, higher pay, and benefits under federal affirmative action guidelines. As early as 1974, ULP president Milton Washington warned that affirmative action was insufficient to promote "large scale" African American employment. "With rising inflationary costs," he said, African American unemployment was "even more pronounced than before." Moreover, the "hammer of Affirmative Action" had started to dissipate as white resistance set in. Washington described the unemployment rate among the city's black population as "catastrophic" and urged the mayor to use the Comprehensive Education and Training Act (CETA) to develop public works programs and "get people working again."[4] In 1982 the Pennsylvania legislature passed Act 75, which terminated public assistance for large numbers of poor and working-class residents of the state. Signed into law by Republican governor Richard Thornburgh, this punitive social welfare legislation became known as "Thornfare" among social justice activists. Over the next decade, the dismantling of the New Deal social welfare state intensified, and it finally collapsed with passage of the Republican-sponsored Personal Responsibility and Work Opportunities Act, known as "welfare to work." Signed into law by Democratic president Bill Clinton in 1996, the new law fundamentally altered the local and national context of social service.[5]

The ULP's fortunes as a social service agency also dwindled with the passing of the old industrial order and the welfare state. In 1981 it had an operating budget of $4 million, but that figure dropped to $2 million in 1983 as the industrial economy plummeted. This occurred during the waning years of Arthur Edmunds's directorship, and he recalled, "It was a shock to all of us, and particularly to younger staff members who knew nothing of the depression years, when—in 1982—it became apparent that the depressed economy and the massive layoffs in the mills would cause a shortfall in the United Way funds." The agency faced an "across the board cut" in 1982 and another in 1983. Pledges for social service work fell $3 million short of the league's goal, and it reduced staff through "attrition" and "salary cuts." As Edmunds put it, "Everybody worked harder for less money."[6]

Near the end of the century, the Pittsburgh branch continued to labor under a $350,000 debt, which it eventually retired by instituting a series of stringent cost-cutting measures under the leadership of chief fiscal officer Vincent Lepera. These measures included giving up space under its lease agreement with United Way, "rebidding" its contract with insurers of its employees' health benefits package, and renegotiating with funders to cover overhead costs through grants. The proportion of revenue from government grants and contracts had dropped from a high of about 80 percent during the late 1970s and early 1980s to 64 percent, while contributions from fund-raising drives and private sources had increased from only 8 percent in 1995 to 20 percent by 1999. United Way funding had stabilized at about 15 percent of the budget.[7] It was only in 1997 that the ULP announced a financial turnaround. At a meeting on the Carnegie Mellon University campus, assistant treasurer Craig Campbell declared that the fiscal year ending 30 June was "one of the strongest financial performances of the Urban League ever." The league's revenue, including a total of 42 percent of its budget from Allegheny County, exceeded expenses by nearly $127,700.[8]

As the economy bottomed out, the welfare state dissipated, and the ULP's social service staff declined, the branch launched a $3 million fund-raising campaign to secure a new headquarters in downtown Pittsburgh. Despite an optimistic feasibility study and extensive appeals to USX, Alcoa, and other corporate and foundation giants, the building campaign failed. Edmunds and Bush later summed up the matter in their history of the ULP: "Our efforts to carry out this major capital campaign failed, largely because we lacked the resources to engage full-time professional fund-raising counsel and because, at the time, neither the foundation and corporate community nor our own Board was willing to support such a large capital project." Once the capital campaign collapsed, the ULP moved from its central office at 200 Ross Street to 1 Smithfield Street, "the first major relocation of the League in nearly four decades."[9]

Despite its failed capital campaign, the ULP intensified its quest for up-to-date research on the changing status of the city's black community in the depths of the deindustrializing era. Near the beginning of Leon Haley's tenure as president and CEO in 1985, the organization conducted needs assessments for municipal and county social service agencies and collaborated with the University of Pittsburgh's Institute for the Study of the Black Family to address poverty and family fragmentation among low-income black residents. In March 1986 the organization planned a Black Family Summit with a major focus on the needs of households headed by black women.[10] In 1994, following Haley's retirement, Esther Bush returned to the city of her birth and took the reins of the Urban League of Pittsburgh after a stellar career in the Urban League movement in Hartford, Connecticut, and New York City. Within the first year of her arrival, Bush joined the University of Pittsburgh's Benchmark Advisory Committee of the Center for Social and Urban Research (CSUR).[11]

Over the next decade and a half, a series of benchmark studies by the CSUR documented the dire straits of Pittsburgh's black community during the closing years of the twentieth century and the beginning of the new millennium. A 1995 report underscored the poverty of African Americans in Pittsburgh compared with fifty other municipalities nationwide. It revealed that Pittsburgh housed "one of the poorest, most economically disadvantaged black populations of any larger city in the U.S."[12] It had the highest percentage of black men aged twenty-five to thirty-four "not in the labor force" (just over 30 percent) and the third highest percentage of unemployed black women in the same age group (about 35 percent). Pittsburgh had the nation's highest poverty rate for African Americans eighteen to sixty-four years of age (35 percent) and, among major cities, the second highest percentage of children living in poverty (nearly 57 percent).[13]

The ULP reported a modest increase in African American employ-ment during the "economic boom" of the 1990s, but blacks continued to be overrepresented in "low wage" occupations and underrepresented in "higher-salary" blue- and white-collar jobs. Although white unemploy-ment in the Pittsburgh metropolitan region had dropped to about 5 per-cent as the new century began, African American unemployment remained high at 12 percent.[14] In her first report of the new millennium, Bush sadly concluded, "There remains this stubborn issue of disparity. The chasm between the haves and have nots remains wide and deep. Too few black families in this region are able to hoist themselves up the economic ladder from the uncertainties and limitations of the lower class to the abundance and relative security of the middle class."[15] Many promising black profes-sionals had left the city for other places.[16]

New research on housing, health care, and education told a similar tale. Unequal access to places to live, heal, and educate their children took a heavy toll on the postindustrial black urban community. Allegheny County's black suburban population increased by nearly 20 percent during the 1960s and 22 percent during the 1970s.[17] Still, despite this expansion of the black suburban population, the Urban League's housing director declared, "If you're African American, you stand a 50 percent chance of being discrimi-nated against every time you enter the [Pittsburgh] market for any kind of housing service." African Americans filed an increasing number of com-plaints with the local branch office, the Fair Housing Partnership, and other organizations charged with monitoring and eradicating racial discrimination in the housing market.[18]

At the turn of the new millennium, the Urban League of Pittsburgh reported "alarming health disparities" between blacks and whites in the region. African Americans died "at younger ages and, in some age catego-ries, at more than three times the rate of their white neighbors from pre-ventable ailments such as heart disease and prostate cancer." The African American infant mortality rate was 3.6 times higher than that among whites, the incidence of homicides among young black males (aged fif-teen to nineteen) was 46 times higher, venereal disease rates for both males and females were about 50 percent higher, and the rate of new AIDS cases was nearly 7 percent higher among blacks than whites.[19] In 2001 the branch invited economist Ralph Bangs to produce a series of "black papers" on "the leading causes of death of black men and women, infant mortality, rates of firearm injuries and fatalities, and rates of sexually transmitted diseases."[20] Bangs's research revealed that African American deaths from cancer, heart disease, and stroke were two to three times higher than the goals set by the nation's 2000 Healthy People program.[21] While black people were overrepresented in all major disease and death statistics, they were grossly underrepresented in total inpatient admissions to the region's hospitals.[22] When one doctor kindly agreed not to charge a poor patient who could not afford to pay, the woman declared, "When a doctor refuses money . . . you usually start driving a good bargain with the undertaker."[23]

African American students also faced a steep climb to obtain the necessary education and training to qualify for jobs in the city's changing economy. The ULP documented the persistence of racial inequality in virtually every aspect of the public school system: almost 70 percent of black students and 54 percent of all students could not read at their grade level, nearly 20 percent of black students and 13 percent of white students failed to graduate from high school, and about 22 percent of black students and 15 percent of white students dropped out of college.[24] The ULP regularly protested the region's racially segregated and unequal schools as a fundamental part of the crisis confronting black youth. In late 1994 and early 1995 the agency helped modify a Pittsburgh public schools redistricting proposal that would have eliminated busing as a means of integrating the schools. Under the rubric "(Re)segregation IS NOT an Option," the league participated in an extensive publicity campaign. ULP board president Dianne Green not only supported the campaign but also helped underwrite it. The effort included two forums (featuring nationally renowned speakers such as Charles V. Willie of Harvard University as well as local experts) and resulted in a revamping of the proposal to "create three new neighborhood schools but did not eliminate busing for integration."[25]

The Pittsburgh public schools failed even the most promising African American students, particularly those living in public housing projects. In an interview with journalist Douglas Heuck, Urban League counselor Bob Carter revealed that the schools permitted some of the ablest black students to fall through the cracks: At St. Clair Village "last year, a senior with a 'B' average approached him at 3 p.m.—four hours before his graduation ceremony. 'He didn't have the slightest idea what he was going to do after he graduated.' . . . His counselors and teachers hadn't even discussed the possibility of going to college or getting him into a training program."[26] In education, as in other areas of African American life at century's end, the ULP reported "little improvement in reading achievement among low-income, low-skill children [both black and white] in public schools" across Allegheny County. Moreover, although African Americans constituted just over half of all public school students, they accounted for 70 percent of school suspensions (often described by ULP officials as "push-outs" instead of "drop-outs"), undercutting their prospects for graduation and admission to college or technical training programs.[27]

Setting an Agenda for the New Age

Against the broader backdrop of deteriorating class and race relations, the ULP forged a variety of new programs designed to alleviate immediate suffering and integrate African Americans into the new economy on an equal footing with their white counterparts. More so than before, however, the league increasingly connected "job creation" with political empowerment and, especially, "wealth creation." By the turn of the new century, it hoped "to build wealth through job training and job readiness skills development." Wealth building, league officials argued, "is anchored in securing employment that will enable an individual to leave poverty and financial instability behind."[28] In other words, despite the organization's emphasis on the "Iron Circle" of inequality, staff members believed that "time is on our side" and pushed forward to develop new programs to assist black families and communities in the Greater Pittsburgh metropolitan region.[29]

Work, Health, and Welfare

As the social welfare state continued to shrink and medical, educational, hospitality, and various services replaced steel and other industries as the region's major employers, the ULP extended its long history of job creation and innovative programs to improve the housing, health, education, and living conditions of black people. It focused on opening up the tourist trade and the expanding "eds and meds" sectors of the postindustrial economy. A comprehensive employment counseling and placement service stood at the center of the ULP's programs. League employment projects served more than 3,500 individuals each year, providing skills assessments, resumé writing assistance, and job referral and placement. In a single year, the ULP placed more than 500 African Americans in jobs totaling $5 million in annual income. Other services included the Comprehensive Youth Competencies Program, On-the-Job Training Program, Transitionally Needy Training Program, Self-Employment Training Program, Seniors in Community Service Program, and Minority Elderly Outreach Program, to name a few.[30]

By century's end, the Greater Pittsburgh Convention and Visitors Bureau reported that, on a daily basis, meeting and convention delegates spent an average of $1.3 million in downtown Pittsburgh. Under the leadership of Bill Foster, the ULP's employment, training, and economic empowerment department established a Hospitality/Leisure Training Institute to broaden African American participation at all levels of this booming segment of the economy. Administered by Pennsylvania State University's World Campus, the hospitality program was soon awarding online associate degrees in management. As Bush put it, the ULP hoped to engage a variety of philanthropic, educational, corporate, and governmental bodies "to redouble efforts to include all of the human capital in our region in the prosperity of the 21st century."[31]

In the spring of 1996 Esther Bush joined the board of directors of the University of Pittsburgh Medical Center (UPMC) Health System, the city's largest employer, and reinforced the push for jobs in the health care industry—the most promising area of economic growth in the region. As chair of the organization's Committee on Diversity, Bush firmly advocated for African American patients, students, physicians, nurses, and employees in UPMC's newly devised "Diversity Strategic Plan."[32] The ULP also published a Black Leadership Directory and pressed for greater African American access to high-paying managerial and professional jobs across all areas of the economy, lucrative government and corporate service contracts, and appointments to decision-making boards of government, civic, philanthropic, and corporate organizations.[33]

Job creation in the postindustrial economy was closely intertwined with the development of welfare-to-work programs for families displaced from industrial firms and state-supported social services. By century's end, as the city, state, and nation ended "welfare as we know it," the local branch stepped up to alleviate the harsh transition from welfare to work. Beginning gradually during the 1970s, these programs expanded during the 1980s and 1990s under CETA, the Job Training and Partnership Act (JTPA), the Joint Welfare Initiative's Transitionally Needy Training (TNT) Program, and the Career Advancement Network (CAN).[34] League employment and self-employment projects included a Re-entry Assistance Management Program for previously incarcerated residents aged twenty-one to forty.[35]

The ULP signed a contract with the Department of Federal Programs "to provide recruitment, assessment, counseling, care management, life skills, basic skills, occupational training, job development and placement services, referral, support services, and work experience" to an estimated 100 eligible welfare recipients and "transitionally needy" (TNT Program). The ULP also proposed to provide "entrepreneurial training" to an additional fifteen clients of the TNT Program. They would be trained under the league's Self-Employment Training (SET) Program, an intensive fifteen- to eighteen-week course designed "to take participants through a career transition process, business skills development workshops, business plan development, resource development and financing, and other related phases" of business development. The goal was for participants "to become successful owners of micro-businesses which will be located preferably within the enterprise zones of Allegheny County and City of Pittsburgh." Upon completion of this course, the participants were eligible to apply for start-up loans from the league's "$100,000 revolving loan fund."[36]

During the 1970s and 1980s the ULP established a new School-to-Industry Program and strengthened ties between the high school curriculum and the business and industrial sectors' workforce requirements. In 1984 the ULP received funding from a national philanthropic foundation and created the Business and Finance Academy at Westinghouse High School on the East Side. Designed as a "drop-out prevention strategy," the Westinghouse program had soon enrolled more than 180 students who received a "combination of traditional and vocationally relevant courses and summer work experience for entry level jobs or post-secondary schooling." The Board of Education eventually absorbed this program into its New Futures Initiative, receiving funds from the Annie E. Casey Foundation to support "at risk" young people.[37] The branch also administered the Youth Employment Services (YES) under CETA and its successor JTPA. This program provided services to "out-of-school" Allegheny County youth. In addition, the ULP conducted programs for seventeen- to twenty-one-year-olds under JTPA for both the city of Pittsburgh and Allegheny County. In 1987 the ULP secured a contract with the Pennsylvania Department of Commerce to conduct the SET Program, one of only three such projects in the state. By 1991, seventeen of the original sixty-three participants had started their own businesses, including four individuals who had been on welfare, eight who had been underemployed, and five who had been unemployed.[38]

The Career Advancement Network helped welfare recipients, mainly women, move into wage-earning jobs following the dismantling of the New Deal welfare system. Although the Urban League joined other social service organizations and activist groups in protesting the disproportionately destructive impact of the new antiwelfare state on African Americans, it applauded the successes of some welfare-to-work programs such as CAN. The branch highlighted the experiences of Valerie Lauw, president of the Northview Heights Estates parents' support group. Lauw, now forty years old, had been a teenage mother; she had been living in a homeless shelter with her two daughters, aged four and ten, when she enrolled in the Northview Heights Family Support Center's program. Lauw eventually became a transportation specialist for the program, helping other participants get to their appointments "for housing, legal assistance, and support programs" and putting them "on the road to self-sufficiency."[39]

As the ULP addressed the challenges of unemployment and the transition from welfare to work, it also created a variety of programs to improve the housing, health, and diets of poor and working-class black families. By the early 1990s, the ULP had helped tens of thousands of clients and was "known primarily for its housing services, which offer help in meeting crisis situations (evictions, foreclosure and potential homelessness) as well as assistance in finding affordable housing, home maintenance, budgeting and tenant-landlord negotiations." With funds obtained from a federal community development block grant, the agency initiated "a comprehensive housing counseling program" in Pittsburgh and Allegheny County, and by the early 1990s, it was widely "recognized as the premier service of its kind in the region." During its first fifteen years of existence, the housing counseling program had served more than 10,000 African American families.[40] However, under the impact of the declining social welfare state, the ULP reported the "most drastic cuts in city and county funding" for its "housing counseling services," whereas the demand for such services was "great and increasing." As government funding dissipated, Barbara Baulding, director of the league's housing program, obtained foundation support and spearheaded the development of a vigorous housing counseling and location service, Operation Home, and a rental assistance program. The latter program compensated landlords for housing "homeless and near homeless" men, women, and children who were ULP clients. Twenty-first-century housing initiatives included the Phoenix Rise Homeless Prevention and Rapid Re-housing Program and the one-year Self-Sufficient, Trained, Active and Resourceful (STARS) Program to aid black female heads of households and provide rental supplements and budget workshops "to prevent eviction and homelessness."[41]

League housing programs enabled some black families to repair their credit, move out of rental units, and purchase their own homes. In one year, ULP housing programs helped nearly 700 families move into new homes, enabled 800 children to avoid placement in homeless shelters, prevented another 500 people from being evicted from their homes, and stopped nearly thirty-five utility cutoffs and more than twenty foreclosures. During the housing crisis of 2007, when banks repossessed more than 2.3 million homes nationwide, the ULP developed new programs to forestall foreclosure. Its foreclosure specialist Robert Reeves helped several families save their homes. One Fayette County couple testified: "We are confident that without [Urban League] counsel and assistance, we would not have received the modification offer from our mortgage company and most likely would have gone into foreclosure."[42] In addition to a variety of programs focused on the private rental and real estate markets, the branch operated the Public Housing Improvement Program. In collaboration with the city's ACTION-Housing agency, this program provided skills instruction, case management, and counseling services to

public housing residents. In 2003–2004 the Public Housing Improvement Program helped some 870 children avoid homeless shelters or foster care. Moreover, in partnership with the Housing Authority of the City
of Pittsburgh, the ULP provided home-ownership counseling for Section
8 recipients and low-income public housing residents, with an eye toward
moving public housing tenants into their own homes.[43]

Innovative health and nutrition initiatives reinforced the ULP's campaign to improve housing and living conditions for black residents. The
organization rejected the notion that "significant biological differences
between races/ethnicities" make "one racial/ethnic group more suscep-
tible than another to disease in general." Instead, the branch's health
studies and policy recommendations treated race or ethnicity as a "racial
construct with powerful social effects" on the health care of African Americans. The ULP provided health services in collaboration with the Greater
Pittsburgh Literacy Council, the Metropolitan Baptist Church (which
sponsored a Minority National Health Week), the American Diabetes
Association (which held a diabetes expo for minority group communities), and the March of Dimes Premature Birth Impact Summit, to name
a few.[44]

In 2009–2010 the Urban League of Pittsburgh opened a Health Education Office (HEO) and announced a new health initiative called Newer
Thrusts in Health Care. The HEO underscored ongoing problems in the
city's health care system, including "critical shortages of physicians, dentists
and other specialized" health care providers; "continued defects" in the use
of medical facilities and services; and the rising costs of medical care in general. Formed in collaboration with the University of Pittsburgh's School of
Nursing and its Clinical and Translational Science Institute, the HEO
served more than 600 clients in its first year. Under the leadership of Kafui
Agbemenu, a registered nurse and PhD student in nursing at the University of Pittsburgh, the HEO offered basic health screenings for blood pressure, weight, and cancer. The center also provided preventive care services,
including flu shots, nutrition classes, and CPR training.[45]

Closely intertwined with its health care programs, the ULP developed food support projects to feed poor and working-class black families.
The Hunger Services staff and the project's health advocate developed a
nutrition program for young people to improve their "understanding of

nutrition and of food selection and preparation." This program included the expert advice of dietician Judy Dodd from the Nutrition Science Department of the University of Pittsburgh, nutrition classes taught by a graduate student in the field, and a demonstration of food art by students from the Pennsylvania Culinary Institute. By 2010–2011, the Hunger Services Pantry, located at the ULP's Wood Street office, had provided emergency food supplies to nearly 800 families.[46]

In the meantime, the league's annual Thanksgiving food distribution program had emerged as "one of the most successful food programs in the region." Established in 2004 in collaboration with volunteers from the Allegheny County Attorneys against Hunger campaign, the Thanksgiving program had increased its services to 400 people citywide. Under the direction of Hunger Services Program manager Jim Jackson, it also assisted refugees from Iraq, Iran, and Somalia. Some forty attorneys and their families volunteered to distribute the food. One attorney expressed not only the great satisfaction he felt from feeding the city's neediest citizens but also the impact it had on his family. "We live in Sewickley," his son said, "but this was real." It brought tears to the father's eyes when he realized that this was the first time his son understood the difference between his life of privilege and the lives of people who struggle every day. Other projects, including the Supplemental Nutritional Assistance Program (SNAP) and Step Down, encouraged healthy food purchases and preparation to facilitate better health among working-class and poor families.[47]

Funded by a combination of public and private foundation money, ULP programs addressed a wide range of needs and served an increasingly diverse constituency—able-bodied men and women in the prime of life, previously incarcerated individuals, single-parent families, and senior citizens. But programs designed to address the educational challenges and life chances of black youth took priority. Building a foundation for higher education among young people became a key pillar of the ULP's work in the late twentieth and early twenty-first centuries. According to Bush, this emphasis reflected "the priority placed on services for children" by the National Urban League, the local branch's board, and the creators of the organization's "strategic plan" for the new millennium.[48] The ULP reinforced its focus on youth with the publication of *The State of Black Youth in Pittsburgh* (1999) in collaboration with the University of Pittsburgh.[49]

Education, Youth Services, and Politics

In the wake of growing street-level violence involving black youth, the Urban League joined forces with the NAACP and a broad range of other organizations to encourage young people to seek jobs. With a mix of government and private foundation funding, the Urban League of Pittsburgh launched a series of work programs in 1990. Modeled on Depression-era New Deal programs, these projects employed young black men and women, but especially young men aged sixteen to nineteen, during the summer months. Executive director Arthur J. Edmunds later recalled, "[We] created teams of young men who learned construction skills from adult trainers and put them to use in creating 'signature' projects in public area playgrounds" in Braddock, Northview Heights, Clairton, the South Side, and the North Side.[50]

Even as the agency created job opportunities for black youth, it also encouraged African American children to stay in school and excel in their studies. The Negro Education Emergency Drive (NEED), established in the early 1960s, persisted through the late twentieth century and provided more than $300,000 in scholarships each year to help needy black students advance their education.[51] By century's end, these efforts revolved around the ULP's new youth development department as well as the Campaign for African American Achievement, the Thurgood Marshall Achievers Society, the National Achievers Society, a local chapter of the NUL's Incentives to Excel and Succeed project, and the African American Achievement Trust.[52] The ULP's youth development department was established partly with funds bequeathed by Dianne Green, former president of the board of directors. Following her untimely death in 1997, the ULP established the youth development department to honor Green's life and memorialize her commitment to improving the lives of African American youth.[53]

In 2010–2011 the branch announced the creation of the African American Achievement Trust (AAAT) following a meeting of some 107 representatives of civic, religious, governmental, and other groups interested in the education of African Americans and other low-income residents of Pittsburgh. The AAAT, a coalition of African American leaders in the city, focused on building "a culture of academic equity and excellence for Pittsburgh's Black Youth." The AAAT's mission statement noted, "Out of deep and abiding love for our African American children, families, and communities, the African American Achievement Trust is committed to advocacy for excellence in education and equity in outcomes in Greater Pittsburgh."[54] Another group, the Thurgood Marshall Achievers Society, adopted the slogan "Achievement Matters" and honored black youth for "doing the right thing." The project reported some 600 student achievers by century's end.[55] At the same time, the ULP addressed the issues of teen pregnancy and single female heads of households in cooperation with the Junior League of Pittsburgh, the Allegheny County Health Department, the March of Dimes, and Pittsburgh's Black Woman Health Network.[56]

In their testimonials on the value of the Urban League's services, black students praised the agency's achievement programs in the Pittsburgh public schools. One student credited the ULP's postsecondary preparation program for making school "tolerable and even a bit exciting." "Every Monday," the student said, "you provided words of inspiration that would play through my mind throughout the entire day. Also, the lessons you provided concerning time and stress management have been most helpful." Another participant underscored the program's impact on students' motivation to pursue higher education and improve their life chances: "You make me want to do more with my life. You make me want to go to college to be a better person."[57]

The ULP's education programs were not limited to the public schools. It vigorously opposed and helped defeat a school "voucher" program that would have used public funds to support tuition in private and parochial schools. But it embraced the creation of charter schools as being consistent with its pioneering efforts to establish alternative schools to enhance the education of African Americans.[58] In August 1998 the Urban League's charter school opened in the building that formerly housed B'nai Israel Synagogue in East Liberty. Under the leadership of Ramon Duardo, director of the ULP's education department, and with a grant from the US Department of Education, the school was established as a nonprofit entity separate from the ULP. Duardo also spearheaded the movement against a school redistricting plan and the organization's proposal to the governor's KIDS II program. In its second year, the charter school served 100 students in grades K–4 and, owing to excessive demand, instituted a lottery to fill available spaces at the school. At the turn of the century, the school continued to expand under the leadership of Janet Bell. By 2005–2006, the charter school's first graduates had entered the appropriate grades in the public schools, and many were continuing their education in some of the region's most elite private schools, including the Ellis School, Frick International Academy, Winchester Thurston School, and Shadyside Academy.[59]

To address the mounting problems of gangs, drugs, and violence, the ULP identified "an end to violence" as a major priority. During her tenure on the Urban League board (1992–1997), Dianne Green, senior vice president for Duquesne Light Company, also served on the steering committee of the Youth Crime Prevention Council. Organized by Frederick Thieman, US attorney for the western Pennsylvania region, the Youth Crime Prevention Council dovetailed with the ULP's energetic campaign to raise public awareness about the crisis of black youth violence. Under the leadership of Barbara Baulding, this effort, dubbed "It Takes a Whole Community to Raise a Child," opened on 4 March 1995 with the airing of a prime-time television documentary on youth violence and the ULP's efforts to address the issue. Based on the disproportionate concentration of African American poverty in Pittsburgh's public housing projects, the branch targeted Northview Heights and St. Clair Village for "intensive attention."[60]

Programs at Northview Heights and St. Clair Village included a peer tutoring program; Linkages, a program funded by the Association for the Advancement of Science to encourage student interest in math and science; and the Home Instruction Program for Pre-school Youngsters (HIPPY), a collaboration among the ULP, the National Council of Jewish Women, and the Board of Education to train low-income mothers to be their children's primary education caregivers. Under the leadership of Bob Carter, the ULP also launched a "black male outreach" initiative at St. Clair Village. This outreach effort served an estimated thirty-five young males aged twelve to eighteen. It not only addressed youth unemployment but also used a "streetworker approach" to investigate the youth drug trade, gangs, and unemployment.[61] Twenty-nine-year-old Carter, who had a BA in political science from Morris Brown College in Atlanta, provided a role model for these young men. The ULP's work at St. Clair Village gained even greater attention with the creation of the multiagency Pittsburgh Coalition against Substance Abuse (PCASA). Funded by an estimated $500,000 grant from the US Department of Health and Human Services, the PCASA worked with the Office of Substance Abuse and Prevention. The Pittsburgh branch was the only Urban League affiliate in the nation to receive funds under this program. Like other ULP initiatives, the PCASA evolved into an independent agency providing a critical service to the community.[62]

In his work with St. Clair youth, Carter also initiated field trips outside the projects, organized a "Manhood Retreat" (with "No TVs no radios. Just some real communication") and a sports/antidrug program, represented students in trouble with school officials or the juvenile courts, and held a popular "recognition banquet" to honor young people in the project. Neither the black nor white press gave the banquet much coverage, but Carter recalled that "it was a beautiful evening. The kids were just bubbling. . . . And that bothered me—I felt that when it's a drug bust or a robbery; the media swarm up here. They can't wait. But something positive isn't newsworthy." One year, he pushed harder for coverage of the banquet, and "all three newspapers and two television stations covered it." In line with the NUL and ULP approaches to social services in the 1990s, Carter urged established agencies—the Board of Education, the Police Department, and the Health Department—to do their jobs in the housing projects and help resolve some of the difficult challenges confronting poor black communities. As a result of efforts at St. Clair Village and elsewhere in the city to curtail youth violence, the ULP reported a drop in African American crime rates and declared Pittsburgh one the nation's safest cities. In 1995 the city's Health Education Center awarded the Urban League of Pittsburgh its Porter Prize for outstanding contributions to public health.[63]

Integral to its efforts to address the economic and social service needs of the African American community, the ULP took part in the transformation of Pittsburgh's political landscape. The city's grassroots social struggles started to dissipate by the early 1970s, but they did not disappear entirely. As the city was claiming a decline in crime rates, African Americans were reporting a rising incidence of police harassment, brutality, and even death during arrest or while in custody. Following the killing of Jonny Gammage, cousin of the Pittsburgh Steelers' Ray Seals, by the police in suburban Brentwood in 1995, the ULP joined a massive grassroots effort to transform this case into a cause célèbre for police reform. The organization supported African American councilwoman Valerie McDonald's resolution calling for better preemployment screening and training of police officers, as well as stronger mechanisms for overseeing police conduct and "stringent disciplinary action for violation of the police code of conduct." In 1998 the ULP helped gather the thousands of signatures required to put the proposal to create a Citizen Review Board to monitor police conduct on the ballot. The measure passed. ULP president and CEO Esther Bush also wrote an op-ed piece for the *Pittsburgh Post-Gazette* entreating the police to back away from the "increasing use of force," citing Nelson Mandela: "A government which uses force to maintain its rule teaches the oppressed to use force to oppose it."[64] Between 1993 and 1999, no fewer than eight African American men died in confrontations with Pittsburgh police officers.

Following the appearance of Bush's op-ed, Governor Tom Ridge appointed her to the state's Commission on Community Relations and Law Enforcement. The ULP also joined the national movement to pressure President Bill Clinton to host a White House conference on police brutality and to intensify the prosecution of offenders. The Clinton administration responded by urging Congress to allocate $42 million for "ethics and integrity" training for police officers. In a meeting at the National Press Club in Washington, NUL president Hugh B. Price entreated Clinton to use his "bully pulpit . . . to remedy what's wrong in police/community relations" and to lay the groundwork for "reconciliation." Bush attended that meeting "on behalf of the angry, frustrated residents" of Pittsburgh and Allegheny County. "Too many" minority residents in Pittsburgh and elsewhere, she said, "have lost faith in law enforcement officials and the criminal justice system. A sense of outrage and confusion, especially prevalent amongst youngsters, threatens every community with violence." Unfortunately, she concluded, legal acts "to promote justice for Jonny Gammage" had "little impact."[65]

Along with its fight against police brutality, the Urban League helped mobilize increasing numbers of previously neglected poor and working-class voters. In Pittsburgh, as elsewhere, African Americans focused on electing black candidates to public office at all levels of government—municipal, county, state, and national. NUL headquarters adopted voter registration as one of its top four priorities and urged local affiliates to launch concerted efforts to "register low-income voters" across the urban Northeast and Midwest. Stewart Cohen, director of research for the ULP, told a *Courier* reporter that the agency's voter registration campaign built directly on the Urban League's national initiative.[66] Edmunds also cited the local branch's close cooperation with the nationwide voter initiative: "We made a big emphasis on voter registration and got out the vote. . . . We got some local help for that, we got some national help, we got some help from the National Urban League on it."[67]

In 1985 African American candidates lost their bid to gain seats on the City Council, leaving black Pittsburghers without representation on the city's principal governing body for the first time in nearly two decades. After a moment of hesitation, the ULP joined the push to replace the city's at-large election system with election by districts. A coalition of grassroots organizations fueled this movement, including the Coalition for District Elections, the Pittsburgh Alliance for District Elections, the Association of Community Organizations for Reform Now, the Interdenominational Social Action Alliance, the Metropolitan Pittsburgh Crusade for Voters, and several churches. According to Leon Haley, ULP executive director and one of the spokesmen for the alliance, it was "essentially" an "umbrella organization made up of a variety of agencies and organizations . . . to develop an educational campaign for district elections and to state the case for why district elections would be beneficial to Pittsburgh." In May 1987 the voters passed a referendum for district elections, and in the election of 1989 and thereafter, African Americans were represented on the City Council.[68]

The Urban League advanced the cause of African American political engagement when it provided a staff and office space for the Black Political Empowerment Program II. Formed in 1996 under the leadership of former NAACP president Tim Stevens, the program soon registered some 20,000 voters and organized public forums where people could meet political candidates and acquaint them with the needs of the community, giving residents an opportunity to influence the political process.[69]

During the early years of the twenty-first century, the Urban League of Pittsburgh intensified its impact on the Urban League movement nationwide. In July 2003 the Pittsburgh branch hosted the annual NUL conference for the first time in forty-nine years. In her "State of Black Pittsburgh Address," Esther Bush reiterated her earlier announcement that the "soul of this conference" would be to reinforce the Urban League's revitalized mission "to assist African Americans to achieve economic self-reliance, parity, power, and civil rights." By outbidding thirteen other contenders hoping to host the 2003 meeting, the ULP enhanced its profile as a national and even global leader. Corporate, nonprofit, governmental, and community leaders from more than 100 cities converged on Pittsburgh. President George W. Bush addressed the gathering, as did seven of the nine 2004 presidential hopefuls who came to Pittsburgh to talk about their visions for the country in general and for the African American population in particular.[70]

In addition to strengthening its impact on the national Urban League movement, the Pittsburgh branch forged and sustained connections with transnational and global movements for social justice, particularly the fight against South Africa's apartheid regime. David Epperson, chair of the ULP board of directors, later joined the board of the NUL and chaired its Ad hoc Committee on South Africa, which, as he put it, helped "move that cause along."[71]

Under the impact of deindustrialization and restructuring of the urban political economy, the Pittsburgh branch of the Urban League renewed its resolve to fight subtle and not so subtle manifestations of the color line in all aspects of the city's institutional life. Within the context of its own struggle to survive as a viable social service organization amid staff reductions and budget cuts, the branch forged a variety of new and innovative programs to alleviate suffering and assist able-bodied men and women obtain work, achieve home ownership, and educate their children for success in the new urban political economy.

The ULP also had a hand in transforming Pittsburgh's political landscape. The league facilitated the emergence of a new politics, allowing blacks to take power through the established electoral process, and it helped mobilize previously neglected segments of the African American electorate. In

Pittsburgh, as elsewhere, African Americans focused on electing black candidates to public office at all levels of government. Again, the Urban League movement shaped the quality of African American life through political no less than philanthropic, interracialist, and economic processes.[72]

Although Pittsburgh stopped short of electing its first African American mayor, the ULP's political activities reinforced the nationwide impetus to take power at the local and state levels and laid the groundwork for a stronger voice in national politics, as symbolized by the election and reelection of Barack Obama, the first US president of African descent. When the triumph of Donald Trump and the conservative wing of the Republican Party upended the relative optimism of the Obama years, the Pittsburgh branch confronted the shifting political climate head-on. As the organization prepared to celebrate its 100th anniversary in 2018, it expressed disappointment with the state of black Pittsburgh: "African Americans in our region are still suffering negative conditions very similar to those which caused the affiliate to be formed in the first place: scarcity of decent affordable housing; lack of access to effective education and good jobs; disparities in health access and outcomes; and an oppressively inequitable rendering of criminal justice." Even so, the Urban League of Pittsburgh resolved to move forward, developing new initiatives based on the strength, energy, and determination of a new generation of "Young Black Pittsburghers," fortified by the city's awareness that persistent "inequities" are "unacceptable" to the Greater Pittsburgh metropolitan community.[73]

Epilogue

The history of the Urban League of Pittsburgh is more than the tale of one city. It underscores the growth of a vibrant social movement. As past NUL president John Jacobs put it, the ULP mirrors the conditions that brought the national organization into existence, including "the kinds of people—black and white—who created it and struggled to keep it alive."[1] Another past president of the Urban League, Hugh B. Price, accented the role of the Pittsburgh branch in the National Urban League's development "not merely" as a social service organization but also as a "social justice movement."[2] The historic militance of the Pittsburgh branch resonated across other Urban League branches and affiliates nationwide. During the 1930s the Chicago Urban League boldly declared, "The time has come for a more aggressive attitude on the part of Negroes. We, of the Chicago Urban League, realize that fact, and our future programs will be more aggressive than they have been in the past."[3]

Despite its immense contributions to the well-being of black people over more than a century, historical interpretations of the Urban League's legacy remain highly contested. Urban Leaguers readily concede that "devastating inequality gaps" continue to "permeate" American and African American life, leading to ongoing debates about the efficacy of the Urban League's social service and social justice programs.[4] Some scholars—most notably, historian Nancy Weiss—argue that the Urban League was a conservative force that "closely reflected the racial ideology of Booker T. Washington." Others, such as Jesse T. Moore Jr., forcefully maintain that the National Urban League most often echoed the views and injunctions of scholar and activist W. E. B. Du Bois. According to Moore, the organization "enlarged its programs to include sustained political pressure, efforts to reform existing governmental structures, and civil rights" from the outset of the Great Migration.[5] Still others, particularly Touré F. Reed, sidestep

180

the Du Bois–Washington dispute and focus on how the Urban League movement (particularly the Chicago and New York branches) challenged white supremacist thought and social practices but nonetheless created education and job programs that privileged the interests of better-educated middle-class and professional blacks over those of their working-class counterparts.[6]

Whether viewing the Urban League movement as a conservative or a progressive social force, studies accent the destructive impact of the segregationist system on the league's efforts to implement programs of uplift and improvement for poor and working-class newcomers to the city. In his seminal study of the Chicago branch of the Urban League published in 1966, historian Arvarh E. Strickland concluded that the league's deficiencies were fundamentally a product of "an indisposition on the part of a great American city to face one of its major problems—the withholding of economic, social, and political opportunities from the sizable nonwhite segment of its population."[7] Similarly, five years later, Urban League historians Guichard Parris and Lester Brooks wrote that the "tyranny of racism" undermined many of the NUL's plans and programs for the empowerment and uplift of black people and sent scores of them "to unmarked graves." Even more pointedly, they declared, were it not for the ongoing social work and activism of the league, its staff, and its volunteers, hundreds of thousands of newcomers "would have suffered even more from the inevitable consequences of unmitigated black migration."[8]

In addition to documenting the influence of the segregationist system, as well as class and gender biases, this volume calls attention to the impact of unique local conditions on social work and social justice programs and practices. Although the experiences of the Pittsburgh branch overlapped, reinforced, and intersected the larger national Urban League movement, it developed distinctive features of its own. From the outset of its history, the Urban League of Pittsburgh placed substantial emphasis on building bridges between blacks and the predominantly white organized labor movement. Partly because of his labor activism, the ULP's first executive director, John T. Clark, lost his job in Pittsburgh and left to lead the St. Louis branch. Although many Urban League affiliates assigned the lion's share of the fight for equal access to public accommodations and equal justice to organizations such as the NAACP, the ULP frequently took up these issues alongside its ongoing fight for jobs, housing, health care, and education. In the years after World War II, the branch not only helped spearhead a grassroots campaign to desegregate downtown department stores but also organized the movement to desegregate the city's public swimming pools.

In sum, this book offers a unique case study of the Urban League movement outside of New York City, Chicago, and Atlanta. It underscores how the Urban League increasingly merged social research and professional social work with social justice, civil rights, workers' rights, and black power struggles. As such, it illustrates in no uncertain terms that the Urban League movement stood inside and not outside the larger fight to liberate people of African descent from the tyranny of white supremacy on a national and even transnational scale. In conjunction with a plethora of other well-known social justice organizations, the Urban League movement uprooted the Jim Crow order and nudged the nation closer to living up to its democratic promise. But the struggle is far from over. It continues within and well beyond the Greater Pittsburgh metropolitan region.

Acknowledgments

It is a pleasure to acknowledge the many people who made this book possible. In addition to my department head, dean, provost, president, and sponsors of my Giant Eagle Professorship in History and Social Justice at Carnegie Mellon University, I extend special thanks to the librarians and archivists at Carnegie Mellon, the University of Pittsburgh, and the Senator John Heinz History Center. These include Sue Collins, Ona Taylor (retired), Gabrielle Michalek, Katherine Barbera, and Erika Linke at Carnegie Mellon; David Grinnell, coordinator of archives and manuscripts at the Archives Service Center, University of Pittsburgh; and John Paul Deley, director, and Mary Jones, chief librarian, at the Detre Library, Heinz History Center, Pittsburgh. At the University Press of Kentucky, thanks to Anne Dean Dotson and Ila McEntire for their confidence in and support of this book from the initial proposal and writing stages through publication in the Civil Rights and the Struggle for Black Equality in the Twentieth Century series.

Numerous other people provided much-needed support during the research and writing of this book. I am especially grateful to Kenya Boswell, president, BNY Mellon Foundation of Southern Pennsylvania, for her abiding support of our regional research, education, and publication efforts through the Carnegie Mellon Center for Africanamerican Urban Studies and the Economy (CAUSE). This book is also indebted to my assistant Hikari Aday; business manager Natalie Taylor; desktop publishing coordinator and webmaster Jesse Wilson; research associate Clayton Vaughn-Roberson, PhD, at Carnegie Mellon; and copyeditor Linda Lotz.

Colleagues, friends, and students provided indispensable energy and intellectual fuel that propelled *Pittsburgh and the Urban League Movement* forward. Friends and colleagues include, to name only a few, Earl Lewis at the University of Michigan; Laurence Glasco at the University of

183

Pittsburgh; Ralph Proctor at the Community College of Allegheny County; Wendy Goldman, Joel Tarr, Nico Slate, Eric Anderson, and Edda Fields-Black at Carnegie Mellon University; and Andrew Masich, president and CEO of the Senator John Heinz History Center. Recent cohorts of graduate and undergraduate students also moved this study forward through their ongoing intellectual engagement with issues in African American history. This study benefited most recently from conversations with graduate students in my seminar on the African American urban experience: Arko Dasgupta, Wyatt Erchak, Peter Singer, Alex Tabor, Michael White, and Jahanzaib Choudhry. In my course on African Americans, imprisonment, and the carceral state, undergraduate students also contributed to the development of this book: Camila Bodden, Akiri Brown, Sammie Paul, Akwelle Quaye, Linden Runels, Jacqueline Wu, Clarisse Brown, and Lauren Pugeda. I am also grateful to the Dr. Edna McKenzie Branch of ASALH—the Association for the Study of African American Life and History (Pittsburgh)—for an opportunity to present a public lecture on the book ahead of publication.

My deepest gratitude goes to my wife H. LaRue Trotter and the Trotter-14 siblings (now Trotter-12) for their enduring encouragement and support for my scholarship and all else that matters in life. Finally, and in many ways most importantly, thanks to Esther L. Bush, president and CEO of the Urban League of Greater Pittsburgh, for inviting me to write a history of the city's Urban League movement.

Notes

Abbreviations

RAP   Remembering Africanamerican Pittsburgh oral history
                            project, Center for Africanamerican Urban Studies and the
                            Economy (CAUSE), Carnegie Mellon University
ULP Papers, Heinz   Urban League of Pittsburgh Papers, Senator John Heinz
                            History Center, Pittsburgh
ULP Papers, UP   Urban League of Pittsburgh Papers, Archives Service Cen-
                            ter, University of Pittsburgh

Prologue

1. Published accounts of the ULP include a mix of primary and secondary studies. See Arthur J. Edmunds and Esther L. Bush, *Daybreakers: The Story of the Urban League of Pittsburgh, the First Eighty Years* (1983; revised and updated, Pittsburgh: Urban League of Pittsburgh, 1999); Laurence A. Glasco, ed., *The WPA History of the Negro in Pittsburgh* (Pittsburgh: University of Pittsburgh Press, 2004); Dennis Dickerson, *Out of the Crucible: Black Steelworkers in Western Pennsylvania, 1875–1980* (Albany: State University of New York Press, 1986); Peter Gottlieb, *Making Their Own Way: Southern Blacks' Migration to Pittsburgh, 1916–30* (Urbana: University of Illinois Press, 1987); Joe William Trotter Jr., *River Jordan: African American Urban Life in the Ohio Valley* (Lexington: University Press of Kentucky, 1998); Joe William Trotter Jr. and Jared Day, *Race and Renaissance: African Americans in Pittsburgh since World War II* (Pittsburgh: University of Pittsburgh Press, 2010); Joe William Trotter Jr. and Eric Ledell Smith, eds., *African Americans in Pennsylvania: Shifting Historical Perspectives* (College Park: Pennsylvania Historical and Museum Commission and Pennsylvania State University Press, 1997). Also see the PhD dissertations by Ancella Livers, "Defining Ourselves: Gender Construction and the Creation of a Black Community in Pittsburgh, 1925–55" (PhD diss., Carnegie Mellon University, 1998); Fidel Makoto Campet, "Housing in Black Pittsburgh: Community Struggles and the State, 1916–1973" (PhD diss., Carnegie Mellon University, 2011); Jessica Klanderud, "Street Wisdom: African American Cultural and Political Formations in Pittsburgh, 1918–1970" (PhD diss., Carnegie Mellon University, 2011); Adam Lee Cilli, "'The Greatest Good': Black Reformers and the Early Civil Rights Movement

in Pittsburgh, 1915–1945" (PhD diss., University of Maine, 2005). This book also draws on the ULP records housed at the Archives Service Center at the University of Pittsburgh and Pittsburgh's Senator John Heinz History Center (a Smithsonian affiliate), the *Pittsburgh Courier,* the *Pittsburgh Post-Gazette,* and the Remembering Africanamerican Pittsburgh (RAP) oral history project conducted by Carnegie Mellon University's Center for Africanamerican Urban Studies and the Economy (CAUSE). Studies that help place the ULP within a broader national and comparative framework include Guichard Parris and Lester Brooks, *Blacks in the City: A History of the National Urban League* (Boston: Little Brown, 1971); Nancy J. Weiss, *The National Urban League, 1910–1940* (New York: Oxford University Press, 1974); Jesse Thomas Moore Jr., *A Search for Equality: The National Urban League, 1910–1961* (University Park: Pennsylvania State University Press, 1981); Susan D. Carle, *Defining the Struggle: National Organizing for Racial Justice, 1880–1915* (New York: Oxford University Press, 2013); Alonzo N. Smith, *Empowering Communities, Changing Lives: 100 Years of the National Urban League and Black America, 1910–2010* (Virginia Beach, VA: Donning, 2011). There are also a number of biographies about and memoirs by Urban League leaders such as Eugene Kinckle Jones, Whitney Young, and Hugh Price. See Felix L. Armfield, *Eugene Kinckle Jones: The National Urban League and Black Social Work, 1910–1940* (Urbana: University of Illinois Press, 2012); Dennis C. Dickerson, *Militant Mediator: Whitney M. Young, Jr.* (Lexington: University Press of Kentucky, 1998); Nancy J. Weiss, *Whitney M. Young, Jr., and the Struggle for Civil Rights* (Princeton, NJ: Princeton University Press, 1989); Hugh B. Price, *This African-American Life: A Memoir* (Durham, NC: John F. Blair, 2017); Touré F. Reed, *Not Alms but Opportunity: The Urban League and the Politics of Racial Uplift, 1910–1950* (Chapel Hill: University of North Carolina Press, 2008); Arvarh E. Strickland, *History of the Chicago Urban League* (1966; reprint, Columbia: University of Missouri Press, 2001). Studies of other branches of the Urban League include Dennis N. Mihelich, "World War II and the Transformation of the Omaha Urban League," *Nebraska History* 60 (1979): 401–23; Albert S. Broussard, "Perey H. Steele, Jr., and the Urban League: Race Relations and the Struggle for Civil Rights in Post–World War II San Diego," *California History* 83, no. 4 (2006): 7–23; Stuart Mcelderry, "Building a West Coast Ghetto: African-American Housing in Portland, 1910–1960," *Pacific Northwest Quarterly* 92, no. 3 (Summer 2001): 137–48; Njeru Murage, "The Detroit Urban League–Employers Alliance in Wartime Detroit, 1916–1919," *Michigan Historical Review* 26, no. 1 (Spring 2000): 66–104. For a recent review of this larger body of scholarship, see Joe William Trotter Jr., "Appendix: Essay on Sources," in *Workers on Arrival: Black Labor in the Making of America* (Berkeley: University of California Press, 2019).

2. Trotter, *River Jordan,* 96.

3. Reginald A. Johnson, secretary, Industrial Relations Department, ULP, to T. Arnold Hill, NUL, 20 October 1938, NUL Papers, Library of Congress; Report of the Department of Industrial Relations, January and February 1933, NUL Papers.

4. Esther L. Bush, "The State of Black Pittsburgh," 28 October 1999, 6, library of the Urban League of Great Pittsburgh.

1. Quest for Jobs and Housing

1. Paul U. Kellogg, ed., *The Pittsburgh Survey: Findings in Six Volume* (New York: Charities Publication Committee, 1909–1914). For a contemporary historical assessment of the *Pittsburgh Survey*'s social scientific study of the white working class, see Maurine W. Greenwald and Margo Anderson, eds., *Pittsburgh Surveyed: Social Science and Social Reform in the Early Twentieth Century* (Pittsburgh: University of Pittsburgh Press, 1996). Unlike many early-twentieth-century social scientific studies of urban life, *The Pittsburgh Survey* included brief assessments of African American life, but its major aim was to transform popular perceptions of the white immigrant working class. In her essay "The Immigrants Pictured and Unpictured in the Pittsburgh Survey," historian Ewa Morawska concludes that *The Pittsburgh Survey* writers treated the poverty of immigrant workers primarily as a product of "the workers' exploitative and hazardous working conditions and . . . the calculated neglect of landlords" (Greenwald and Anderson, *Pittsburgh Surveyed*, 235).

2. "Constitution of the Association for the Improvement of Social Conditions in the Hill District of Pittsburgh," 1914 Series I, Executive Board Subseries, Administrative Matters, box 7, file folder 320, ULP Papers, UP; Arthur J. Edmunds and Esther L. Bush, *Daybreakers: The Story of the Urban League of Pittsburgh, the First Eighty Years* (1983; revised and updated, Pittsburgh: Urban League of Pittsburgh, 1999), 18.

3. "The Urban League of Pittsburgh," vol. 1, no. 1 (March 1918); one-page background document on the transition of the PCSSN to the ULP, 1918; "Urban League of Pittsburgh, Plan of Work," 1918, box 3, file folders 87, 88, ULP Papers, UP; Edmunds and Bush, *Daybreakers*, 18–21.

4. National-level studies include Guichard Parris and Lester Brooks, *Blacks in the City: A History of the National Urban League* (Boston: Little Brown, 1971); Nancy J. Weiss, *The National Urban League, 1910–1940* (New York: Oxford University Press, 1974); Jesse Thomas Moore Jr., *A Search for Equality: The National Urban League, 1910–1961* (University Park: Pennsylvania State University Press, 1981); Susan D. Carle, *Defining the Struggle: National Organizing for Racial Justice, 1880–1915* (New York: Oxford University Press, 2013); Alonzo N. Smith, *Empowering Communities, Changing Lives: 100 Years of the National Urban League and Black America, 1910–2010* (Virginia Beach, VA: Donning, 2011). Also see "Race Prejudice Can Best Be Combatted through Individual Effort Declares Walter A. May," *Pittsburgh Courier*, 20 January 1923.

5. Weiss, *National Urban League*, 42–43 (emphasis in original).

6. Weiss, *National Urban League*, 112.

7. Edmunds and Bush, *Daybreakers*, 24–27.

8. Excerpt of letter from Eugene K. Jones to S. R. Morsell, 12 September 1917, box 3, file folders 87, 88, ULP Papers, UP; "Additional Notes," *Pittsburgh Courier*, 10 November 1923. For additional background information on the ULP, see the 1918–1920 reports and correspondence of Mrs. George Elliott, women's employment secretary, and T. E. Barton, men's industrial secretary, box 3, file folders 87, 88, ULP Papers, UP.

9. Weiss, *National Urban League,* 123–24.

10. "Urban League of Pittsburgh, Plan of Work," 1918; article 3, "Constitution of the Urban League of Pittsburgh," box 1, file folder 2, ULP Papers, UP.

11. Andrew Buni, *Robert L. Vann of* Pittsburgh Courier: *Politics and Black Journalism* (Pittsburgh: University of Pittsburgh Press, 1974), 59–60; Weiss, *National Urban League,* 123–24; Edmunds and Bush, *Daybreakers,* 20–22, 51.

12. Edmunds and Bush, *Daybreakers,* 72; American Civil Liberties Union, "The Shame of Pennsylvania: The Story of How Pennsylvania Leads the States in Violence and Police Brutality, Prosecutions for Opinion, and War on Strikers and Radicals," 1928, box 18, folder 14, ULP Papers, Heinz.

13. T. Arnold Hill to Clark, 7 April 1926; Clark to Hill, 12 April 1926, box 1, file folder 3, ULP Papers, UP.

14. Edmunds and Bush, *Daybreakers,* 73. As early as January 1920, the leadership of the ULP had changed considerably. Walter A. May remained on as president through 1920, and John D. Fraser remained as treasurer; however, Frances Brown had become secretary, Reverend Trigg was first vice president, and Hezekiah Anderson was second vice president. See Frances Brown to John D. Fraser and other ULP board members, 14 January 1920; John T. Clark to Edwin C. May, 6 November 1922, box 1, file folder 1, ULP Papers, UP.

15. Paul F. Mowbray to Clark, 25 November 1919, box 3, file folders 88, 96, 115, ULP Papers, UP.

16. "Report of Home Economics Worker," May 1919, box 1, file folder 19; box 3, file folders 87, 88, 112, 115, 137; box 5, file folders 237, 238, ULP Papers, UP.

17. Carolyn L. Carson, "And the Results Showed Promise . . . Physicians, Childbirth, and Southern Black Migrant Women, 1916–1930: Pittsburgh as a Case Study," *Journal of American Ethnic History* 14 (Fall 1994): 32–64, reprinted in Joe William Trotter Jr. and Eric Ledell Smith, eds., *African Americans in Pennsylvania: Shifting Historical Perspectives* (University Park: Pennsylvania Historical and Museum Commission and Pennsylvania State University Press, 1997), 340; Edmunds and Bush, *Daybreakers,* 49.

18. Edmunds and Bush, *Daybreakers,* 41; "Executive Board Meeting," 25 May 1920; Clark to Heinz, 10 May 1918; Mrs. George (Elizabeth) Elliott, women's employment secretary, six-month report, 1918, box 1, file folders 1, 19, ULP Papers, UP.

19. Clark to Tyson, 7 November 1925; Jeffries to Allen, 5 November 1926; "Report of the President E. C. May, at the 9th Annual Meeting," 17 January 1927; Francis Tyson to H. B. Wheeler, American Sheet and Tin Plate Company, 8 December 1919, box 1, file folders 2, 3, 4, 19; box 3, file folders 87, 88, 96, 115, ULP Papers, UP. The ULP opened offices at 505 Wylie Avenue in 1918 but had moved to 518 Wylie Avenue, near Fifth Avenue, by late 1922. See Clark to May, 6 November 1922; Edmunds and Bush, *Daybreakers,* 21, 35. Initially, the State Department of Labor and Industry rejected as "impractical" the ULP's request to hire a black examiner to help handle the large number of black job applicants. Only after the ULP launched its own very successful independent employment service did the state agree to collaborate.

20. "Executive Board Meeting," 25 May 1920; "Minutes of Social Workers," 6 January 1922; Elliott, six-month report, 1918, box 1, file folder 19; box 3, file folders 87, 88, 115, 127, ULP Papers, UP.

21. Elliott, six-month report, 1918; Clark to A. L. Humphrey, Westinghouse Air Brake Company, Wilmerding, PA, 28 November 1919; "Meeting of Mechanics," 5 February 1918, box 1, file folder 19; box 3, file folders 87, 88, 115, 137, ULP Papers, UP; "Article on Steel Industry," ca. 1922–1923, box 3, file folders 110, 114, 117, 135, ULP Papers, UP.

22. Clark to H. M. Reed, 31 July 1920, box 3, file folder 110, ULP Papers, UP.

23. "Executive Board Meeting," 25 May 1920; Clark to Reed, 31 July 1920.

24. "Visit to New Castle," ca. 1920; Clark to Donora Steel Company, 30 August 1918; Clark to John Johnson, Johnstown, PA, 21 November 1921; Clark to J. A. Gruber, Carnegie Steel, 5 July 1919; Clark to D. Cameron, foreman, Wheeling Mold and Foundry Company, Wheeling, WV, 26 February 1920, box 1, file folders 1, 19; box 3, file folders 87, 88, 115, 137, ULP Papers, UP. In September 1920 the city's black residents, under the auspices of the Invincible Club of Ten, invited W. E. B. Du Bois to address the group at the First Christian Church of New Castle. Mrs. Lettie B. Williams served as chair of the sponsoring committee, which included eight other married women.

25. "Minutes of the Executive Board," 21 March 1923, box 1, file folder 2, ULP Papers, UP; "Executive Board Meeting," 25 May 1920; "Study of Certain Industries in which Negroes Work and Their Progress over a Ten Year Period," 12 December 1927; "Special Problems of Negro Workers in Pittsburgh," 6 April 1929, box 1, file folders 4, 24; box 3, file folder 142, ULP Papers, UP; Joe William Trotter Jr. and Jared Day, *Race and Renaissance: African Americans in Pittsburgh since World War II* (Pittsburgh: University of Pittsburgh Press, 2010), 30.

26. "Minutes of Social Workers," 6 January 1922; Clark to A. L. McLaughlin, 4 January 1921, box 3, file folders 89, 104, ULP Papers, UP; Edmunds and Bush, *Daybreakers*, 39–43.

27. "Report," January 1920; "Minutes of Executive Board Meeting," 17 November 1921; "Points to Present to Churches by Representative of the Negro Emergency Relief Committee," ca. 1922; "Minutes, Executive Bd.," 12 October 1926, box 1, file folders 1, 3, 23, ULP Papers, UP. In 1922 the ULP offered its services as a "clearinghouse for temporary relief" among black residents. As late as October 1926, the ULP continued to provide fuel to needy families from its Brewer Coal Fund.

28. "Minutes of Executive Board," 18 January 1922; "Executive Secretary's Report," March 1922; "A June Note, Executive Board Members of Urban League," ca. June 1922; "Minutes of the Executive Board," 21 March 1923 and 9 February 1926; "Materials to Study for Annual Meeting," ca. 1925, box 1, file folders 1, 2, 3, ULP Papers, UP; A. C. Thayer, "Report of the Board of Directors of the Urban League of Pittsburgh," September 1927, box 1, file folder 4, ULP Papers, UP.

29. Clark to Edwin C. May, 1 August 1924; E. C. May to Members of the ULP Board, 12 September 1924, box 1, file folders 2, 21; box 3, file folder 89; box 5, file folder 205, ULP Papers, UP.

30. Thayer, "Report of the Board of Directors," September 1927; "Study of Certain Industries in which Negroes Work," 12 December 1927.

31. "Local Urban League Plans 'Negro Industry Week': T. Arnold Hill Makes Return Engagement," *Pittsburgh Courier,* 25 February 1928; "One of 'Big Three' Here Wednesday," *Pittsburgh Courier,* 14 April 1928; "Urban League 'Big Three' Make Fine Impression Here," *Pittsburgh Courier,* 28 April 1928 (reporting on the visit of NUL officers L. Hollingsworth Wood, president; Eugene Kinckle Jones, executive secretary; and Oswald Garrison Villard, treasurer and grandson of William Lloyd Garrison); "T. Arnold Hill of New York to Visit City: Director of Industrial Relations of National Urban League to Be Guest," *Pittsburgh Courier,* 12 May 1928 (Hill was scheduled to speak at the ULP offices, the YWCA, the Rotary Club, and possibly on KDKA radio); "Urban League to Fete T. A. Hill: Public Is Invited," *Pittsburgh Courier,* 15 December 1928. John T. Clark also regularly reported on the status of the Urban League movement in Pittsburgh at national meetings, such as the one in Kansas City in 1923, where he delivered a talk on "how to find opportunities for the skilled workers." See "National Urban League Holds Yearly Meeting: Vital Topics Discussed," *Pittsburgh Courier,* 27 October 1923; "Better Jobs for Workers Being Sought," *Pittsburgh Courier,* 13 October 1923.

32. "Memoranda of Interviews Held during Week of December 3, 1928, between Parties Mentioned below and T. Arnold Hill," box 1, file folder 5, ULP Papers, UP.

33. "Memoranda of Interviews Held during Week of December 3, 1928."

34. "Article on Industry," ca. 1922–1923, box 1, file folders 1, 2, ULP Papers, UP.

35. "Article on Industry," ca. 1922–1923.

36. Excerpts from "A Study of Occupational and Numerical Progress of the Negro in Certain Industries," ca. 1928, box 1, file folder 5, ULP Papers, UP.

37. "Observations on Physical and Recreational Needs of the Negro Miners Made at the Mining Camps at Library, Imperial, George, and Moon Run, Pa.," July 1927; John T. Clark, "A June Note, Executive Board Members of Urban League," ca. June 1922; "Study of Certain Industries in which Negroes Work," 12 December 1927; "Special Problems of Negro Workers in Pittsburgh," 6 April 1929, box 1, file folders 1, 4, 5, ULP Papers, UP.

38. "Article on Industry," ca. 1922–1923.

39. Clark to James Hemphill, 8 May 1923; ULP to L. H. Burnett, 18 January 1924; Clark to A. L. McLaughlin, 25 June 1923, box 1, file folder 2, ULP Papers, UP; "Incident at J & L in Woodlawn," ca. June 1926, box 1, file folder 3, ULP Papers, UP.

40. See Maurice Moss to John T. Clark, 26 September 1935, includes copy of "Causes of Negro Migration from the South," excerpt of letter received from a family in Atlanta, GA, box 1, file folder 11; box 3, file folders 133, 155, ULP Papers, UP.

41. "Article on Industry," ca. 1922–1923.

42. Edmunds and Bush, *Daybreakers,* 41; "Executive Board Meeting," 25 May 1920; Clark to Heinz, 10 May 1918, box 3, file folders 87, 88, ULP Papers, UP; "Executive Board Meeting," 26 May 1920, box 1, file folder 1, ULP Papers, UP.

43. "Miss Lowndes Will Make Special Survey of Local Social Problems of Groups," *Pittsburgh Courier,* 31 July 1926.

44. Grace S. Lowndes, "Report," 15 June–15 August 1927, box 1, file folder 4, ULP Papers, UP.

45. Lowndes, "Report," 15 June–15 August 1927.

46. Edmunds and Bush, *Daybreakers,* 21.

47. ULP annual report, "The Fifteenth Year, 1918–1932," ULP Branch Files, NUL Papers, Library of Congress, cited in Trotter and Day, *Race and Renaissance,* 236n56; "Negro Settlement Workers in Plants," *Pittsburgh Gazette Times,* 13 February 1921; Edmunds and Bush, *Daybreakers,* 21, 37; Dennis Dickerson, *Out of the Crucible: Black Steelworkers in Western Pennsylvania, 1875–1980* (Albany: State University of New York Press, 1986), 105; "The Urban League Scholarship Is Awarded to Local Youth: Gerald E. Allen, Pitt Graduate, Studying for Masters Degree," *Pittsburgh Courier,* 23 October 1926; "Canton Urban League Head in Pittsburgh," *Pittsburgh Courier,* 26 November 1927.

48. Carson, "And the Results Showed Promise," 340; Edmunds and Bush, *Daybreakers,* 37, 49; "Executive Board Meeting," 27 April 1920, box 1, file folder 1, ULP Papers, UP.

49. Edmunds and Bush, *Daybreakers,* 47–49.

50. "Executive Board Meeting," 2 March 1920; John T. Clark to Mary E. Bakewell, 4 March, 3 May 1920; Clark to Bayard H. Christy, 25 and 31 August, 2 November 1920, box 1, file folders 2, 3, 4, 19; box 3, file folders 87, 88, 96, 115, ULP Papers, UP.

51. ULP [Clark] to Standard Steel Car Corporation, 13 March 1918, box 3, file folders 87, 88, ULP Papers, UP; Edmunds and Bush, *Daybreakers,* 39, 65–66.

52. "Nat'l Urban League Ends Fifth Session: Secretaries Describe Work of Branches in Thirty-Three Cities," *Pittsburgh Courier,* 6 November 1920; "Pittsburgh Urban League Hears National Delegate," *Pittsburgh Courier,* 29 January 1921; "Interesting Meetings Feature Urban League Conference: Race Conference of Unique Interest," *Pittsburgh Courier,* 14 April 1928 (meeting held in Philadelphia); "Courier Feature Writer Pittsburgh Visitor," *Pittsburgh Courier,* 28 April 1928 (on New York City–based *Courier* writer Floyd J. Calvin's visit to Pittsburgh after attending the NUL meeting in Philadelphia).

53. "Article on Industry," ca. 1922–1923.

54. "Article on Industry," ca. 1922–1923; "Minutes of Executive Board Meeting," 1922–1923, box 1, file folders 1, 2, 20, 21; box 3, file folder 89, ULP, UP; "Report of the Ind. Dept.," April and May 1920, January, February, and March 1929, box 3, file folders 89, 96, 110, 114, 136, 142, 145, ULP, UP. For an excellent description of the tedious process of job-placement work, see Virginia M. Woodson, "Report of Emp. Dept. for Months of Jan., Feb., and Mar. 1929," box 1, file folders 5, 26, ULP Papers, UP. For detailed records of black women's employment in department stores, see "Report of Women's Employment Secretary," November 1918, box 3, file folders 87, 88, 137, ULP Papers, UP. "Special Problems of Negro Workers in Pittsburgh," 6 April 1929, offers information on how coal mining helped offset the loss of steel industry jobs for black workers during the mid to late 1920s.

55. Edmunds and Bush, *Daybreakers,* 37, 42–43; Parris and Brooks, *Blacks in the City,* xxx.

56. Peter Gottlieb, *Making Their Own Way: Southern Blacks' Migration to Pittsburgh, 1916–30* (Urbana: University of Illinois Press, 1987), 172; Sterling D. Spero and Abram L. Harris, *The Black Worker: The Negro and the Labor Movement* (1930; reprint, New York: Atheneum, 1968), 258–59; "Study of Certain Industries in which Negroes Work," 12 December 1927; A. C. Thayer to T. A. Hill, 29 February, 1928, NUL Records, Industrial Relations Department, Local Affiliates file, series 4: "Synopsis of Interview," 1, Blankehorn Collection, Library of Congress; "Houston, Pennsylvania, About Two Miles East of Cannonsburg," ca. October 1925, box 3, file folder 89; box 1, file folder 2, ULP Papers, UP; Edmunds and Bush, *Daybreakers,* 73.

57. Hill to Clark, 7 April 1926; Clark to Hill, 12 April 1926, box 1, file folder 3, ULP Papers, UP; "Report of the President E. C. May, at the 9th Annual Meeting," 17 January 1927; "Specific Service Rendered through Workers," ca. 1925; Jeffries to Allen, director of the Columbus, Ohio, Urban League, 5 November 1926; "General Outline of Industrial Program for 1926," box 3, file folders 129, 89; box 1, file folders 2, 3, 4, ULP Papers, UP. Clark routinely cooperated with a variety of agencies on research projects involving the city's black population. At the outset of 1926, he assisted Mrs. H. L. Johnson of the US Department of Labor when she carried out a study of industrial conditions among black workers in Pittsburgh. In addition to Clark, Johnson consulted Grace Lowndes, John Carter Robinson, and Miss A. L. Stoner, supervisor of the Negro Department of the State Employment Bureau, among others. See "Mrs. H. L. Johnson Spends Week in City Studying Industrial Conditions," *Pittsburgh Courier,* 30 January 1926. In 1925 the ULP contemplated setting up its own independent industrial department and employment service "separate from the State," contingent upon receiving sufficient financial support from firms in the area. The ULP also insisted that job placements should be controlled by the organization creating the jobs.

58. "Pittsburgh Tenders Reception to Local Urban League Head Alonzo Thayer," *Pittsburgh Courier,* 24 September 1927; "Local Urban League Secretary Finishes First Year's Work," *Pittsburgh Courier,* 9 June 1928; "Minutes of the Executive Board," 8 June 1927, box 3, file folder 129; box 1, file folder 4, ULP Papers, UP. At the same time, Tyson asked Thayer to consult a thesis written by ULP social work fellow Gerald E. Allen on the quality of African American life in the coal camps of western Pennsylvania. See G. E. Allen, "The Negro Coal Miner in the Pennsylvania District" (MA thesis, University of Pittsburgh, 1927).

59. "Report of Exec. Sec. for Oct. 1928," box 1, file folder 5, ULP Papers, UP; "Report of the Executive Sec. for the Period Covering Oct. and Nov. 1927," submitted 13 December 1927, box 3, file folder 129; box 1, file folder 4, ULP Papers, UP; "Minutes of the Executive Board," 8 June 1927, box 1, file folders 1, 4, 5, ULP Papers, UP; "Observations on Physical and Recreational Needs of Negro Miners," July 1927; "General Welfare Plan Submitted to the Pittsburgh Coal Company: Supplementary to the Study of Physical and Recreational Conditions of the Negro in the Mines," 16 September 1927; "Minutes of the Executive Board," 8 June 1927, box 1, file folders 1, 4, 5, ULP Papers, UP; Gottlieb, *Making Their Own Way,* 193, 197.

60. "Staff Members Entertain Urban League Secretary," *Pittsburgh Courier*, 21 December 1927; "R. Maurice Moss of Baltimore to Head Local Urban League," *Pittsburgh Courier*, 9 November 1929.

61. "Industrial and Civic Report," September 1927, box 1, file folders 4, 24, 36, ULP Papers, UP; Alonzo Thayer, "September Report: To the Board of Directors, ULP," ca. September 1927, ibid.; "Local Urban League Secretary Resigns: Alonzo Thayer Will Take Post in Chicago, Baltimore Man May Come Here," *Pittsburgh Courier*, 19 October 1929. As discussed later, particularly in chapter 2, the ULP's success was thanks in part to the extraordinary work of women staffers such as Grace Lowndes, civic and industrial secretary; Virginia Woodson, head of girls' club work; and Georgine Pearce, director of the home and school visitor program.

62. Trotter and Day, *Race and Renaissance*, 10, 12–13; Dickerson, *Out of the Crucible*, 46–47; Carson, "And the Results Showed Promise," 340–41; Clark to the Donora Steel Co., 30 August 1918, box 1, file folder 19; box 3, file folders 87, 88, 115, 137, ULP Papers, UP; "Report of Home Economics Worker," May 1922; "Trip to New Castle, Penna.," ca. 1920, box 3, file folders 110, 114, 117, 135, ULP Papers, UP; "Materials to Study for Annual Meeting," ca. 1925, box 3, file folder 89; box 1, file folder 2, ULP Papers, UP.

63. "Memoranda of Interviews Held during Week of December 3, 1928, between Parties Mentioned below and T. Arnold Hill," box 1, file folder 5; box 3, file folder 129, ULP Papers, UP.

64. "Report of the Home Economics Worker," February, March, April, May, June, July, and August 1919, and February, April, May, and July 1921, box 1, file folders 2, 3, 4, 19; box 3, file folders 87, 88, 96, 115, ULP Papers, UP; "Minutes of the Exec. Bd. Meeting," 18 April 1923, box 1, file folder 2; box 3, file folders 89, 104, ULP Papers, UP. The board suggested that the committee "take up the health problem in a community way," including contacting the Tuberculosis Association for assistance.

65. Edmunds and Bush, *Daybreakers*, 21, 43. On Pittsburgh's zoning legislation, see Anne Lloyd, "Pittsburgh's 1923 Zoning Ordinance," *Western Pennsylvania Magazine* 57, no. 3 (July 1974): 289–305; Gottlieb, *Making Their Own Way*, 190; "Economic Program of Pittsburgh Urban League," 21 February 1920, box 1, file folder 19; box 3, file folders 96, 110, 114, 117, ULP Papers, UP.

66. "Materials to Study for Annual Meeting," ca. 1925, box 1, file folders 2, 3, 4, 19; box 3, file folders 87, 88, 96, 115, ULP Papers, UP; Clark to the Donora Steel Co., 30 August 1918; Clark to Robert E. Newcomb, Worthington Pump and Machinery Corporation, 29 July 1919, box 1, file folders 2, 3, 4, 19; box 3, file folders 87, 88, 96, 115, ULP Papers, UP.

67. "Observations on Physical and Recreational Needs of Negro Miners," July 1927; Clark to Cameron, 26 February 1920, box 1, file folders 2, 3, 4, 19; box 3, file folders 87, 88, 96, 110, 114, 117, 131, ULP Papers, UP.

2. Promise and Limits

1. Dennis Dickerson, *Out of the Crucible: Black Steelworkers in Western Pennsylvania, 1875–1980* (Albany: State University of New York Press, 1986), 78.

2. "Report of the Home Economics Worker," April, May, and August 1919, box 1, file folder 19; box 3, file folders 87, 88, 96, 112, 115, 137; box 5, file folders 237, 238, ULP Papers, UP; "Report of the Home Economics Worker," February, May, and July 1920, box 1, file folder 1; box 3, file folders 89, 96, 110, 114, 117, 131, ULP Papers, UP; "Report of Home School Visitor," April 1926; "Report of the Home Economics Worker," April 1926 (citing educational improvements among the children of one poor family), box 1, file folders 3, 23, ULP Papers, UP; "Memo to Mr. Moss," n.d. (ca. 1930), box 1, file folders 6, 34; box 3, file folder 132, ULP Papers, UP; "Home Economics Report," July 1922 and April 1921, box 1, file folders 1, 19, 20; box 3, file folders 89, 119, 114, 131, ULP Papers, UP; Arthur J. Edmunds and Esther L. Bush, *Daybreakers: The Story of the Urban League of Pittsburgh, the First Eighty Years* (1983; revised and updated, Pittsburgh: Urban League of Pittsburgh, 1999), 33.

3. "Materials to Study for Annual Meeting," ca. 1925, box 1, file folders 2, 22; box 3, file folder 89, ULP Papers, UP; "Observations on Physical and Recreational Needs of the Negro Miners Made at the Mining Camps at Library, Imperial, George, and Moon Run, Pa.," July 1927, box 1, file folders 4, 24; box 3, file folder 142, ULP Papers, UP.

4. Edmunds and Bush, *Daybreakers*, 22, 33, 67–68. The ULP forged ties with diverse hospitals and health care organizations in the Pittsburgh area, including St. Francis, St. Margaret's, Passavant, Homeopathic, West Penn, Mercy, Allegheny General, and Magee Women's Hospital. See "League Program for 1925," ca. 1925, box 1, file folders 2, 22; box 3, file folder 89, ULP Papers, UP. In December 1928 the ULP reported plans to develop a library containing books on African American life and history. In the same report, it urged the health committee to explore the possibility of cooperating with the YMCA and YWCA on a joint Health Week campaign, rather than holding three separate events. See "Report of Exec. Sec. for Dec. 1928," box 1, file folders 5, 25, 36; box 2, file folder 81; box 3, file folder 142, ULP Papers, UP.

5. "Health Program Planned by Urban League," *Pittsburgh Courier*, 5 May 1928; "Urban League Health Week May 20–26," *Pittsburgh Courier*, 9 May 1928.

6. Carolyn L. Carson, "And the Results Showed Promise . . . Physicians, Childbirth, and Southern Black Migrant Women, 1916–1930: Pittsburgh as a Case Study," *Journal of American Ethnic History* 14 (Fall 1994): 339.

7. "Minutes of Exec. Bd.," 8 June 1927, box 1, file folders 4, 24; box 3, file folder 142, ULP Papers, UP; "Health Program Planned by Urban League," *Pittsburgh Courier*, 5 May 1928; "Minutes of the Exec. Bd. Meeting," 14 May 1924, box 1, file folders 2, 21; box 3, file folder 89; box 5, file folder 205, ULP Papers, UP; Carson, "And the Results Showed Promise," 342. The organization also aided in the distribution of fruit and flowers to the ill in homes and hospitals in the city and cooperated with agencies studying housing conditions among blacks.

8. "Social Workers Announce Fine 1927–28 Program," *Pittsburgh Courier*, 19 November 1927. Officers involved in this work included C. T. Green, president; Georgine R. Pearce, secretary; and J. A. Williams, chair of the program committee.

9. Carson, "And the Results Showed Promise," 342; "Report of Home Economics Worker," April 1921, box 1, file folders 1, 19, 20; box 3, file folders, 89, 110, 114,

131, ULP Papers, UP; "'Healthier Babies—Stronger Mothers': Slogan of Urban League Health Week," *Pittsburgh Courier*, 12 May 1928; Jessica Klanderud, "Street Wisdom: African American Cultural and Political Formations in Pittsburgh, 1918–1970" (PhD diss., Carnegie Mellon University, 2011), 46–47.

10. "'Healthier Babies—Stronger Mothers'"; Klanderud, "Street Wisdom," 46–47; "Minutes of the Exec. Bd. Meeting," 14 May 1924.

11. Adam Lee Cilli, "'The Greatest Good': Black Reformers and the Early Civil Rights Movement in Pittsburgh, 1915–1945" (PhD diss., University of Maine, 2005), 60; Peter Gottlieb, *Making Their Own Way: Southern Blacks' Migration to Pittsburgh, 1916–30* (Urbana: University of Illinois Press, 1987), 191; Daisy Lampkin, chair, "Meeting of Home and Community Committee of Urban League," 13 December 1928, box 1, file folders 5, 25, 36; box 2, file folder 81; box 3, file folder 142, ULP Papers, UP; Edmunds and Bush, *Daybreakers*, 47–49.

12. "Minutes of Executive Board," 9 November 1926 and 7 September 1927, box 1, file folders 3, 4, 24, ULP Papers, UP. In December 1928 the ULP reported plans to develop a library containing books on African American life and history. See "Report of Exec. Sec. for Dec. 1928"; "History of Camp James Weldon Johnson, 1939–1958," box 5, file folder 201, ULP Papers, UP.

13. "R. Maurice Moss of Baltimore to Head Local Urban League," *Pittsburgh Courier*, 9 November 1929; Edmunds and Bush, *Daybreakers*, 63–64.

14. "Report of the President, E. C. May, 9th Annual Meeting," 17 January 1927, box 1, file folders 4, 24; box 3, file folder 142, ULP Papers, UP.

15. Edmunds and Bush, *Daybreakers*, 66–68; "Report of Home Economics Worker," April 1921.

16. John T. Clark to Francis B. Tyson, 11 May 1922, box 1, file folders 1, 20; box 3, file folder 89, ULP Papers, UP; Payton Rose to Exec. Bd., 3 November 1925, box 1, file folder 4, ULP Papers, UP; Edmunds and Bush, *Daybreakers*, 66–68; "Report of Home Economics Worker," April 1921; "Special Committee on Hospital Plans," September 1930, box 1, file folders 6, 34; box 3, file folder 132, ULP Papers, UP.

17. Cilli, "'The Greatest Good,'" 61; Gottlieb, *Making Their Own Way*, 197.

18. Carson, "And the Results Showed Promise," 319, 340, 344–48, 354.

19. Edmunds and Bush, *Daybreakers*, 34–35; Georgine R. Pearce, assisted by Grace Lowndes, "A Study of the Families of the New Registrants in the Public Schools of the Hill District, from Sept. 1927 to Dec. 1927," box 18, folder 18, ULP Papers, Heinz.

20. "A June Note: Executive Board Members of Urban League," ca. June 1922, box 1, file folders 1, 20; box 3, file folder 89, ULP Papers, UP; Edmunds and Bush, *Daybreakers*, 34–35, 66.

21. "League Program for 1925"; "Urban League Holds Essay Contest Here," *Pittsburgh Courier*, 15 December 1922.

22. See excerpt of "Day's Work for the Pittsburgh Urban League," in Edmunds and Bush, *Daybreakers*, 53–54.

23. "Home Economics Report," March 1921, box 1, file folders, 1, 19, 20; box 3, file folders 89, 110, 114, 131, ULP Papers, UP; "A June Note: Executive

Board Members of Urban League," ca. June 1922; "Radio Flames," *Pittsburgh Courier*, 7 July 1923 (reporting on a ULP-sponsored graduation party for eighth-grade students); John T. Clark to Executive Board Members of Urban League, 11 June 1927, box 1, file folders 4, 24; box 3, file folder 142, ULP Papers, UP.

24. "Memoranda of Interviews Held during Week of December 3, 1928, between Parties Mentioned below and T. Arnold Hill," box 1, file folders 5, 25, 36; box 2, file folder 81; box 3, file folder 142, ULP Papers, UP; "Report of Home and School Visitor," October 1930, box 1, file folders 6, 34; box 3, file folder 132, ULP Papers, UP.

25. "Memoranda of Interviews Held during Week of December 3, 1928."

26. A. Thayer, "Sept. Report to the Board of Directors," September 1927, box 1, file folders 4, 24; box 3, file folder 142, ULP Papers, UP; Alonzo C. Thayer, "Summary of Interview with Mr. Frank Leavitt on Trade Opportunities for Colored Boys," 21 September 1927, ibid.

27. Cilli, "'The Greatest Good,'" 98.

28. Cilli, "'The Greatest Good,'" 98; Joe William Trotter Jr. and Jared Day, *Race and Renaissance: African Americans in Pittsburgh since World War II* (Pittsburgh: University of Pittsburgh Press, 2010), 23; Andrew Buni, *Robert L. Vann of* Pittsburgh Courier: *Politics and Black Journalism* (Pittsburgh: University of Pittsburgh Press, 1974), 67–69, 343n59 (statements of Lewin and Lampkin).

29. See "Minutes, Executive Board Meeting," 8 December 1920, May 1919, August 1919, box 1, file folders 1, 19; box 3, file folders 87, 88, 89, 96, 110, 112, 114, 115, 131; box 5, file folders 237, 238, ULP Papers, UP; "Executive Secretary's Report," March 1922, box 1, file folders 1, 20; box 3, file folder 89, ULP Papers, UP; "Executive Board Meeting," 14 May 1924; E. C. May to Rev. C. B. Allen, 4 April 1924; "Minutes, Urban League Executive Board," 10 November 1925, box 1, file folders 2, 21; box 3, file folder 89; box 5, file folder 205, ULP Papers, UP; Trotter and Day, *Race and Renaissance,* 23; Margaret C. "Peg" Albert, director of public information, to history team, 1 August 1983 (referring to September 1925 news clipping about Mrs. Leona Carter's case), box 18, folder 21, ULP Papers, Heinz; Edmunds and Bush, *Daybreakers,* 47; John T. Clark to Francis Stewart, 19 November 1925, box 1, file folders 2, 22; box 3, file folder 89, ULP Papers, UP.

30. "Minutes, Executive Board Meeting," 8 December 1920; "Executive Secretary's Report," March 1922; "Minutes, Urban League Executive Board," 10 November 1925; "Miss Lowndes Will Make Special Survey of Local Social Problems of Groups," *Pittsburgh Courier,* 31 July 1926.

31. See "Morals Court," box 18, file folder 8, ULP Papers, Heinz; "Minutes, Executive Board Meeting," 8 December 1920, May 1919, August 1919; "Executive Secretary's Report," March 1922; "Executive Board Meeting," 14 May 1924; E. C. May to Rev. C. B. Allen, 4 April 1924; "Minutes, Urban League Executive Board," 10 November 1925; John T. Clark to Francis Stewart, 19 November 1925; Trotter and Day, *Race and Renaissance,* 23; Edmunds and Bush, *Daybreakers,* 47.

32. "Girl's Work," ca. 1921–1922, box 1, file folders 1, 19, 20; box 3, file folders 89, 110, 114, 131, ULP Papers, UP; "A June Note: Executive Board Members of

Urban League," ca. June 1922. See also Gottlieb, *Making Their Own Way*, 191–92; Edmunds and Bush, *Daybreakers*, 22.

33. "Report of the Executive Secretary for the Period Covering Oct. and Nov. 1927," box 1, file folders 4, 24; box 3, file folder 142, ULP Papers, UP; Alonzo Thayer, "September Report: To the Board of Directors, ULP," ca. September 1927, ibid.; "Girls Find Happiness in Work and Play with Urban League Advisor Miss Virginia Woodson," *Pittsburgh Courier*, 5 May 1928. See also Gottlieb, *Making Their Own Way*, 191–92; Edmunds and Bush, *Daybreakers*, 22.

34. See "Minutes, Executive Board Meeting," 8 December 1920, May 1919, August 1919; "Executive Secretary's Report," March 1922; "Executive Board Meeting," 14 May 1924; E. C. May to Rev. C. B. Allen, 4 April 1924; "Minutes, Urban League Executive Board," 10 November 1925; Trotter and Day, *Race and Renaissance*, 23; Edmunds and Bush, *Daybreakers*, 47.

35. Gottlieb, *Making Their Own Way*, 191–92; Edmunds and Bush, *Daybreakers*, 22.

36. "Annual Report of Home and School Visitor," 1 January–31 December 1927, box 1, file folder 24; box 3, file folder 142 ULP Papers, UP; "Home Economics Report," 1921 (on earlier visitations of selected schools), box 1, file folders 1, 19, 20; box 3, file folders 89, 110, 114, 131, ULP Papers, UP; "Minutes of Exec. Bd.," 8 June 1927; "Report of the President, E. C. May, at the 9th Annual Meeting," 17 January 1927; Thayer, "September Report: To the Board of Directors, ULP," ca. September 1927; Edmunds and Bush, *Daybreakers*, 64; Gottlieb, *Making Their Own Way*, 192. Also see appendix to "Annual Report of Home and School Visitor," 1 January–31 December 1927.

37. "Minutes of Exec. Bd.," 8 June 1927; "Report of the President, E. C. May, at the 9th Annual Meeting," 17 January 1927; Thayer, "September Report: To the Board of Directors, ULP," ca. September 1927; "Annual Report of Home and School Visitor," 1 January–31 December 1927; Edmunds and Bush, *Day breakers*, 64; Gottlieb, *Making Their Own Way*, 192. Also see appendix to "Annual Report of Home and School Visitor," 1 January–31 December 1927.

38. Edmunds and Bush, *Daybreakers*, 126–27.

39. ULP to Taggert, cited in Cilli, "'The Greatest Good,'" 42n65; Marcus Garvey, UNIA, to Shelton Hale Bishop, 31 December 1921, box 1, file folders 1, 19, 20; box 3, file folders 89, 110, 114, 131, ULP Papers, UP; "Minutes of the Meeting of the Executive Board," 21 December 1921, ibid.; "Minutes of the Exec. Bd.," 17 September 1924, box 1, file folders 2, 21; box 3, file folder 89; box 5, file folder 205, ULP Papers, UP; Cilli, "'The Greatest Good,'" 42–43; Clark to All Committee Members, 22 March 1922; "A June Note: Executive Board Members of Urban League," ca. June 1922; "Minutes of Executive Board Meeting," 21 June 1922; Clark to Albert Hufschmidt, 29 March 1922, box 1, file folders 1, 20; box 3, file folder 89, ULP Papers, UP.

40. "Minutes of the Exec. Bd. Meeting," 20 September 1922, box 1, file folders 1, 20; box 3, file folder 89, ULP Papers, UP.

41. "Hill District Disturbance," 16 July 1927, box 1, file folders 4, 24; box 3, file folder 142, ULP Papers, UP; "Report of the Executive Secretary for the Period Covering Oct. and Nov. 1927."

42. Buni, *Robert L. Vann*, 49, 338n27, 123–25.

43. Daisy E. Lampkin, president, Lucy Stone League of Republican Women Voters of Allegheny County, to John T. Clark, 21 February 1922, box 1, file folders 1, 20; box 3, file folder 89, ULP Papers, UP; Clark to All Committee Members, 22 March 1922; "A June Note: Executive Board Members of Urban League," ca. June 1922; Clark to Hufschmidt, 29 March 1922; "Minutes of Executive Board Meeting," 21 June 1922.

44. Alonzo Thayer to Daisy Lampkin, 1 October 1928, box 1, file folders 5, 25, 36; box 2, file folder 81; box 3, file folder 142, ULP Papers, UP; "Memo to Mr. Moss," n.d.

45. Clark to All Committee Members, 22 March 1922; "A June Note: Executive Board Members of Urban League," ca. June 1922; "Minutes of Executive Board Meeting," 21 June 1922; Clark to Hufschmidt, 29 March 1922.

46. "Mrs. Alice West Dies," *Pittsburgh Courier,* 23 March 1929.

47. Ancella Livers, "Defining Ourselves: Gender Construction and the Creation of a Black Community in Pittsburgh, 1925–55" (PhD diss., Carnegie Mellon University, 1998), 131; Clark to Edwin C. May, 1 August 1924, box 1, file folders 2, 21; box 3, file folder 89; box 5, file folder 205, ULP Papers, UP; "Mrs. C. Jeffries Resigns Position with Urban League: After 38 Years of Service," *Pittsburgh Courier,* 25 February 1961.

48. "Minutes, ULP Annual Meeting," 30 January 1922; "Minutes of Executive Board Meeting," 15 February 1922, box 1, file folders 1, 20; box 3, file folder 89, ULP Papers, UP; Clark to Edwin C. May, 1 August 1924, box 1, file folders 2, 21; box 3, file folder 89; box 5, file folder 205, ULP Papers, UP; "Mrs. C. Jeffries Resigns Position with Urban League"; Edmunds and Bush, *Day breakers,* 74–76, 77–79.

49. Edmunds and Bush, *Daybreakers,* 75–76; Jeffries to Allen, 5 November 1926, box 1, file folders 3, 23, ULP Papers, UP.

50. Diane R. Powell, "Tracing 65 Years of Pittsburgh's Urban League History," *Pittsburgh Courier,* 26 November 1983.

51. See "Report of the Home Economics Worker," June 1919, box 1, file folder 19; box 3, file folders 87, 88, 96, 113, 115, 137; box 5, file folders 237, 238, ULP Papers, UP; "Minutes of the Executive Board," 21 March 1923, box 1, file folders 2, 21; box 3, file folders 89, 104, ULP Papers, UP.

52. "Report of Home Economics Worker," February 1919, box 1, file folder 19; box 3, file folders 87, 88, 96, 115, 137; box 5, file folders 237, 238, ULP Papers, UP.

53. Trotter and Day, *Race and Renaissance,* 26–27; "Report of Exec. Sec. to Board of Dir.," September 1927, box 1, file folders 4, 24; box 3, file folder 142, ULP Papers, UP. In September 1927 the ULP reported the reopening of its job-placement service.

54. Grace S. Lowndes, "Report," 15 June–15 August 1927, box 1, file folders 4, 24; box 3, file folder 142, ULP Papers, UP.

55. John T. Clark to Edwin C. May, 6 November 1922, box 1, file folders 1, 20; box 3, file folder 89, ULP Papers, UP; ULP Exec. to Mr. L. H. Burnette, 18 January 1924, box 1, file folders 2, 21; box 3, file folder 89; box 5, file folder 205, ULP Papers, UP; "Executive Board Meeting," 27 April 1920, box 1, file folder 1; box 3, file folders 89, 96, 110, 114, 117, 131, ULP Papers, UP.

56. "Race Prejudice Can Best Be Combatted through Individual Effort Declares Walter A. May," *Pittsburgh Courier*, 20 January 1923; Tyson to Clark, 15 July 1923, box 1, file folders 2, 21; box 3, file folders 89, 104, ULP Papers, UP.

57. T. Arnold Hill to Clark, 7 April 1926; Clark to Hill, 12 April 1926, box 1, file folders 3, 23, ULP Papers, UP; "Minutes, Executive Board Meeting," 9 February, 23 March, 22 September 1926, box 1, file folders 3, 23, ULP Papers, UP; "Minutes of Exec. Bd.," 8 June 1927.

58. Bayard Christy to John Clark, 2 November 1920, box 1, file folder 1; box 3, file folders 89, 96, 110, 114, 117, 131, ULP Papers, UP; "Where the Fault Lies," news clipping, ibid.

59. "Executive Board Meeting," 2 March 1920; John T. Clark to Mary E. Bakewell, 4 March, 3 May 1920; Clark to Bayard H. Christy, 25 and 31 August, 2 November 1920, box 1, file folder 1; box 3, file folders 89, 96, 110, 114, 117, 131, ULP Papers, UP.

60. "Urban League Said to Be in Dire Straits: Resignation of Women Employees Discloses Alleged Difficulties," *Pittsburgh Courier*, 6 September 1924; "Minutes of Executive Board," 22 November 1924, box 1, file folders 2, 21; box 3, file folder 89; box 5, file folder 205, ULP Papers, UP.

61. John T. Clark, letter to the editor, *Pittsburgh Courier*, 13 September 1924; "Minutes of Executive Board," 22 November 1924.

62. Clark to Christy, 25 August 1920; "Where the Fault Lies," news clipping; "Outline of Campaign for Funds among the Colored Citizens of Pittsburgh Urban League," 13 December 1927, box 1, file folders 4, 24; box 3, file folder 142, ULP Papers, UP.

63. "Minutes, Executive Board Meeting," 18 May 1921; "Minutes, ULP Annual Meeting," 30 January 1922; "Minutes of the Executive Board," 19 November 1924; "Minutes of the Annual Meeting," 16 February 1925; "Outline of Campaign for Funds among the Colored Citizens of Pittsburgh Urban League," 13 December 1927; "Minutes, Exec. Bd.," 16 February 1925, box 1, file folders 2, 22; box 3, file folder 89, ULP Papers, UP; "Local Urban League Launches $5,000 Drive: Slogan 'League Needs Pittsburgh,'" *Pittsburgh Courier*, 5 February 1927; "Urban League Here to Be 'Sold' to Negro Citizens: Campaign for Memberships Begins November 18," *Pittsburgh Courier*, 29 October 1927; "Urban League Membership Drive Opens This Friday," *Pittsburgh Courier*, 19 November 1927; "Urban League Campaign Shows Rapid Progress: Workers Entertained at League Headquarters," *Pittsburgh Courier*, 26 November 1927; "Urban League Units Plan Joint Festival," *Pittsburgh Courier*, 13 October 1928.

64. "Minutes of Executive Board," 15 February 1922; "National Urban League Holds Yearly Meeting: Vital Topics Discussed," *Pittsburgh Courier*, 27 October 1923. On this occasion, Hollingsworth described the work of the NUL as a "noble but unpopular cause."

65. Margaret C. "Peg" Albert, ULP history summaries, 20 September 1925, box 18, folder 21, ULP Papers, Heinz.

66. "Urban League Art Exhibit," *Pittsburgh Courier*, 7 March 1928; "Urban League Holds First Annual Display," *Pittsburgh Courier*, 31 March 1928; "Local Urban League Secretary Finishes First Year's Work," *Pittsburgh Courier*, 9 June 1928;

"Local Organization Accommodates Urban League for Annual Meeting Jan. 16: Luncheon to Precede Program," *Pittsburgh Courier,* 5 January 1929.

67. "Amateurs Entertain in 'Revue,'" *Pittsburgh Courier,* 2 May 1925; "Editor Believes that Race's Industrial Art Shows Its Industrial Advance," *Pittsburgh Courier,* 22 January 1927.

68. "Urban League Presents Free Movie Show," *Pittsburgh Courier,* 9 March 1929; Rob Ruck, *Sandlot Seasons: Sport in Black Pittsburgh* (Urbana: University of Illinois Press, 1987), 35–36, 37.

69. Edmunds and Bush, *Daybreakers,* 36.

3. Surviving the Depression

1. "Report of Department of Industrial Relations, Jan. and Feb. 1933," box 1, file folders 10, 28, 30, ULP Papers, UP.

2. Alonzo Thayer, "Report of the Executive Secretary for the Period Covering October and November 1927," 13 December 1927, and "Study of Certain Industries in Which Negroes Work and Their Progress over a Ten Year Period," 18 December 1927; Grace S. Lowndes, "Report, June 15 to August 15, 1927," box 1, file folders 4, 24; box 3, file folder 142; box 4, file folder 59, ULP Papers, UP; Joe William Trotter Jr. and Jared Day, *Race and Renaissance: African Americans in Pittsburgh since World War II* (Pittsburgh: University of Pittsburgh Press, 2010), 28, 203.

3. "Report, Industrial Relations Department," October 1930; "Report of Industrial Committee," June, July, August 1930; "Industrial Relations Department Tentative Outline of Activities," ca. 1930, box 1, file folders 6, 26, 34; box 2, file folder 55; box 3, file folders 132, 135; box 4, file folder 158, ULP Papers, UP; "Summary of Minutes of Exec. Bd. Meeting," 14 January 1931, box 1, file folders 7, 27, 34; box 2, file folder 55; box 3, file folders 132, 135, ULP Papers, UP.

4. Grace S. Lowndes, "Report of Civic Secretary," October 1930, box 1, file folders 6, 26, 34; box 2, file folder 55; box 3, file folders 132, 135; box 4, file folder 158, ULP Papers, UP.

5. Georgine R. Pearce, "Report of Home and School Visitor," October 1930, box 1, file folders 6, 26, 34; box 2, file folder 55; box 3, file folders 132, 135; box 4, file folder 158, ULP Papers, UP.

6. "Minutes, Executive Board Meeting," 18 April 1933, box 1, file folders 9, 28, 35, 55, 109, 133, 135; box 4, file folder 158, ULP Papers, UP.

7. "Report of Industrial Relations Secretary," December 1930, box 1, file folders 6, 26, 34; box 2, file folder 55; box 3, file folders 132, 135; box 4, file folder 158, ULP Papers, UP.

8. Lawrence W. Showers, "Is Urban League Failing in Service to Local Community? Hill Housing Situation Commands Its Attention," *Pittsburgh Courier,* 15 September 1934; "Hill Negroes and the Civilian Conservation Corps," ca. October 1934, box 1, file folders 10, 21, 30; box 2, file folder 55; box 3, file folders 90, 109, 133, 155, ULP Papers, UP.

9. "Hill Is Named as Lett's Successor," news clipping, *Pittsburgh Courier,* ca. November 1934; "Lett Slated for Newark Position," news clipping, *Pittsburgh Courier,*

ca. November 1934; Ruth Bowen, general secretary, Social Service Bureau, Lansing, Michigan, to Eugene Kinckle Jones, 9 January 1929, box 1, file folders 5, 13, 31; box 2, file folders 55, 84; box 3, file folders 91, 109, 129, 133, 134, 135, 144, 151, 153, 155, 156; box 7, file folder 321, ULP Papers, UP; "Reception for Urban League Executives," *Pittsburgh Courier,* 29 March 1930 (reporting on plans to present Maurice Moss and Harold Lett to the community; Moss had arrived in January, and Lett in March 1930); "City Mourns Death of Maurice Moss," *Pittsburgh Courier,* 15 November 1958; "Omegas and Businessmen Entertain Thayer: Executive Secretary of Urban League Bid Fond Farewell," *Pittsburgh Courier,* 11 January 1930 (one event took place in the private home of Carter T. Collins [Omegas], and the other took place at the Centre Avenue YMCA [businessmen]); Arthur J. Edmunds and Esther L. Bush, *Daybreakers: The Story of the Urban League of Pittsburgh, the First Eighty Years* (1983; revised and updated, Pittsburgh: Urban League of Pittsburgh, 1999), 81. Although there were significant changes in the ULP's male leadership, there was significant continuity in the female leadership of Christina Jeffries and Grace Lowndes.

10. "Industrial Committee Report," 11 April 1933; "Minutes of the Executive Board Meeting," 22 May 1933; H. A. Lett, industrial secretary, to 146 white pastors, 2 May 1933, box 1, file folders 10, 28, 30, ULP Papers, UP.

11. "Report of Department of Industrial Relations, Jan. and Feb. 1933."

12. "Local Urban League Gets Busy in Job Seeking Campaign: H. A. Lett Announces Week's Program Here in Nationwide Vocational Opportunity Campaign," *Pittsburgh Courier,* 12 April 1930.

13. "R. Maurice Moss to Head Local Urban League: Will Assume Duties Here December 15th," *Pittsburgh Courier,* 9 November 1929; "Summary of Minutes of the Executive Board Meeting," 18 November 1930; Maurice Moss to ULP Board, 12 December 1930, box 1, file folders 6, 26, 34; box 2, file folder 55; box 3, file folders 132, 135; box 4, file folder 158, ULP Papers, UP.

14. "Report of the Industrial Relations Department," October 1930.

15. "Successful Vocational Conference Opens 'Activities Month' Program: William S. Howell Points up Interest of Negroes in Mining Villages in Series of Exhibitions and Conferences," *Pittsburgh Courier,* 20 May 1939; "State Officials Attend Community Welfare's Confab at Library: Seventy Five Delegates Take Part in Interesting Day Session and Discuss Problems," *Pittsburgh Courier,* 17 June 1933. Cf. "Women's Civic Clubs of Pittsburgh Coal Company in Confab: Annual Conference at Westland and Van Meter October 30 and November 1st," *Pittsburgh Courier,* 27 October 1934.

16. "Minutes, Executive Board Meeting," 18 April 1933.

17. "Report, Industrial Relations Department," October 1930; "Report of Industrial Committee," June, July, August 1930; "Industrial Relations Department Tentative Outline of Activities," ca. 1930, box 1, file folders 6, 26, 34; box 2, file folder 55; box 3, file folders 132, 135; box 4, file folder 158, ULP Papers, UP.

18. "Industrial Committee Report," 11 April 1933; "Minutes of the Executive Board Meeting," 22 May 1933; Lett to 146 white pastors, 2 May 1933.

19. Showers, "Is Urban League Failing in Service to Local Community?"; "Hill Negroes and the Civilian Conservation Corps."

20. Showers, "Is Urban League Failing in Service to Local Community?"; "Hill Negroes and the Civilian Conservation Corps," ca. October 1934.

21. Fidel Makoto Campet, "Housing in Black Pittsburgh: Community Struggles and the State, 1916–1973" (PhD diss., Carnegie Mellon University, 2011), 128.

22. Campet, "Housing in Black Pittsburgh," 143.

23. "Fair Share of CWA Jobs Given to Race: Nearly 12% of Jobs Go to Race, Lead in Exams," *Pittsburgh Courier,* 27 January 1934.

24. "Negro Clients of the Allegheny County Transient Bureau," October 1934; "CCC Camps," October 1934, box 1, file folders 10, 21, 30; box 2, file folder 55; box 3, file folders 90, 109, 133, 155, ULP Papers, UP.

25. "Minutes of Executive Board Meeting," 20 November 1934; R. Maurice Moss, "The Pittsburgh Urban League Studies of the Negro Worker in Pittsburgh," ca. 1934 (on study methodology); Edgar G. Brown, "Federal Emergency Relief Administration," 3 December 1934; "Minutes of Executive Board Meetings," 17 March 1934, box 1, file folders 10, 21, 30; box 2, file folder 55; box 3, file folders 90, 109, 133, 155, ULP Papers, UP. For a review of progress at the national level, see Eugene Kinckle Jones, executive secretary, national office, to branches, 1 January 1938, box 1, file folders 14, 32, 35; box 2, file folders 55, 79, 84, 90; box 3, file folders 90, 109, 126, 133, 144, 151, 153 155, 156, ULP Papers, UP.

26. "Minutes of Executive Board Meeting," 21 November 1933, box 1, file folders 10, 28, 30, ULP Papers, UP; "Minutes of the Executive Board," 16 January, 20 February 1934, box 1, file folders 10, 21, 30; box 2, file folder 55; box 3, file folders 90, 109, 133, 155, ULP Papers, UP.

27. "Negro Clients of the Allegheny County Transient Bureau," October 1934; "CCC Camps," October 1934.

28. R. M. Moss to Edward M. Jones, administrator, WPA, Harrisburg, PA, 10 October 1936; William E. Hill to Mrs. H. D. Stark, president, Congress of Women's Clubs and Clubs of Western Pennsylvania, 10 October 1936, box 1, file folders 12, 30; box 2, file folders 55, 84; box 3, file folders 109, 133, 135, 144, 155, ULP Papers, UP.

29. "Negro Art Center in Hill Would Create Jobs for Twenty Artists," *Pittsburgh Courier,* 5 April 1941; R. M. Moss to Board Members, 23 April 1941; ULP, "Executive Board Meeting," 17 June 1941, box 1, file folders 17, 33, 35, 44; box 2, file folder 90; box 3, file folders 55, 90, ULP Papers, UP. In the spring of 1941 the ULP reported that the WPA office abruptly terminated Pennsylvania's recreation and adult education programs.

30. "Race Holding Its Own in Recovery," *Pittsburgh Courier,* 19 May 1934.

31. Edmunds and Bush, *Daybreakers,* 18–21.

32. ULP, "Executive Secretary to Advisory Committee," 18 March 1937; "Hill Is Named as Lett's Successor," box 1, file folders 13, 31; box 2, file folders 55, 84; box 3, file folders 91, 109, 129, 133, 134, 135, 144, 151, 153, 155, 156; box 7, file folder 321, ULP Papers, UP; Edmunds and Bush, *Daybreakers,* 141, 144–45. Edmunds and Bush note that a coterie of young black professionals, including ULP officers, and their white collaborators used this method of collecting data to initiate

discussion and action on a wide range of issues during the 1950s and 1960s (141). Also see "Urban League Head Makes Local Survey: Ira DeA Reid, Director of Research and Investigation," *Pittsburgh Courier*, 19 October 1929; "Ira DeA Reid Tells of Fight for Skilled Race Workers: Industrial Secretary of N.Y. Urban League," *Pittsburgh Courier*, 28 May 1927.

33. ULP annual report, "The Fifteenth Year, 1918–1932," box 1, file folders 8, 27, 35; box 2, file folder 55; box 3, file folders 133, 135, ULP Papers, UP.

34. R. M. Moss to ULP Board, 14 August 1934, box 1, file folders 13, 31; box 2, file folders 55, 84; box 3, file folders 91, 109, 129, 133, 134, 135, 144, 151, 153, 155, 156; box 7, file folder 321, ULP Papers, UP.

35. "Urban League 'Fellows' Keep up Fine Record," *Pittsburgh Courier*, 24 September 1932; Moss to ULP Board, 2 January 1932; CV of Ira deAugustine Reid, ca. 7 March 1934, box 1, file folders 13, 31; box 2, file folders 55, 84; box 3, file folders 91, 109, 129, 133, 134, 135, 144, 151, 153, 155, 156; box 7, file folders 321, 329, ULP Papers, UP; "Urban League Sec'y Feted in Pittsburgh," *Pittsburgh Courier*, 9 April 1938; "Urban League Will Celebrate Twentieth Year of Activity: Members of Original Committee Will Be Guests," *Pittsburgh Courier*, 3 May 1930.

36. "Urban League Will Move into Larger Quarters March 1st: Local Branch to Be Comfortably Housed at 43 Fernando Street," *Pittsburgh Courier*, 17 February 1934. See also "Minutes of Executive Board," 16 January, 20 February 1934.

37. This and the following section are based on Fidel Campet's excellent dissertation on the subject. See Campet, "Housing in Black Pittsburgh," 126–37. In December 1939 the Hill District Community Council's president, Harold Lavine, announced the appointment of council members Minnie Birk, Health Nursing Association; Mary D. Weinbert, Irene Kaufmann Settlement House; and June Webber, Tuberculosis League. See "Hill Council Names Health Committee," *Pittsburgh Courier*, 16 December 1939.

38. Campet, "Housing in Black Pittsburgh," 128.

39. "75 Waiters Finish Urban 8-Week Course," *Pittsburgh Courier*, 14 March 1931; R. Maurice Moss to ULP Board, 23 August 1930, box 1, file folders 6, 7; box 3, file folder 132; box 4, file folder 158, ULP Papers, UP.

40. "Building Workers Institute Planned by Urban League," *Pittsburgh Courier*, 15 October 1932.

41. "Urban League Classes to End Soon," *Pittsburgh Courier*, 12 December 1931.

42. "Memorandum on Proposals for a Household Training Center in Pittsburgh," 15 January 1937, box 1, file folders 5, 13, 31; box 2, file folders 55, 84; box 3, file folders 91, 109, 129, 133, 134, 135, 144, 151, 153, 155, 156; box 7, file folder 321, ULP Papers, UP; Mrs. David Arter, president of ULP board, "Domestic Service: A Profession," radio address, KDKA, 3 November 1936; "National Committee on Household Employment," *Bulletin*, December 1936, box 1, file folders 12, 30; box 2, file folders 55, 84; box 3, file folders 109, 133, 135, 144, 155, ULP Papers, UP; "Progress Report: The First Year of the Philadelphia Institute on Household Occupations, 2005 Fine Street, Feb. 1937–1938," box 1, file folders 14, 32, 35;

box 2, file folders 55, 79, 84, 90; box 3, file folders 90, 109, 126, 133, 144, 151, 153 155, 156, ULP Papers, UP; "National Council on Household Employment," accessed online, 30 December 2018. For a helpful discussion of the New Deal's funding of household training courses, see Victoria W. Wolcott, *Remaking Respectability: African American Women in Interwar Detroit* (Chapel Hill: University of North Carolina Press, 2001), 231–32.

43. Moss to Jones, 10 October 1936; Hill to Stark, 10 October 1936.

44. "Memorandum on Proposals for a Household Training Center in Pittsburgh," 15 January 1937; Arter, "Domestic Service: A Profession," 3 November 1936; "National Committee on Household Employment"; "Progress Report: The First Year of the Philadelphia Institute on Household Occupations."

45. "Pittsburgh Labor College: Extension Courses," and Pittsburgh Labor College to R. M. Moss, 14 October 1936, box 1, file folders 12, 30; box 2, file folders 55, 84; box 3, file folders 109, 133, 135, 144, 155, ULP Papers, UP; Selma Robinson, "Maids in America," *Reader's Digest*, September 1936.

46. "The Joint Board-Staff Meeting," 21 January 1937, box 1, file folders 13, 31; box 2, file folders 55, 84; box 3, file folders 91, 109, 129, 133, 134, 135, 144, 151, 153, 155, 156; box 7, file folder 321, ULP Papers, UP. Some employers interviewed half a dozen or more women and declined to hire any of them. Other employers refused to pay women the wage rate cited over the phone when they showed up to work.

47. Household Employment Committee, "Proposals for a Voluntary Agreement in Household Employment: Prepared by the Pittsburgh Committee on Employment," 1936–1937; Arter, "Domestic Service: A Profession," 3 November 1936; "Nineteenth Annual Meeting: Urban League of Pittsburgh," 16 February 1937, box 1, file folders 5, 13, 31; box 2, file folders 55, 84; box 3, file folders 91, 109, 129, 133, 134, 135, 144, 151, 153, 155, 156; box 7, file folder 321, ULP Papers, UP.

48. See "Phil Murray Urges Negro Workers to Join Great Steel Industry Union," *Pittsburgh Courier*, 13 February 1937.

49. T. Arnold Hill to branches, 3 and 16 April 1934, box 2, file folder 55; box 3, file folders 90, 109, 133, 155, ULP Papers, UP.

50. William E. Hill, ULP industrial secretary, to W. W. Clements, president, Pennsylvania Railroad Company, 4 December 1937; "Red Caps and the Fair Labor Standards Act," ca. 1938–1939, box 1, file folders 14, 32, 35; box 2, file folders 55, 79, 84, 90; box 3, file folders 90, 109, 126, 133, 144, 151, 153 155, 156, ULP Papers, UP. For 1939, see also box 1, file folders 15, 152.

51. "Minutes of the Executive Board Meeting," 16 April 1940; memorandum, Industrial Relations Department, 26 February 1940, box 1, file folders 16, 33, 61; box 2, file folder 84; box 3, file folders 144, 151, 155, ULP Papers, UP; R. Maurice Moss to Reginald Johnson, 19 January 1938, box 1, file folders 14, 32, 35; box 2, file folders 55, 79, 84, 90; box 3, file folders 90, 109, 126, 133, 144, 151, 153 155, 156, ULP Papers, UP.

52. "Industrial Committee Meeting," 20 October 1937, box 1, file folders 13, 31; box 2, file folders 55, 84; box 3, file folders 91, 109, 129, 133, 134, 135, 144, 151, 153, 155, 156; box 7, file folder 321, ULP Papers, UP.

53. R. Maurice Moss to Francis Tyson, 9 January 1931; Moss to ULP Board, 2 January 1932; CV of Reid, ca. 7 March 1934; Moss to ULP Board, 14 August 1934; T. Arnold Hill to R. M. Moss, 2 January 1936 (update on national programs); Wilbur Maxwell, Community Fund, to R. M. Moss, 27 January 1926; Status of Community Fund, Friends of the Soviet Union, to R. M. Moss, 18 February 1936; Joint Committee on the WPA to R. M. Moss, 6 October 1936, box 1, file folders 12, 30; box 2, file folders 55, 84; box 3, file folders 109, 133, 135, 144, 155, ULP Papers, UP.

54. "Workers Seek to Organize Forces," *Pittsburgh Courier,* 26 January 1935.

55. "Urban League Workers' Council Is Progressing," *Pittsburgh Courier,* 18 August 1934.

56. "Memorandum on Proposals for a Household Training Center in Pittsburgh"; Arter, "Domestic Service: A Profession," 3 November 1936; "National Committee on Household Employment"; "Progress Report: The First Year of the Philadelphia Institute on Household Occupations."

57. "Pittsburgh Labor College: Extension Courses"; Pittsburgh Labor College to R. M. Moss, 14 October 1936; Robinson, "Maids in America."

58. ULP, "The Fifteenth Year, 1918–1932"; Trotter and Day, *Race and Renaissance,* 30.

59. "Resolution: To the National Negro Congress in Chicago, Feb. 14, 1936"; "Minutes: Pittsburgh Council, National Negro Congress," 16 May 1936; John P. Davis, national secretary, NNC, to local NNC chapters, 10 July 1936; Roger Laws, secretary, Pittsburgh NNC, to John P. Davis, 19 October 1936 (seeking to change the date of Davis's scheduled visit to Pittsburgh), box 1, file folders 12, 13, 31; box 2, file folders 55, 85; box 7, file folders 321, 329, ULP Papers, UP.

60. See "Phil Murray Urges Negro Workers to Join Great Steel Industry Union"; Fred Abbott, executive secretary, Friends of the Soviet Union (US section, Pittsburgh), to R. M. Moss, 18 February 1936 (Abbott urged Moss to appoint a delegate to travel to the Soviet Union and suggested that William Hill would be an excellent candidate); memorandum, Industrial Committee of the ULP, 28 February 1936 (unanimously approving Hill's selection to be a guest of the Soviet Trade Unions and asking the board to grant him a leave of absence), box 1, file folders 12, 30; box 2, file folders 55, 84; box 3, file folders 109, 133, 135, 144, 155, ULP Papers, UP.

61. "Local Urban League Heads Are Renamed," *Pittsburgh Courier,* 24 January 1931; Claude Boddie, prison inmate, to ULP, 19 March 1936; ULP Industrial Committee, "Activities, 1936," in "Nineteenth Annual Meeting: Urban League of Pittsburgh," 16 February 1937; Moss to the Community Fund, 14 August 1934, box 1, file folders 10–13, 29–31; box 2, file folders 55, 85; box 3, file folder 90; box 7, file folders 321, 329, ULP Papers, UP.

62. Virginia M. Woodson, "Report of Girls Club Worker," October 1930, box 1, file folders 6, 26, 34; box 2, file folder 55; box 3, file folders 132, 135; box 4, file folder 158, ULP Papers, UP.

63. ULP, "The Fifteenth Year, 1918–1932."

64. "Basketball Game to Be Feature of Urban League Recreation Program: Director Berry Plans to Display Activities at 'Y' Friday January 20," *Pittsburgh Courier*, 4 January 1939.

65. R. Maurice Moss, "The Urban League of Pittsburgh: A Statement Concerning Camp [James Weldon Johnson]," 27 July 1938, box 1, file folders 14, 32, 35; box 2, file folders 55, 79, 84, 90; box 3, file folders 90, 109, 126, 133, 144, 151, 153 155, 156, ULP Papers, UP.

66. ULP, "Report," 18 March 1937, box 1, file folders, 12, 13, 31; box 2, file folders, 55, 85; box 7, file folders 321, 329; box 10, file folder 468, ULP Papers, UP.

67. "Noted Speakers, Fine Exhibit Planned at Big Urban Meeting," *Pittsburgh Courier*, 23 January 1932; "Urban League Scores in Annual Meeting: Name New Officers," *Pittsburgh Courier*, 6 February 1932; Ivory Cobb and Willette Preston, "Fifth Ave. High School," *Pittsburgh Courier*, 6 February 1932 (on student artwork at the ULP's annual exhibit).

68. "Nineteenth Annual Meeting: Urban League of Pittsburgh," 16 February 1937; "From Day to Day: With Mary McLeod Bethune," *Pittsburgh Courier*, 13 March 1937.

69. "Report of Department of Industrial Relations, Jan. and Feb. 1933," ULP Branch Files, NUL Papers, Library of Congress; Trotter and Day, *Race and Renaissance*, 30.

70. "Dr. Mordecai W. Johnson Pleases Local Audiences in Fine Address: Bishop Mann Presents Speaker at Urban League's Second Annual Religious Service," *Pittsburgh Courier*, 21 December 1935.

71. "Noted Chicagoan to Speak at Meeting in Pittsburgh Urban League," *Pittsburgh Courier*, 10 January 1931; "Local Urban League Heads Are Renamed," *Pittsburgh Courier*, 24 January 1931 (announcing Mary McDowell's illness and cancellation of her engagement in Pittsburgh; the Reverend Robert F. Galbreath of Bellvue replaced her).

72. "Editor Carter Scores in Fine Speech Here: Set Postal Meet Plans," *Pittsburgh Courier*, 25 April 1931.

73. George E. Barbour, "42 Year History of Community Service: Pittsburgh Urban League Cites Outstanding History," *Pittsburgh Courier*, 16 April 1960; "Report of Department of Industrial Relations, Jan. and Feb. 1933."

74. "Report of Department of Industrial Relations, Jan. and Feb. 1933."

75. "Atty. Tabor Speaks at Urban League Service on Sunday," *Pittsburgh Courier*, 3 November 1934.

76. Lett to 146 white pastors, 2 May 1933; Lett to community leaders, 20 April 1933.

77. "Interest High in Race Relations Programs in Local Churches," *Pittsburgh Courier*, 17 February 1934.

78. R. Maurice Moss to Senators J. J. Davis (PA), J. Guffey (PA), and others, 26 February 1936; E. P. Costigan (Col.), US Senate office, to Moss, 28 February 1936, box 1, file folders 12, 30; box 2, file folders 55, 84; box 3, file folders 109, 133, 135, 144, 155, ULP Papers, UP. Costigan thanked Moss for the ULP's support of the anti-lynching measure.

79. "National Urban League Conference Meets Here," *Pittsburgh Courier*, 9 April 1932; "Epoch-Making Urban League Confab Ended," *Pittsburgh Courier*, 21 May 1932; "Nat'l Urban League Regional Confab Here Next Month: Fifteen Branches Will Be Guests of Local Body February 15th and 16th," *Pittsburgh Courier*, 26 January 1935 (T. Arnold Hill was scheduled to preside at the gathering); ULP, "Executive Secretary to Advisory Committee," 18 March 1937.

80. "Resolution: To the National Negro Congress in Chicago, Feb. 14, 1936"; "Minutes: Pittsburgh Council, National Negro Congress," 16 May 1936; Davis to local NNC chapters, 10 July 1936; Laws to Davis, 19 October 1936.

81. T. Arnold Hill, acting executive secretary, to R. Maurice Moss, 8 February 1936, box 1, file folders 12, 30; box 2, file folders 55, 84; box 3, file folders 109, 133, 135, 144, 155, ULP Papers, UP.

82. "Minutes of Executive Board Meeting," 20 November 1934; Moss, "Pittsburgh Urban League Studies of the Negro Worker in Pittsburgh"; Brown, "Federal Emergency Relief Administration," 3 December 1934; "Minutes of Executive Board Meetings," 17 March 1934; Eugene Kinckle Jones to branches, 1 January 1938. The Lett-Hill study focused on the experiences of blacks in some 731 firms, where nearly 75 percent of blacks (mostly men) worked in the manufacturing and mining sectors of the economy; women labored mainly in department stores, hotels, and hospitals, supplemented by a few female employees in clothing and laundry firms.

83. ULP, "The Fifteenth Year, 1918–1932"; "Executive Board Meeting," 17 June 1941, box 1, file folders 17, 33, 35, 44; box 2, file folder 90; box 3, file folders 55, 90, ULP Papers, UP.

84. "Report of Department of Industrial Relations, Jan. and Feb. 1933."

85. ULP, "Report," 18 March 1937.

4. Establishing a New Social Service Regime

1. ULP annual report, "The Fifteenth Year, 1918–1932," box 1, file folders 8, 27, 35; box 2, file folder 55; box 3, file folders 133, 135, ULP Paper, UP.

2. "Report of Department of Industrial Relations, Jan. and Feb. 1933," box 1, file folders 10, 28, 30, ULP Papers, UP.

3. Joe William Trotter Jr. and Jared Day, *Race and Renaissance: African Americans in Pittsburgh since World War II* (Pittsburgh: University of Pittsburgh Press, 2010), 33–34.

4. Trotter and Day, *Race and Renaissance*, 33–34.

5. "Plan for Study of Consumer Pressure Programs among Negroes as a Source for Employment," ca. early 1930s; "Consumer Pressure as an Employment Program for Urban League," ca. 1930s, box 1, file folders 6, 26, 34; box 2, file folder 55; box 3, file folders 132, 135; box 4, file folder 158, ULP Papers, UP; "Summary of Minutes of Exec. Bd. Meeting," 14 January 1931, box 1, file folders 7, 27, 34; box 2, file folder 55; box 3, file folders 132, 135, ULP Papers, UP. See Pauline Redmond, "Race Relations on the South Side of Pittsburgh as Seen through Brashear Settlement" (MA thesis, University of Pittsburgh, 1936), for a good description of the black community and work on the South Side.

6. "Committee Meeting, Consumers League," 7 September 1937; Beatrice Bayless, secretary, Housewives League, 15 September, 22 October 1937, box 1, file folders 5, 13, 31; box 2, file folders 55, 84; box 3, file folders 91, 109, 129, 133, 134, 135, 144, 151, 153, 155, 156; box 7, file folder 321, ULP Papers, UP. At one meeting, Lampkin supported the idea of a housewives' consumer organization "to run parallel" with "a men's trade association." The organization adopted the name Housewives Cooperative League. The ULP left no stone unturned in its advocacy for black workers. It suggested that black undertakers could help open jobs for blacks at the National Casket Company, which, it reported, "employs no Negroes." Moss underscored the need to create more skilled and professional training opportunities for young black workers. Among 731 firms surveyed, 327 hire no blacks at all. "Minutes of Executive Board Meeting," 15 May 1934 (includes "Preliminary Report on Survey" of black employment in Pittsburgh since World War I), box 1, file folders 10, 21, 30; box 2, file folder 55; box 3, file folders 90, 109, 133, 155, ULP Papers, UP.

7. "Housewives League Plans Mass Meeting: Editor Vann Enthuses Large Group in Fine Speech—Mrs. Fannie B. Peck Speaker at Mass Meet Sept. 19," *Pittsburgh Courier,* 10 September 1932.

8. [Mrs.] P. Hills, "Resolution: To the National Negro Congress in Chicago, Feb. 14, 1936"; "Minutes: Pittsburgh Council, National Negro Congress," 16 May 1936; John P. Davis, national secretary, NNC, to local NNC chapters, 10 July 1936; Roger Laws, secretary, Pittsburgh NNC, to John P. Davis, 19 October 1936 (Laws sought to change the date of Davis's visit to Pittsburgh), box 1, file folders 12, 30; box 2, file folders 55, 84; box 3, file folders 109, 133, 135, 144, 155, ULP Papers, UP. See also "Special Problems of Negro Workers in Pittsburgh," 6 April 1929, box 1, file folders 5, 25, 26; box 2, file folder 81; box 3, file folders 136, 142, 145; box 5, file folders 5, 158, ULP Papers, UP; Trotter and Day, *Race and Renaissance,* 30.

9. "Dr. C. Howard Marcy to Address the Annual Meeting," *Pittsburgh Courier,* 20 January 1934.

10. ULP, "Executive Secretary to Advisory Committee," 18 March 1937, box 1, file folders 13, 31; box 2, file folders 55, 84; box 3, file folders 91, 109, 129, 133, 134, 135, 144, 151, 153, 155, 156; box 7, file folder 321, ULP Papers, UP. This report also included subcommittee reports by the recreation and civic committees.

11. "Executive Secretary to Advisory Committee," 18 March 1937. Board member Mrs. Raymond Kaufman supported the idea of a black hospital as an expedient that paralleled the struggle for Jewish health care in the city. Also see "Special Committee on Hospital Plans," 22 September 1930, box 1, file folders 6, 26, 34; box 2, file folder 55; box 3, file folders 132, 135; box 4, file folder 158, ULP Papers, UP; "Summary of Minutes of Exec. Bd. Meeting," 14 January 1931 (including a ULP hospital report).

12. Arthur J. Edmunds and Esther L. Bush, *Daybreakers: The Story of the Urban League of Pittsburgh, the First Eighty Years* (1983; revised and updated, Pittsburgh: Urban League of Pittsburgh, 1999), 116–17.

13. See Darlene Clark Hine, *Black Women in White: Racial Conflict and Cooperation in the Nursing Profession, 1890–1950* (Bloomington: Indiana University Press,

1989), 199. Philadelphia developed two black hospitals: Frederick Douglass Memorial and Mercy Hospital. See David McBride, *Integrating the City of Medicine: Blacks in Philadelphia Health Care, 1910–1965* (Philadelphia: Temple University Press, 1989).

14. "Hill District Health Clinic," in "Minutes of Executive Board Meeting," 18 March 1941, box 1, file folders 17, 33, 35, 44; box 2, file folder 90; box 3, file folders 55, 90, ULP Papers, UP.

15. R. M. Moss to Board, 4 April 1941, box 1, file folders 17, 33, 35, 44; box 2, file folder 90; box 3, file folders 55, 90, ULP Papers, UP.

16. ULP, "Summary of the Minutes of Executive Board Meeting," 15 April 1941, box 1, file folders 17, 33, 35, 44; box 2, file folder 90; box 3, file folders 55, 90, ULP Papers, UP.

17. "Record Crowd Attends Urban League's Anniversary Meeting," *Pittsburgh Courier,* 11 February 1933.

18. ULP, "The Fifteenth Year, 1918–1932."

19. "Select Citizens to Probe School Situation Here: Teacher Drive Waxes Warm," *Pittsburgh Courier,* 12 March 1932.

20. "Report of Industrial Committee," June, July, August 1930; "Industrial Relations Department, Tentative Outline of Activities," ca. 1930; "Report of Industrial Relations Department, September 1930 [1931?], box 1, file folders 6, 26, 34; box 2, file folder 55; box 3, file folders 132, 135; box 4, file folder 158, ULP Papers, UP.

21. "Urban League Scholarship Committee to Give Concert as Annual 1941 Event: Concert, March 8th in Stephen Foster Memorial Hall Will Feature Cream of Pittsburgh's Young Artists," *Pittsburgh Courier,* 15 February 1941; "Committee Confident of Large Crowd at Urban League Artists' Concert," *Pittsburgh Courier,* 8 March 1941; "Urban League Plans Annual Meeting Here," *Pittsburgh Courier,* 27 December 1930; "Interest Growing in Benefit Show to Be Given by Urban League," *Pittsburgh Courier,* 16 April 1932.

22. Adam Lee Cilli, "'The Greatest Good': Black Reformers and the Early Civil Rights Movement in Pittsburgh, 1915–1945" (PhD diss., University of Maine, 2005), 180–81. For a discussion of the ULP's research agenda, see Cilli, 82; Ancella Livers, "Defining Ourselves: Gender Construction and the Creation of a Black Community in Pittsburgh, 1925–55" (PhD diss., Carnegie Mellon University, 1998), 120–21; Trotter and Day, *Race and Renaissance,* 33.

23. "Executive Secretary to Advisory Committee," 18 March 1937.

24. Edmunds and Bush, *Daybreakers,* 98–100; "R. I. Wilson Is New Head of Urban League," *Pittsburgh Courier,* 21 February 1931; "Merechal-Neil Ellison to Wed: Pittsburgh Urban League Education Secretary to Marry William Arthur Young in Philly—To Live in Pittsburgh," *Pittsburgh Courier,* 23 December 1939. Ellison and Young both received degrees from the University of Pennsylvania—she in sociology and guidance, and he in social sciences.

25. "To Present Problem to School Board Here after Urban Confab," *Pittsburgh Courier,* 2 January 1932. Following a meeting at the Urban League offices in December 1931, a committee chaired by Daisy Lampkin discussed the lack of black teachers

in public schools, discrimination in the Frick Training School for Teachers, and the need for a black vocational counselor. Ivory Cobb, "Makes Plea for Negro Vocational Counselors in Pittsburgh Schools," *Pittsburgh Courier*, 19 December 1931.

26. "Urban League History Class Goes over Big," *Pittsburgh Courier*, 25 November 1933. Also see "Another Pitt Ph.D.: Warrant M. Banner, Research Director of Urban League, Awarded Degree in Economics," *Pittsburgh Courier*, 15 July 1939. Banner's thesis was titled "The Housing of Negro Families in Greater New York." See "St. Louis Youth Gets Fellowship at Pitt," *Pittsburgh Courier*, 9 August 1930, on the ULP fellow for 1930–1931.

27. T. Arnold Hill, director, Department of Industrial Relations, NUL, to Reginald A. Johnson, 1 March 1939; R. Maurice Moss, executive secretary, ULP, to T. Arnold Hill, director, Industrial Relations Department, NUL, 1 March 1939, box 1, file folders 14, 32, 35; box 2, file folders 55, 79, 84, 90; box 3, file folders 90, 109, 126, 133, 144, 151, 153 155, 156, ULP Papers, UP. For 1939, see box 1, file folders 15, 152.

28. Hill to Johnson, 1 March 1939; Moss to Hill, 1 March 1939; "Annual Meeting of League: Variety of Discussions Feature Youth Rally," *Pittsburgh Courier*, 4 March 1939. The vocational committee of the ULP planned an East End youth rally at the Lincoln School Community Center for 7:00 p.m. on 6 March. The gathering would include talks on youth, the church, and marriage and family problems.

29. "Job Advice Bureau Set up by League: George Culberson at Herron Hill Junior High, Miss Marechal-Neil Ellison to Help Youth with Job Problems," *Pittsburgh Courier*, 21 January 1939.

30. R. Maurice Moss to Executive Board, 21 February 1941, box 1, file folders 17, 33, 35, 44; box 2, file folder 90; box 3, file folders 55, 90, ULP Papers, UP. Moss also urged support for the scholarship committee's benefit concert at Foster Memorial Hall, mentioned earlier.

31. Trotter and Day, *Race and Renaissance*, 40–41.

32. "Discuss Post-War Problems: Urban League Executives Say 'Negro Must Not Become Beggar Again': Serious Men Delegates and Visitors at Annual National Urban League Conference Held at Camp James Weldon Johnson, Florence, Pa. Over-Weekend," *Pittsburgh Courier*, 12 September 1942.

33. T. Arnold Hill, director, Department of Industrial Relations, NUL, to R. Maurice Moss, 29 November 1937, box 1, file folders 13, 31; box 2, file folders 55, 84; box 3, file folders 91, 109, 129, 133, 134, 135, 144, 151, 153, 155, 156; box 7, file folder 321, ULP Papers, UP.

34. "Unemployed Workers Urged to Register: Many New Jobs Available," *Pittsburgh Courier*, 15 March 1941.

35. R. Maurice Moss to membership, 6 March 1941 (announcing upcoming visit of Robert Weaver); Moss to citizens, 2 April 1941; "Minutes of Defense Meeting," 15 October 1940 (called by the NAACP and the Urban League at Grace Memorial Church), box 1, file folders 16, 17, 33, 34; box 2, file folders 44, 61, ULP Papers, UP.

36. Moss to Community Fund, 14 August 1934, box 1, file folders 10, 11, 29, ULP Papers, UP; "Report on the Work of the Free Loan Association," 1 June–1 October 1940; memorandum from Thomas Barton, chairman, Small Loan Subcommittee,

to subcommittee members, 26 February 1940; memorandum from R. M. Moss to Executive Board, 21 February 1941; "ULP Executive Board Meeting," 17 June 1941; "Minutes of Executive Board," 16 April 1940 (the industrial committee agreed to set up a fund to help pay union dues for poor and working-class blacks), box 1, file folders 16, 17, 33, 34; box 2, file folders 44, 61, ULP Papers, UP.

37. Harold M. Parker, Johnstown, PA, affidavit of complaint against American Bridge Company to FEPC, 5 February 1943, FEPC Papers, Library of Congress; George E. DeMar, secretary, Department of Industrial Relations, ULP, to P. T. Fagan, area director, War Manpower Commission, 25 May 1943, FEPC Papers.

38. F. Marie Thompson to Geo. E. DeMar, 29 May 1943, NUL Papers, Library of Congress. For an excellent table of job placements, see ULP, Employment Department, 1 January–31 December 1928, ULP Papers, UP.

39. Parker affidavit, 5 February 1943; DeMar to Fagan, 25 May 1943.

40. George E. DeMar, secretary, Department of Industrial Relations, to Lawrence Cramer, FEPC and War Manpower Commission, 7 December 1942; DeMar to R. J. Greenly, chair of personnel, Carnegie-Illinois Steel Corporation, 4 May 1943; DeMar to office of the president, H. J. Heinz Company, 6 June 1943; Moss to H. J. Heinz, president, H. J. Heinz Company, 25 May 1943; H. J. Heinz to E. Maurice Moss, executive secretary, ULP, 1 June 1943, box 1, file folder 18; box 2, file folders 56, 57; box 3, file folders 92, 139, 155; box 5, file folder 204; box 6, file folder 265; ULP Papers, UP.

41. Lester B. Granger, assistant executive secretary, NUL, to George E. DeMar, industrial relations secretary, ULP, 14 November 1941; [George DeMar] to Granger, 10 December 1941, box 1, file folders 16, 17, 33, 34; box 2, file folders 44, 61, ULP Papers, UP.

42. "Meeting of the Workers' Council," 5 February 1942; ULP Industrial Department, "Workers Institute," 1940, box 1, file folder 18; box 2, file folder 56, ULP Papers, UP; "Workers' Schools in Western Pennsylvania," annual report, 1937–1938, 22 May 1938, box 1, file folders 5, 13, 31; box 2, file folders 55, 84; box 3, file folders 91, 109, 129, 133, 134, 135, 144, 151, 153, 155, 156; box 7, file folder 321, ULP Papers, UP.

43. "Meeting of the Workers' Council," 5 February 1942; "Workers Institute," 1940; "Workers' Schools in Western Pennsylvania," 22 May 1938.

44. "The Negro Worker's Housing Worry," 10 February 1943, box 2, file folder 56; box 5, file folder 204; box 6, file folder 265, ULP Papers, UP.

45. "Minutes, Industrial Relations Committee," 19 May 1944, box 2, file folder 56; box 3, file folders 92, 93, 101; box 6, file folder 265; box 9, file folder 436, ULP Papers, UP.

46. Edmunds and Bush, *Daybreakers*, 113–15.

47. "Minutes of Executive Board Meeting," 18 March 1941; Ralph E. Koger, "Three Outstanding Social Workers Accept New Jobs," *Pittsburgh Courier*, 17 March 1945.

48. "Minutes of Executive Board Meeting," 18 March 1941; Koger, "Three Outstanding Social Workers Accept New Jobs."

49. "Urban League Opposes Local FEPC Campaign: Organization Questions Legality of a Pittsburgh Fair Employment Practices Committee and Points out that Subpoenas and Enforcement Powers Would Be Limited," *Pittsburgh Courier,* 22 December 1945.

50. "Talk O'Town: To Grace Lowndes," *Pittsburgh Courier,* 22 January 1944; "Miss Grace Lowndes Honored by Pittsburgh League," *Pittsburgh Courier,* 17 June 1944; "Committee Confident of Large Crowd at Urban League Artists' Concert," *Pittsburgh Courier,* 8 March 1941.

51. "ULP Board and Staff Dinner Meeting," 27 September 1938, box 1, file folders 14, 32, 35; box 2, file folders 55, 79, 84, 90; box 3, file folders 90, 109, 126, 133, 144, 151, 153, 155, 156, ULP Papers, UP.

52. Trotter and Day, *Race and Renaissance,* 26–27; Cilli, "'The Greatest Good,'" 61; Livers, "Defining Ourselves," 131. For a discussion of ULP leadership changes, see Edmunds and Bush, *Daybreakers,* 78–79.

53. Edmunds and Bush, *Daybreakers,* 75–76, 228–29.

54. Fidel Makoto Campet, "Housing in Black Pittsburgh: Community Struggles and the State, 1916–1973" (PhD diss., Carnegie Mellon University, 2011), 183.

55. Campet, "Housing in Black Pittsburgh," 183, 187; Peter Gottlieb, *Making Their Own Way: Southern Blacks' Migration to Pittsburgh, 1916–30* (Urbana: University of Illinois Press, 1987), 197.

56. "Monster Community Song Fest to Be Staged at Greenlee Field: Urban League and the Pittsburgh Courier Sponsor Large Song and Musical Fete Aug 2 . . . 1,000 Voices and an Orchestra of 200 Pieces to Feature—Arter Is Director," *Pittsburgh Courier,* 16 July 1932. Also see "Urban League Community Choir Prepares Annual Presentation: Concert Will Be Held in Stephen Foster Memorial Auditorium," *Pittsburgh Courier,* 18 October 1941.

57. Trotter and Day, *Race and Renaissance,* 23; Cilli, "'The Greatest Good,'" 42–43, 180–81; Andrew Buni, *Robert L. Vann of* Pittsburgh Courier: *Politics and Black Journalism* (Pittsburgh: University of Pittsburgh Press, 1974), 59–60.

5. Combating Inequality in the Postwar City

1. "Proceedings: Ninth Annual Institute on Human Relations—The Supreme Court Decision and Discrimination in Our Community," 21 February 1955, William Penn Hotel, Pittsburgh.

2. "Proceedings: Ninth Annual Institute on Human Relations."

3. Joe William Trotter Jr. and Jared Day, *Race and Renaissance: African Americans in Pittsburgh since World War II* (Pittsburgh: University of Pittsburgh Press, 2010), 52–53.

4. "Annual Report of the ULP for 1951," NUL Papers, Library of Congress.

5. "Annual Report of the ULP for 1951"; Trotter and Day, *Race and Renaissance,* 49.

6. Trotter and Day, *Race and Renaissance,* 61.

7. Arthur J. Edmunds and Esther L. Bush, *Daybreakers: The Story of the Urban League of Pittsburgh, the First Eighty Years* (1983; revised and updated, Pittsburgh: Urban League of Pittsburgh, 1999), 126–27.

8. "Proceedings: Ninth Annual Institute on Human Relations."

9. ULP, "32nd Annual Meeting," 15 May 1950, NUL Papers; "Annual Report of the ULP for 1951."

10. "Irving Finley, of Urban League, Discusses Upgrading, Union Activity, League Structure," *Pittsburgh Courier,* 22 July 1950.

11. Guichard Parris and Lester Brooks, *Blacks in the City: A History of the National Urban League* (Boston: Little, Brown, 1971), 333–34; Dennis C. Dickerson, *Out of the Crucible: Black Steelworkers in Western Pennsylvania, 1875–1980* (Albany: State University of New York Press, 1986), 205–10; Edmunds and Bush, *Daybreakers,* 116–17.

12. Dickerson, *Out of the Crucible,* 205–10; Edmunds and Bush, *Daybreakers,* 116–17.

13. "Annual Report of the ULP for 1955," NUL Papers.

14. "Annual Report of the ULP for 1954," NUL Papers.

15. "Annual Report of the ULP for 1951."

16. "Brown's Bill Wins 'First Round,'" *Pittsburgh Courier,* 31 March 1945.

17. "Annual Report of the ULP for 1951"; "Caravan of Pittsburghers Ready for FEPC Hearings," *Pittsburgh Courier,* 24 March 1945; Edmunds and Bush, *Daybreakers,* 116–17; Trotter and Day, *Race and Renaissance,* 49, 60; "Brown's Bill Wins 'First Round.'"

18. Trotter and Day, *Race and Renaissance,* 59–60.

19. "Urban League Opposes Local FEPC Campaign," *Pittsburgh Courier,* 22 December 1945.

20. Trotter and Day, *Race and Renaissance,* 59–60.

21. "Local FEPC Fight On: Leaders' Views Differ," *Pittsburgh Courier,* 8 December 1945; "Local FEPC Law Urged," *Pittsburgh Courier,* 24 November 1945.

22. "Annual Report of the ULP for 1955."

23. Dickerson, *Out of the Crucible,* 205–10; "Annual Report of the ULP for 1951"; "Annual Report of the ULP for 1954"; "Annual Report of the ULP for 1955"; Trotter and Day, *Race and Renaissance,* 52–53.

24. Trotter and Day, *Race and Renaissance,* 64; "Annual Report of the ULP for 1955."

25. Edmunds and Bush, *Daybreakers,* 140.

26. Edmunds and Bush, *Daybreakers,* 139–40.

27. Hugh B. Price, *This African-American Life: A Memoir* (Durham, NC: John F. Blair, 2017), 2.

28. Fidel Makoto Campet, "Housing in Black Pittsburgh: Community Struggles and the State, 1916–1973" (PhD diss., Carnegie Mellon University, 2011), 266, 269–70, 272, 277–82.

29. "Annual Report of the Urban League of Pittsburgh for 1951."

30. "Annual Report of the ULP for 1951."

31. "Annual Report of the ULP for 1954."

32. "Annual Report of the ULP for 1955."

33. Trotter and Day, *Race and Renaissance,* 49, 64; Dickerson, *Out of the Crucible,* 205–10.

34. Dickerson, *Out of the Crucible*, 205–10.

35. "Irving Finley, of Urban League, Discusses Upgrading, Union Activity, League Structure."

36. Quoted in Jessica Klanderud, "Street Wisdom: African American Cultural and Political Formations in Pittsburgh, 1918–1970" (PhD diss., Carnegie Mellon University, 2011), 135.

37. Campet, "Housing in Black Pittsburgh," 261–63; Trotter and Day, *Race and Renaissance*, 69, 71–72.

38. "Annual Report of the ULP for 1954"; Albert W. Bloom, "Big Untapped Housing Market Here for Negro Housing," *Pittsburgh Post-Gazette*, 1 February 1954.

39. "Annual Report of the ULP for 1955."

40. Klanderud, "Street Wisdom," 136–37, 143.

41. Trotter and Day, *Race and Renaissance*, 66.

42. "Annual Report of the ULP for 1955."

43. Campet, "Housing in Black Pittsburgh," 266, 269–70, 272, 277–82. Black-owned real estate firms enhanced African Americans' access to the private housing market in the city.

44. Pittsburgh Commission on Human Relations, "Time Is Running Out," 1967 annual report, City of Pittsburgh.

45. Leon L. Haley, "Housing and You," *Pittsburgh Courier*, 1 January 1966.

46. Campet, "Housing in Black Pittsburgh," 322–23, 325–27, 339–54. Also see Donald C. Stevens Jr., "The Role of Nonprofit in Urban Development: A Case Study of ACTION-Housing Inc. of Pittsburgh" (PhD diss., Carnegie Mellon University, 1987).

47. "Stanton Land Company, Corporation, and Francis X. Totten, Plaintiffs vs. City of Pittsburgh, the Commission on Human Relations of the City of Pittsburgh, Louis Mason Jr., Executive Director of the Commission on Human Relations, and David W. Craig, Solicitor of the City of Pittsburgh, and Oswald J. Nickens, Defendants, No. 1741, in Equity, in the Court of Common Pleas of Allegheny County, Pennsylvania; "Nickens Housing Case Verdict Will Be Handed Down This Fall," *Pittsburgh Courier*, 2 August 1963.

48. Campet, "Housing in Black Pittsburgh,"332–33; "Anti Trust Suit Hits Pgh. Multilist: Byrd and NAACP LDF Represent Realtor," *Pittsburgh Courier*, 8 April 1967; James McCarron, "Negro Wins Realty Berth: Multilist Eliminating Bias from By-laws," *Pittsburgh Press*, 3 October 1968. See Ervin Dyer, "The Sweet Life . . . Sugar Top," *Pittsburgh Post-Gazette*, 17 July 2005, on the elite Hill District neighborhood of Robert Lavelle and others.

49. Pittsburgh Commission on Human Relations, "Time Is Running Out."

50. "Annual Report of the ULP for 1954." During the closing decades of the twentieth century, ULP housing programs included the Housing Information Program, Housing Counseling Services, Housing Assistance Program, Fair Housing Program, Emergency Shelter Program, and Public Housing Improvement Program. See Edmunds and Bush, *Daybreakers*, 182–86.

51. Bryn J. Hovde, *Report on Population Movement and Housing Trends* (Pittsburgh: Civic Unity Council, 1950).

52. Dickerson, *Out of the Crucible*, 205–10.

53. "Annual Report of the ULP for 1955."

54. Edmunds and Bush, *Daybreakers*, 133; Trotter and Day, *Race and Renaissance*, 75–76.

55. ULP, "32nd Annual Meeting," 15 May 1950; "Annual Report of the ULP for 1951."

56. "Annual Report of the ULP for 1954."

57. "Annual Report of the ULP for 1954." Also see "Annual Report of the ULP for 1955."

58. "Annual Report of the ULP for 1955"; "Public to Hear Gaines Bradford," *Pittsburgh Courier*, 21 March 1959; Trotter and Day, *Race and Renaissance*, 84–85.

59. ULP, "32nd Annual Meeting," 15 May 1950.

60. Hovde, *Report on Population Movement and Housing Trends*.

61. "Annual Report of the ULP for 1955"; Trotter and Day, *Race and Renaissance*, 84–85.

62. Thomas A. Henney, "Urban League Hits Doctor Inequality," *Pittsburgh Post-Gazette*, 10 July 1963; Henry W. Pierce, "Negro MD Plight '1 More Problem,'" *Pittsburgh Post-Gazette*, 11 July 1963; "League Backs Pgh. Hosp. in Med. Center Row," *Pittsburgh Courier*, 14 October 1967; "Annual Report of the ULP for 1955."

63. "Annual Report of the ULP for 1954."

64. "Annual Report of the ULP for 1955."

65. ULP, "32nd Annual Meeting," 15 May 1950; "Annual Report of the ULP for 1951."

66. ULP, "32nd Annual Meeting," 15 May 1950.

67. Edmunds and Bush, *Daybreakers*, 135–36, 143–44, 160; "Annual Report of the ULP for 1954." Over a twenty-year period, beginning with its inception in the 1960s, the program awarded grants to some 18,000 students.

68. ULP, "32nd Annual Meeting," 15 May 1950; "Pittsburgh Urban League Fellowship," *Pittsburgh Courier*, 17 March 1956.

69. "Annual Report of the ULP for 1954"; "Annual Report of the ULP for 1955"; Edward W. Schwerle, "A Study of the Administrative Decentralization in the Pittsburgh Public Schools" (PhD diss., University of Pittsburgh, 1973), 22–33.

6. Navigating Civil Rights and Black Power Struggles

1. Joe William Trotter Jr. and Jared Day, *Race and Renaissance: African Americans in Pittsburgh since World War II* (Pittsburgh: University of Pittsburgh Press, 2010), 58–59.

2. "Plans to 'Work on' Department Stores," *Pittsburgh Courier*, 3 February 1945.

3. "Stores Study Negro Clerk," *Pittsburgh Courier*, 6 December 1947.

4. "'Hire More Negroes at Arena!'—NAACP," *Pittsburgh Courier*, 7 October 1961.

5. "Courier, NAACP, NALC Mass Protest Wins; Arena to Improve Job-Hiring Policy," *Pittsburgh Courier*, 28 October 1961. Also see "Kaufmann's Pledges to Upgrade Negroes," *Pittsburgh Courier*, 2 December 1961.

6. Arthur J. Edmunds and Esther L. Bush. *Daybreakers: The Story of the Urban League of Pittsburgh, the First Eighty Years* (1983; revised and updated, Pittsburgh: Urban League of Pittsburgh, 1999), 128–31.

7. Trotter and Day, *Race and Renaissance*, 91, 96–98, 103, 117, 121.

8. Ralph Proctor, *Voices from the Firing Line: A Personal Account of the Pittsburgh Civil Rights Movement*, 2nd ed. (Pittsburgh: Introspec Press, 2014), 311.

9. Proctor, *Voices from the Firing Line*, 312, 313.

10. Community Renewal Program, *A Report on Social Problems in Urban Renewal* (Pittsburgh: Department of City Planning, 1965). Also see "Urban Renewal Impact Study Ready Here," *Pittsburgh Press*, 23 June 1963; "Fight for Urban Survival: Crises Challenging County to Tackle Future in New Way," *Pittsburgh Press*, 24 June 1963; "Fight for Urban Survival: Redevelopment Needs a 'Face Lift,' More Coordination," *Pittsburgh Press*, 25 June 1963; "Fight for Survival: More Negro Leaders Needed to Equalize Housing and Jobs," *Pittsburgh Press*, 6 June 1963.

11. "Negro American Labor Council Member Wants to Know about Civic Arena Jobs," *Pittsburgh Courier*, 16 September 1961.

12. Proctor, *Voices from the Firing Line*, 312, 313.

13. Arthur Edmunds, interview by Jared N. Day, 24 August 2007, RAP.

14. Proctor, *Voices from the Firing Line*, 311, 312. Proctor voluntarily left the ULP after a year because, as he put it, "I was certain that my militancy would eventually cause me to become an ex-employee." Proctor nonetheless described the ULP's relationship with the grassroots black social movement during Edmunds's tenure as substantially collaborative and cooperative.

15. David Epperson, interview by Jared N. Day, ca. August 2007, RAP.

16. Esther Bush, interview by Ben Houston, 7 August 2007, RAP.

17. "County Promises Blasted," *Pittsburgh Courier*, 28 June 1969.

18. "Three Rivers Stadium Faces Work Stoppage," *Pittsburgh Courier*, 9 August 1969.

19. "Massive 'Black Monday' Protest Set," *Pittsburgh Courier*, 15 November 1969. African American activists lamented the dearth of black employees at all Sears stores: 59 of 599 at the East Liberty store, 12 of 469 at Penn Center, 9 of 307 at the Fifty-First Street service center, 13 of 408 at Baldwin, 5 of 393 at Greensburg, 64 of 693 at the North Side location, 19 of 599 at South Hills, and 16 of 444 at West Mifflin.

20. "UBPC, Sears Set Meeting," *Pittsburgh Courier*, 10 January 1970; "Sears Now Ready for Negotiations," *Pittsburgh Courier*, 13 December 1969; "List of Demands to Sears," *Pittsburgh Courier*, 20 December 1969; "Sears Boycott Ends, HRCP Plays Key Role," *Pittsburgh Courier*, 28 March 1970.

21. Edward W. Schuerle, "A Study of the Administrative Decentralization in the Pittsburgh Public Schools" (PhD diss., University of Pittsburgh, 1973), 69, 70, 74, 76, 144–45.

22. Edmunds and Bush, *Daybreakers*, 149–50; Arthur J. Edmunds, executive director, Leon Haley, assistant executive director, and Mildred L. Wade, director of programs, "An Educational and Medical Program for School-Age Pregnant Girls,"

ca. 27 January 1978, in cooperation with the Pittsburgh Board of Education, Allegheny County Health Department, and Magee-Women's Hospital, box 122, folder 5, ULP Papers, Heinz; Susan Downs Pettigrew, "Urban League Statement on Pittsburgh Educational-Medical School," presented to Board of Education 15 April 1975, box 122, folder 7, ULP Papers, Heinz; Leon L. Haley, ULP President and CEO, to Joseph M. Hohman, Director, Department of Development, Allegheny, 4 October 1991, box 26, folder 5, ULP Papers, Heinz.

23. Schuerle, "Study of Administrative Decentralization in Pittsburgh Public Schools," 24–25, 28–29.

24. "Urban League Supports Pittsburgh School Board: Wendell Freeland, President; Ronald Davenport, Chairman of Education Committee; and Arthur J. Edmunds, Executive Director," *Pittsburgh Courier*, 21 August 1965; "Urban League Backs School Mixing Plan," *Pittsburgh Courier*, 3 June 1967.

25. "Community Applauds School Hiring Policy," *Pittsburgh Courier*, 7 March 1964.

26. Ralph Proctor, "Racial Discrimination against Black Teachers and Black Professionals in the Pittsburgh Public School System, 1834–1973" (PhD diss., University of Pittsburgh, 1979), 174.

27. Schuerle, "Study of Administrative Decentralization in Pittsburgh Public Schools," 69, 70, 74, 76, 144–45; "Education Department, 1968," and "Statement of Education or Crisis in Public Education—A Call for Effective Schooling," 11 February 1969, box 87, folder 1, ULP Papers, Heinz.

28. "Statement of Education or Crisis in Public Education," 11 February 1969.

29. Hugh B. Springer, "The Dynamics of Policy Formation in Urban Schools: Pittsburgh's Education Park/Great High Schools Concept" (PhD diss., University of Pittsburgh, 1973), 155.

30. "Urban League Supports Pittsburgh School Board"; "Urban League Backs School Mixing Plan."

31. Fidel Makoto Campet, "Housing in Black Pittsburgh: Community Struggles and the State, 1916–1973" (PhD diss., Carnegie Mellon University, 2011), 14–15, 244, 251–59, 339–50, 364–67; "The Woman behind CASH," *Pittsburgh Courier*, 26 August 1967.

32. "Urban League to Help in Minority Housing," *Pittsburgh Courier*, 24 December 1966; "Fair Housing Program Starts," *Pittsburgh Courier*, 16 September 1967 (on the launch of Operation Equality); Campet, "Housing in Black Pittsburgh," 296–98; James V. Cunningham, "The Rising Urban Neighborhood," press release, 22 March 1964, ACTION-Housing Inc., personal files of J. V. Cunningham; James Frazier, interview by Fidel Campet, ca. August 2007, RAP.

33. Campet, "Housing in Black Pittsburgh," 296–98, 364–65, 367–89, 417–19; "Fair Housing Program Starts"; Frazier interview; Milton Washington, interview by RAP staff, ca. August 2007, RAP.

34. Pittsburgh Commission on Human Relations, "Time Is Running Out," 1967 annual report, City of Pittsburgh; Edmunds and Bush, *Daybreakers*, 133–34; Trotter and Day, *Race and Renaissance*, 80–88, 102.

35. "Urban League Backs Project in West End," *Pittsburgh Courier,* 18 November 1967; Campet, "Housing in Black Pittsburgh," 286–89.

36. Community Renewal Program, *Report on Social Problems in Urban Renewal.* Also see the *Pittsburgh Press* articles cited in note 10.

37. Campet, "Housing in Black Pittsburgh," 286–87.

38. Proctor, *Voices from the Firing Line,* 317, 320.

39. Edmunds and Bush, *Daybreakers,* 144–45, 170–72, 174–77, 184.

40. Kenneth J. Heineman, "Model City: The War on Poverty, Race Relations, and Catholic Social Activism in 1960 Pittsburgh," *Historian* 65 no. 4 (2003): 889–91.

41. Edmunds interview; Peter Schrag, "Pittsburgh: The Virtues of Candor," in *The Politics of Urban Education,* ed. Marilyn Gittell and Alan G. Hevesi (New York: Frederick A. Praeger, 1969), 207, 208, 209–10; Edmunds and Bush, *Daybreakers,* 153.

42. "Annual Report of the ULP for 1955," NUL Papers, Library of Congress; Edmunds and Bush, *Daybreakers,* 5, 12, 75–76, 131–33, 146, 228–39.

43. "Urban League to Honor Barton, Mrs. Jeffries," *Pittsburgh Courier,* 7 March 1953; Edmunds and Bush, *Daybreakers,* 75–76, 228–29, 227–31.

44. "Store Heads 'Mum' about Race Issue," *Pittsburgh Courier,* 24 October 1947; Edmunds and Bush, *Daybreakers,* 122, 167, 230.

45. Proctor, *Voices from the Firing Line,* 311.

46. Proctor, *Voices from the Firing Line,* 321, 325.

47. Proctor, *Voices from the Firing Line,* 314, 317, 320–21, 325; Bob McCarthy, *Malice toward None: Remembering Pittsburgh Mayor Joe Barr* (Pittsburgh: Dorrance, 2002), 1–5, 18.

48. Edmunds and Bush, *Daybreakers,* 12, 132.

7. Confronting Decline and Facilitating Renaissance

1. Esther L. Bush, "The State of Black Pittsburgh," 28 October 1999, 6, library of the Urban League of Greater Pittsburgh.

2. Joe William Trotter Jr. and Jared Day, *Race and Renaissance: African Americans in Pittsburgh since World War II* (Pittsburgh: University of Pittsburgh Press, 2010), 141–43.

3. Trotter and Day, *Race and Renaissance,* 144–46.

4. Althea Fonville, "Urban Problems Concern Urban League," *Pittsburgh Courier,* 19 October 1974; Esther Bush, interview by Ben Houston, 7 August 2007, RAP.

5. Joe William Trotter Jr., *The African American Experience* (Boston: Houghton Mifflin, 2001), 613–14.

6. Arthur J. Edmunds and Esther L. Bush, *Daybreakers: The Story of the Urban League of Pittsburgh, the First Eighty Years* (1983; revised and updated, Pittsburgh: Urban League of Pittsburgh, 1999), 170–71, 176, 191, 209.

7. Edmunds and Bush, *Daybreakers,* 210, 212.

8. Deepak Karamcheti, "Urban League Recaptures Financial Support: Allegheny County Support Level at 42 Percent," *Pittsburgh Courier,* 22 November 1997.

9. Leon L. Haley, ULP President and CEO, to USX, Alcoa, and other corporate leaders, 19 January 1989, box 2, folders 6–7; box 18, folder 21, ULP Papers, Heinz; "Preliminary Building Proposal for ULP," July 1986, box 37, folder 1, ULP Papers, Heinz; Edmunds and Bush, *Daybreakers,* 191.

10. See ULP, "Minority Economic Development Needs Assessment, for Allegheny County Department of Development and City of Pittsburgh's Urban Redevelopment Authority," 30 June 1986, box 37, folder 1, ULP Papers, Heinz; Sonya Johnson-Reid, "Haley Orchestrates Local Urban League Face Lift," *Pittsburgh Courier,* 14 December 1945; "Edmunds to Retire," *Pittsburgh Courier,* 29 September 1984.

11. "Esther Bush to Head Urban League of Pittsburgh," *Pittsburgh Courier,* 8 October 1994; Tresha N. Wade, "Time Is on Our Side: Despite 'Ugly Realities" the Urban League Believes the Region Holds Great Promise for Blacks," *Pittsburgh Courier,* 20 November 1999.

12. Edmunds and Bush, *Daybreakers,* 189.

13. Ralph L. Bangs and Jan Hyun Hong, *Black and White Economic Conditions in the City of Pittsburgh: A Benchmarks Special Report* (Pittsburgh: University Center for Social and Urban Research, 1995), 7.

14. ULP Report, 1999, 5–6. All ULP reports cited here are located in the library of the Urban League of Greater Pittsburgh.

15. ULP Report, 2001, 10–11.

16. ULP Report, 2000, 4.

17. Sabrina Deitrick, "Cultural Change in Pittsburgh: A Demographic Analysis at City and County Scales" (working paper, 2015), 80.

18. ULP Report, 1999, 8–9; Jim McKinnon, "Ex-Foes Unite against Sanders Agreement," *Pittsburgh Post-Gazette,* 4 May 1999.

19. ULP Report, 2000, 8–9, 15–19.

20. Hesalyn Hunts, Ralph Bangs, and Ken Thompson, "The Health Status of African Americans in Allegheny County: A Black Paper for the Urban League of Pittsburgh," January 2002; Trista N. Sims, "Health Problems among African American Women Age 35–64 in Allegheny County: A Black Paper for the Urban League of Pittsburgh," January 2002. These papers may be found at the University of Pittsburgh's Center on Race and Social Problems.

21. ULP Report, 2001, 14–15.

22. Hunts, Bangs, and Thompson, "Health Status of African Americans in Allegheny County"; Sims, "Health Problems among African American Women."

23. ULP Report, 2002, 7; ULP Report, 2003, 10.

24. ULP Report, 1999, 2–3, 4–5; ULP Report, 2003, 6–7.

25. Edmunds and Bush, *Daybreakers,* 204. Also see University of Pittsburgh Race Segregation Assistance Center, Ogle Duff, director, "The Pros and Cons of Busing in Pennsylvania," January 1982, box 53, folder 13, ULP Papers, Heinz; Carl Morris, "Education, Not Integration, No. 1 Black Priority," *Pittsburgh Post-Gazette,* 1 April 1979, box 59, folder 26, ULP Papers, Heinz.

26. Douglas Heuck, "Tender Casualties: Children Are the First Victims of Bitter Conditions," *Pittsburgh Press,* 9 March 1990.

27. ULP Report, 1999, 2–3, 4–5; ULP Report, 2003, 6–7.

28. ULP Report, 2002, 3.

29. Wade, "Time Is on Our Side."

30. "Transitionally Needy Program, Amendment, Narrative," box 26, folders 4, 5, ULP Papers, Heinz (also see box 13, folders 7–9; box 16, folders 2, 4, 11; box 26, folder 10); Leon L. Haley, ULP President and CEO, to Joseph M. Hohman, Director, Department of Development, Allegheny, 4 October 1991, box 26, folder 5, ULP Papers, Heinz; Diane I. Daniels, project manager, "Self-Employment (SET) Program, Quarterly Report," for the period 1 December 1989–April 1990, 22 June 1990, box 25, folders 14, 15, ULP Papers, Heinz.

31. Esther L. Bush, "Keynote Address: The State of Black Pittsburgh," ULP annual meeting and conference, 28 October 1999, 7–8; E. L. Bush, "Keynote Address: The Pittsburgh Movement for Change," ULP annual meeting and conference, 26 September 2003.

32. Edmunds and Bush, *Daybreakers,* 217, 225.

33. Edmunds and Bush, *Daybreakers,* 217, 225. Also see Harvey Adams and Leon Haley, conveners, Pittsburgh African American Leadership Summit, 2 March 1993; African American Leadership Forum meeting, Hill House, 5 February 1993; "Summary of the Meeting, African American Leadership Forum," 5 February 1993, box 13, folder 13, ULP Papers, Heinz.

34. Edmunds and Bush, *Daybreakers,* 152–53, 155–57, 182.

35. ULP Report, 2005–2006, 15.

36. "Transitionally Needy Program," appendix a; Dionne M. Pannell, "Urban League Statewide Program Helps to Build Communities through Business," *Pittsburgh Courier,* ca. December 1988–January 1989, news clipping, box 160, folder 1, ULP Papers, Heinz.

37. "Transitionally Needy Program," appendix a; "Pittsburgh School-to-Work Transition Project," ca. January 1984, box 84, folder 12, ULP Papers, Heinz.

38. "Transitionally Needy Program"; Haley to Hohman, 4 October 1991.

39. Trotter and Day, *Race and Renaissance,* 178–79, 186–87.

40. "Transitionally Needy Program," appendix a; Haley to Hohman, 4 October 1991.

41. ULP annual report, "Housing Counseling Services," 1 June 1976–31 May 1977, box 213, folder 5, ULP Papers, Heinz; "Transitionally Needy Program," appendix a; Haley to Hohman, 4 October 1991; Edmunds and Bush, *Daybreakers,* 213; ULP Report, 2000, 13; ULP Report, 2001, 16–17; ULP Report, 2003, 9; ULP Report, 2004, 8–9; ULP Report, 2004–2005, 19; ULP Report, 2009–2010, 9–10; ULP Report, 2010–2011, 15.

42. ULP Report, 2000, 13; ULP Report, 2001, 16–17; ULP Report, 2003, 9; ULP Report, 2004, 8–9.

43. ULP Report, 2003, 9; ULP Report, 2004, 8–9; ULP Report, 2004–2005, 19; ULP Report, 2010–2011, 15. Also see ULP/ACTION-Housing trainer's report, "Public Housing Improvement Program," 1988–89, box 135, folder 11, ULP Papers, Heinz; Housing Authority, City of Pittsburgh, "Blueprints for Our Future," 1993,

box 213, folder 4, ULP Papers, Heinz. In 2005 federal authorities called for $1 billion worth of cuts in the Section 8 Housing Choice Voucher Program.

44. Hunts, Bangs, and Thompson, "Health Status of African Americans in Allegheny County"; Sims, "Health Problems among African American Women."

45. "Urban League Adopts New Health Program," *Pittsburgh Courier*, 1 March 1969. The *Courier* reported that the ULP aimed to strengthen its role as a "health advisory" resource for "individuals, groups, and communities" interested in improving the health of the city's minority and poor communities. In July 1969 the *Courier* reported on the selection of Dorothy Bellas to serve as cochair and citizen representative on the Health Advisory Council of Community Action Pittsburgh. Her appointment represented a growing grassroots challenge to health organizations dominated by elites and professionals. "Woman to Help Guide Health Program Here," *Pittsburgh Courier*, 19 July 1969. See also ULP Annual Report, 2005–2006, 14; ULP Annual Report, 2006–2007, 14; ULP Annual Report, 2009–2010, 14; ULP Annual Report, 2010–2011, 14, 15.

46. ULP Report, 2005–2006, 14; ULP Report, 2006–2007, 14; ULP Report, 2009–2010, 14; ULP Report, 2010–2011, 14, 15.

47. ULP Report, 2005–2006, 14; ULP Report, 2010–2011, 15–17; ULP Report, 2006–2007, 14; ULP Report, 2009–2010, 14; ULP Report, 2010–2011, 14–17.

48. Edmunds and Bush, *Daybreakers*, 182, 213–14.

49. Trotter and Day, *Race and Renaissance*, 178–79, 186–87.

50. Edmunds and Bush, *Daybreakers*, 189. Also see "Youths Get Summer-Job Help," *Pittsburgh Post-Gazette*, ca. June 1981; "City Plan Targets Teen Jobs, Litter," *Pittsburgh Press*, 1 June 1982, news clippings, box 160, folder 2, ULP Papers, Heinz.

51. Haley to Hohman, 4 October 1991.

52. ULP Report, 1999, 12–14.

53. Edmunds and Bush, *Daybreakers*, 205–8, 215.

54. ULP Annual Report, 2007–2008, 5, 6, 17. Other programs included the Early College and Career Awareness Program and the Science, Technology, Engineering, and Math (STEM) Program.

55. Trotter and Day, *Race and Renaissance*, 178–79, 186–87.

56. Sonya Johnson, "Teen Pregnancy Prevention Focus of Survey," *Pittsburgh Courier*, 11 May 1985.

57. ULP Report, 2007–2008, 5, 6, 17; Allegheny County Health Department, "Problems of Teenage Pregnancy in Allegheny County, 1982–1986," 29 October 1987, box 124, folder 7, ULP Papers, Heinz.

58. See the discussion in chapter 6 and in Edmunds and Bush, *Daybreakers*, 205–8, 215.

59. Edmunds and Bush, *Daybreakers*, 205–8, 215; ULP Report, 2000, 14; ULP Report, 2005–2006, 23; ULP Report, 2007–2008, 5, 6, 17.

60. Urban League of Pittsburgh Priority Program, FY 1990–91, St. Clair Village Training and Employment Project, 8 November 1989, box 25, folder 14, ULP Papers, Heinz; Y. Denise Caldwell, activities director, to Alice Carter, director, "Urban

League Northview Program Update," 17, 27 August 1990; "Agreement, by and between City of Pittsburgh and the Urban League of Pittsburgh," ca. 12 September 1991, box 25, folder 15, ULP Papers, Heinz; Leon L. Haley, application summary sheet, Community Development Block Grant, 12 September 1990, box 40, folder 1, ULP Papers, Heinz; "Urban League of Pittsburgh, African American Community Summit on Violence," box 8, folder 10, ULP Papers, Heinz; Edmunds and Bush, *Daybreakers,* 187–88, 189–90.

61. "Transitionally Needy Program"; Haley to Hohman, 4 October 1991.

62. Edmunds and Bush, *Daybreakers,* 187–88, 189–90.

63. Heuck, "Tender Casualties."

64. Edmunds and Bush, *Daybreakers,* 200.

65. Edmunds and Bush, *Daybreakers,* 197–98, 200–201; "Clinton Urged to Examine Police Misconduct," *Pittsburgh Courier,* 20 November 1996.

66. Diane R. Powell, "Groups Mass Voter Drive," *Pittsburgh Courier,* 21 August 1982.

67. Arthur Edmunds, interview by Jared N. Day, 24 August 2007, RAP.

68. Marty Wills, "Urban League Supports District Elections," *Pittsburgh Courier,* 31 January 1987; Trotter and Day, *Race and Renaissance,* 151–53, 189–93; Marty Willis, "Black Groups Unify around District Elections Effort," *Pittsburgh Courier,* 11 April 1987.

69. Edmunds and Bush, *Daybreakers,* 213.

70. Bush, "State of Black Pittsburgh," 2003; Sonya M. Toler, "Pittsburgh Attracts National Urban League Convention," *Pittsburgh Courier,* 26 October 2002; Edmunds and Bush, *Daybreakers,* 220–22.

71. David Epperson, interview by Jared N. Day, ca. August 2007, RAP.

72. For insight into the impact of shifting political and economic conditions on the politics of Pittsburgh's black community, see the series of special articles in the *Pittsburgh Post-Gazette:* Clarke Thomas, "Pittsburgh Blacks Making Progress, Suffering Setbacks for over 2 Centuries," 1 June 1981; "City Blacks: Victims of Lawless, and the Law," 22 June 1981; "Pittsburgh: Someplace Not so Special" and "Jobs Slowly Open up for Minorities," 6 July 1981; "Poll: No Single Leader Speaks for Blacks" and "On Black Pittsburgh," 20 July 1981.

73. ULP annual report, "Empowering Communities, Changing Lives," 2016–2017.

Epilogue

1. John E. Jacobs, preface to first edition, Arthur J. Edmunds and Esther L. Bush, *Daybreakers: The Story of the Urban League of Pittsburgh, the First Eighty Years* (1983; revised and updated, Pittsburgh: Urban League of Pittsburgh, 1999), 8.

2. Hugh B. Price, preface to second edition, Edmunds and Bush, *Daybreakers,* 2.

3. St. Clair Drake and Horace R. Cayton, *Black Metropolis: A Study of Negro Life in a Northern City,* vols. 1 and 2 (1945; revised and enlarged, Chicago: University of Chicago Press, 1993), 734.

4. Alonzo N. Smith, *Empowering Communities, Changing Lives: 100 Years of the National Urban League and Black America, 1910–2010* (Virginia Beach, VA: Donning, 2011), 10.

5. Nancy J. Weiss, *The National Urban League, 1910–1940* (New York: Oxford University Press, 1974), 23–24; Jesse Thomas Moore Jr., *A Search for Equality: The National Urban League, 1910–1961* (University Park: Pennsylvania State University Press, 1981), xxi–xxiii, 213. Also see Susan D. Carle, *Defining the Struggle: National Organizing for Racial Justice, 1880–1915* (New York: Oxford University Press, 2013).

6. Touré F. Reed, *Not Alms but Opportunity: The Urban League and the Politics of Racial Uplift, 1910–1950* (Chapel Hill: University of North Carolina Press, 2008), 6–7.

7. Arvarh E. Strickland, *History of the Chicago Urban League* (1966; reprint, Columbia: University of Missouri Press, 2001), 260.

8. Guichard Parris and Lester Brooks, *Blacks in the City: A History of the National Urban League* (Boston: Little Brown, 1971), 472–73. For biographies and memoirs of National Urban League leaders, see Felix L. Armfield, *Eugene Kinckle Jones: The National Urban League and Black Social Work, 1910–1940* (Urbana: University of Illinois Press, 2012); Dennis C. Dickerson, *Militant Mediator: Whitney M. Young, Jr.* (Lexington: University Press of Kentucky, 1998); Nancy J. Weiss, *Whitney M. Young, Jr., and the Struggle for Civil Rights* (Princeton, NJ: Princeton University Press, 1989); Hugh B. Price, *This African-American Life: A Memoir* (Durham, NC: John F. Blair, 2017).

Selected Bibliography

In addition to the works listed below, this book drew on the records of the Urban League of Pittsburgh housed at the Archives Service Center at the University of Pittsburgh and Pittsburgh's Senator John Heinz History Center (a Smithsonian affiliate), the *Pittsburgh Courier,* and the *Pittsburgh Post-Gazette.* Equally important to this book were the recollections of black Pittsburghers participating in the Remembering Africanamerican Pittsburgh (RAP) oral history project conducted by Carnegie Mellon University's Center for Africanamerican Urban Studies and the Economy (CAUSE).

Armfield, Felix L. *Eugene Kinckle Jones: The National Urban League and Black Social Work, 1910–1940.* Urbana: University of Illinois Press, 2012.

Broussard, Albert S. "Perey H. Steele, Jr., and the Urban League: Race Relations and the Struggle for Civil Rights in Post–World War II San Diego." *California History* 83, no. 4 (2006): 7–23.

Campet, Fidel Makoto. "Housing in Black Pittsburgh: Community Struggles and the State, 1916–1973." PhD diss., Carnegie Mellon University, 2011.

Carle, Susan D. *Defining the Struggle: National Organizing for Racial Justice, 1880–1915.* New York: Oxford University Press, 2013.

Cilli, Adam Lee. "'The Greatest Good': Black Reformers and the Early Civil Rights Movement in Pittsburgh, 1915–1945." PhD diss., University of Maine, 2005.

Dickerson, Dennis C. *Out of the Crucible: Black Steelworkers in Western Pennsylvania, 1875–1980.* Albany: State University of New York Press, 1986.

Dickerson, Dennis C. *Militant Mediator: Whitney M. Young, Jr.* Lexington: University Press of Kentucky, 1998.

Edmunds, Arthur J., and Esther L. Bush. *Daybreakers: The Story of the Urban League of Pittsburgh, the First Eighty Years.* 1983. Revised and updated, Pittsburgh: Urban League of Pittsburgh, 1999.

Glasco, Laurence A., ed. *The WPA History of the Negro in Pittsburgh.* Pittsburgh: University of Pittsburgh Press, 2004.

Gottlieb, Peter. *Making Their Own Way: Southern Blacks' Migration to Pittsburgh, 1916–30.* Urbana: University of Illinois Press, 1987.

Klanderud, Jessica. "Street Wisdom: African American Cultural and Political Formations in Pittsburgh, 1918–1970." PhD diss., Carnegie Mellon University, 2011.

Livers, Ancella. "Defining Ourselves: Gender Construction and the Creation of a Black Community in Pittsburgh, 1925–55." PhD diss., Carnegie Mellon University, 1998.

Mcelderry, Stuart. "Building a West Coast Ghetto: African-American Housing in Portland, 1910–1960." *Pacific Northwest Quarterly* 92, no. 3 (Summer 2001): 137–48.

Mihelich, Dennis N. "World War II and the Transformation of the Omaha Urban League." *Nebraska History* 60 (1979): 401–23.

Moore, Jesse Thomas, Jr. *A Search for Equality: The National Urban League, 1910–1961.* University Park: Pennsylvania State University Press, 1981.

Murage, Njeru. "The Detroit Urban League–Employers Alliance in Wartime Detroit, 1916–1919." *Michigan Historical Review* 26, no. 1 (Spring 2000): 66–104.

Parris, Guichard, and Lester Brooks. *Blacks in the City: A History of the National Urban League.* Boston: Little Brown, 1971.

Price, Hugh B. *This African-American Life: A Memoir.* Durham, NC: John F. Blair, 2017.

Reed, Touré F. *Not Alms but Opportunity: The Urban League and the Politics of Racial Uplift, 1910–1950.* Chapel Hill: University of North Carolina Press, 2008.

Smith, Alonzo N. *Empowering Communities, Changing Lives: 100 Years of the National Urban League and Black America, 1910–2010.* Virginia Beach, VA: Donning, 2011.

Strickland, Arvarh E. *History of the Chicago Urban League.* 1966. Reprint, Columbia: University of Missouri Press, 2001.

Trotter, Joe William, Jr. "Appendix: Essay on Sources." In *Workers on Arrival: Black Labor in the Making of America.* Berkeley: University of California Press, 2019.

———. *River Jordan: African American Urban Life in the Ohio Valley.* Lexington: University Press of Kentucky, 1998.

Trotter, Joe William, Jr., and Jared Day. *Race and Renaissance: African Americans in Pittsburgh since World War II.* Pittsburgh: University of Pittsburgh Press, 2010.

Trotter, Joe William, Jr., and Eric Ledell Smith, eds. *African Americans in Pennsylvania: Shifting Historical Perspectives.* College Park: Pennsylvania Historical and Museum Commission and Pennsylvania State University Press, 1997.

Weiss, Nancy J. *The National Urban League, 1910–1940.* New York: Oxford University Press, 1974.

———. *Whitney M. Young, Jr., and the Struggle for Civil Rights.* Princeton, NJ: Princeton University Press, 1989.

Index

Page references in italics indicate illustrations, and t *indicates a table.*

AAAT (African American Achievement Trust), 172–73
ACTION-Housing, 128, 169–70
Activities Month Celebration, 74
Ad hoc Committee on South Africa (NUL), 178
Administrative and Clerical Council (NUL), 153
Advisory Committee, 21, 108
Advisory Council, 62
affirmative action, 4, 142, 160
AFL (American Federation of Labor), 83–84, 106, 108–9, 137
African American Achievement Trust (AAAT), 172–73
Agbemenu, Kafui, 170
AHRCO (Allegheny Housing and Rehabilitation Corporation), 148–50
Albert, Peg, 156
Alexander, William, 17
Allegheny County Attorneys against Hunger, 171
Allegheny County Committee on Community Development, 124
Allegheny County Council on Civil Rights, 128
Allegheny County Emergency Relief Board, 79
Allegheny County Health Department, 173
Allegheny County Labor Council, 122

Allegheny County Race Relations Committee, 107
Allegheny Housing and Rehabilitation Corporation (AHRCO), 148–50
Allen, Alexander ("Joe"), 116, 123–24, 139
Allen, C. B., 37
Allen, Gerald Edgar, 29, 79, 192n58
A. M. Byers, 74
American Bridge, 104
American Civil Liberties Union, 13, 109, 121
American Communist Party, 85–86
American Diabetes Association, 170
American Federation of Labor. *See* AFL
American Sheet and Tin Plate Mill, 17–18
American Steel and Wire, 105
Anderson, J. C., 31
Annie E. Casey Foundation, 168
apartheid, 178
Arter, Mrs. David, 82–83
Arter, S. Nelson, 67, 111
Associated Charities, 10, 12, 64
Association for the Advancement of Science, 174
Association for the Improvement of Social Conditions in the Hill District, 10
Association for the Improvement of the Poor, 20, 72
Association of Community Organizations for Reform Now, 177

Baker, James H., Jr., 79
Bakewell, Mary E., 30, 62–64
Bangs, Ralph, 163–64
Barr, Joe, 156
Barton, Thomas E., 14–15, 20, 37–38, 97, 109, 120–21
basketball, 87
Bath House and Comfort Station (Hill District; Pittsburgh), 45
bathhouses, 44–45, 53
Baulding, Barbara, 169, 174
Beacon Construction, 149–50
Bedford Dwellings (Hill District; Pittsburgh), 80
Bell, Janet, 174
Bellas, Dorothy, 221n45
Bell Telephone, 49–50, 121
Belmar Gardens, 123
Benchmark Advisory Committee (CSUR), 162
Berry, Edwin C., 87, 108
Bethune, Mary McLeod, 88
Better Baby Contests, 42–43
Bieck's Milk, 94
Big Brother/Big Sister programs, 54
Birk, Minnie, 203n37
Black Construction Coalition, 139–40
Black Family Summit, 162
black freedom movement: assault on the gains of, 160; emergence of, 2, 93; escalation/intensification of, 5, 97; segregation challenged by, 111, 143; and the Urban League movement, 135, 140–41, 154–55
black hospital movement, 96–98, 208n11, 209n13
Black Leadership Directory, 166
Black Male Leadership Development Institute, 4
black men: in the military, 116; placement of skilled workers, 15–16; police harassment of, 52; in politics, 56–57, 177–79; research on leading causes of death among, 163–64

black nationalist movement, 55, 137
Black Political Empowerment Program II, 177
black power movement, 135, 139–40, 154–55
Black United Movement for Progress, 139–40
Black Woman Health Network, 173
black women: apartment house work for, 28; clerical/secretarial jobs for, 122; Depression's impact on employment of, 72; discrimination against, at Carnegie-Illinois Steel, 104–5; in domestic service, 16, 82; lack of employment for, 26–28; in laundries, 27; light- vs. dark-skinned, 61; Lowndes surveys socioeconomic conditions for, 27; in manufacturing, 16; "Negress," use of, 58; as prostitutes, 52, 61; protesting discrimination, 138; research on leading causes of death among, 163–64; skilled wartime jobs for, 104; as telephone operators, 49–50; in the ULP, bias against, 58–59; white-collar jobs open to, 49–50
Black Worker, The (Harris and Spero), 79
Bloom, Albert W., 125–26
Bobonis, Regis, 121–22
Boggs and Buhl Company Department Store, 49
Bolden, George, 116
Bond, Mary Peck, 14
Bond, Sadie, 14, 29–30
Bontemps, Arna, 30
Booker T. Washington Hospital and Nurse Training School, 95–96
B&O Railroad, 55
Borland, Wilson S., 106–7
Bowen, Ruth, 73
Boyce, Fred, 56
boycott movement, 93–94
Braddock (Pennsylvania), 19, 172

Bradford, Gaines T., 131, 139
Bradford, James, 152
Brandeis, Louis, 66
Brewer, John, 146
Brewer Coal Fund, 189n27
Brooks, Lester, 32–33, 118, 181
Brotherhood of Railroad Station
    Porters, 84
Brotherhood of Sleeping Car Porters,
    102
Brown, Byrd, 146, 152–53
Brown, Frances, 188n14
Brown, Homer, 81, 85, 100, 103–4,
    109, 120, 125, 130
Brown, Roderick, 46
Brown v. Board of Education of Topeka,
    132–34
Bruce, Clara Burrill, 90
Buchanan, Walter, 37
Buckner, George W., 31
Building Trades Council, 142
building workers institute, 81
Bullock, Matthew, 31
Burnett, L. H., 23
Busch Terminal (Brooklyn), 12
Bush, Esther L.: on affirmative action,
    142; on the Benchmark Advisory
    Committee, 162; on Clark,
    13, 32–33; on the Commission
    on Community Relations and
    Law Enforcement, 176; on the
    Committee on Diversity, 166; on
    data collection, 202–3n32; on
    daybreakers, 30; *Daybreakers,* 156;
    on fundraising, 161–62; on the
    Golden Triangle, 4, 159; on
    inequality, 159, 163; at the NUL
    conference in Pittsburgh, 178; on
    police use of force, 176; on
    prioritizing services for children,
    171; as ULP president and CEO,
    158, 162; on the ULP's early
    priorities, 68; on the UPMC
    board, 166

Bush, George W., 178
Business and Finance Academy
    (Westinghouse High School,
    Pittsburgh), 167–68
Business Week, 118
Butler grocery stores, 76, 93

Calloway, Harold T., 122–23
Calumet City (Pittsburgh), 156
Campaign for African American
    Achievement, 172
Campbell, Craig, 161
Campet, Fidel, 80
Camp James Weldon Johnson (Beaver
    County, Pa.), 45, 87–88, 108
CAN (Career Advancement Network),
    167–68
Cannors, William R., 31
CAPs (Community Action Programs),
    140, 151–52
Careathers, Ben, 86, 121
Career Advancement Network (CAN),
    167–68
Career Conferences, 119
Carnegie-Illinois Steel, 104–5
Carnegie Institute of Technology, 121
Carnegie Steel, 14, 17–19, 23–24, 26,
    30, 36–37, 63
Carroll, Charles H., 62, 97
Carson, Carolyn, 43, 46
Carter, Bob, 164–65, 174–75
Carter, Elmer, 88–89
Carter, John, 192n57
Carter, Leona, 51, 196n29
CASH (Citizens against Slum Housing),
    140, 147
Catholic agencies, 119–20
CCC (Civilian Conservation Corps),
    75–76
Center for Social and Urban Research
    (CSUR), 162
CETA (Comprehensive Education and
    Training Act), 160, 167–68
charter schools, 173–74

Cheney Training School for Teachers (Philadelphia), 51
Chicago Commission on Race Relations, 34
Chicago race riot (1919), 34
Chicago Urban League, 35, 78, 180–81
Children's Service Bureau, 72
Christy, Bayard, 63–64
Cilli, Adam, 100
CIO (Congress of Industrial Organizations), 83, 86, 90, 108–9, 137
Citizen Clergy Coordinating Committee, 147
Citizen Review Board, 176
Citizens against Slum Housing (CASH), 140, 147
Citizens Committee for Integrated Housing, 128
Citizens' Committee on Public Education, 98–99
City Council, 177
Civic Arena (Pittsburgh), 138–39
civic department (ULP), 88, 111
Civic Unity Council, 124, 129, 131–32
Civilian Conservation Corps (CCC), 75–76
Civil Rights Committee (Allegheny County Labor Council), 122
civil rights movement, 135, 138–40, 142–43, 154–55
Civil Works Administration (CWA), 75–77
Clark, John T.: background of, 12; on a black hospital, 46; black population of Pittsburgh surveyed by, 12–14; on black women's lack of employment, 26–27; on black workers' bitterness over discriminatory layoffs, 19–20; capital-labor conflicts navigated by, 13; Leona Carter supported by, 51; vs. Christy, 63–64; on a committee of industrialists, 62; and the

Department of Labor, 192n57; dismissal from the ULP, 13, 33–34, 181; efforts to advance black workers, 16–19; farmwork sought for southern migrants by, 19; on housing, 36, 38–39; on mistreatment of black workers at Jones and Laughlin, 26; on "Negress," 58; at NUL meetings, 31, 190n31; Pickens's meeting with, 48–49; vs. *Pittsburgh Courier*, 64; on racial inequality and injustice, 63; role in establishing the ULP, 12; on single black men, 61; on southern blacks, 12; St. Louis Urban League led by, 13, 33, 181; on student employees, 17; on the Traveler's Aid Society, 30; vs. Tyson, 62–63; vs. ULP board, 63–64; as ULP executive director, 12–13, 188n14; on ULP finances, 21, 65; on ULP member involvement, 64–65; on ULP's committee on health, 46; and unions, 32–33; on vagrancy, 29; welfare workers organized by, 30; on women staffers at ULP, 58–59
Clements, W. W., 84
Clinical and Translational Science Institute (University of Pittsburgh), 170
Clinton, Bill, 160, 176
Coalition for District Elections, 177
coal miners, black: conditions for, 35, 192n58; entrepreneurial, 26; housing for, 38–39; number of, 19, 25, 33; study of, 35; union vs. nonunion, 34–35
coal strikes, 32–34
Cohen, Stewart, 177
Cold War, 116
Coleman, Moe, 156
Collins, Carter T., 201n9
Colored Protective League of Allegheny County, 56

Columbia Hospital (Philadelphia), 132
Columbus School (Pittsburgh), 146
Commission on Community Relations
    and Law Enforcement, 176
Commission on Manpower Utilization
    of the National Association of
    Intergroup Relations Officials, 120
Committee against Discrimination in
    Pittsburgh Department Stores, 137
Committee for Improving the Industrial
    Condition of Negroes in New York,
    2, 11
Committee on Government Contract
    Compliance, 118, 123
Committee on Homeless Men, 73
Committee on Urban Conditions
    among Negroes (New York City),
    2, 11
Community Action Programs (CAPs),
    140, 151–52
Community Sing, 111
Comprehensive Education and Training
    Act (CETA), 160, 167–68
Comprehensive Youth Competencies
    Program, 166
Conference on Negro Industrial
    Welfare Workers (Pittsburgh,
    1920), 30
Congress of Industrial Organizations.
    See CIO
Congress of Women's Clubs, 82
Consumer Pressure as an Employment
    Program for Urban Negroes, 94
Covington, Floyd, 79
Coyne, John B., 100
Cramer, Lawrence, 104
Crawford, B. F., 89
Crucible Steel, 23–24
CSUR (Center for Social and Urban
    Research), 162
Culberson, George, 102
Cullen, Countee, 67
CWA (Civil Works Administration),
    75–77

Daddy Clay, 24
Dancy, John T., 31
Dargan, Goldia, 134
Davenport, Ronald R., 145, 152–53
Davis, John P., 86, 90
Daybreakers (Edmunds and Bush), 156
daybreakers, 30
day care, 53, 153
Defense Manpower Project, 3, 117
DeMar, George E., 103–5
Democratic Party, 57
Department of Federal Programs, 167
Department of Health and Human
    Services, 175
Department of Labor (Pennsylvania),
    15, 34, 62, 188n19
Department of Labor (US), 192n57
Depression (1930s), 71–91; influence
    on the ULP, 2, 71; as
    transformational, 9; unemployment
    relief in Pittsburgh, 71–74. See also
    New Deal; WPA
discrimination, gender, 1, 58–59, 61,
    64, 68, 109–10. See also inequality
discrimination, racial: against black
    health professionals, 45–46;
    boycotts against, 142–43; at
    Carnegie-Illinois Steel, 104–5; in
    defense industries, 102–4; in
    department stores, 137–38, 154,
    182; destructive impact on the
    workforce, 88–89; in education,
    48, 50–51, 100–101, 164 (see also
    education: black teachers); in
    employment, 19–20, 49–50,
    115–21, 156–57; in hospitals,
    95; in housing, 107, 126–30, 150,
    156, 159, 163; by railroads, 55,
    83–84, 104; in theaters, 55; ULP's
    documentation of/fight against,
    2–4, 45–46, 49–51, 55, 58, 68, 75;
    by unions, 16, 32, 76, 83–85, 106,
    116, 123. See also inequality; race/
    ethnicity

Dodd, Judy, 171
domestic service, 5, 16, 19, 82–83,
    204n46
Donora Steel, 36, 38
"Don't Buy Where You Can't Work"
    campaign, 5, 93–94
Dorsey, James A., 45
Dowdy, Richard, 118, 123
drugs, 174–75
Duardo, Ramon, 173
Du Bois, W. E. B., 180–81, 189n24
Duquesne University, 99

Early College and Career Awareness
    Program, 221n54
East Boro Negro Council, 103
East Liberty–Homewood League for
    Civic Improvement, 128
East Liberty neighborhood (Pittsburgh),
    125, 148
economy: boom of the 1990s, 163;
    downturn, 9, 19–20, 161 (see also
    Depression; unemployment);
    manufacturing-based, shift from,
    159–61; recovery era, 20–21
Edmunds, Arthur: on Clark, 13, 32–33;
    on data collection, 202–3n32; on
    daybreakers, 30; Daybreakers, 156;
    on fair employment laws, 140; on
    fundraising, 161–62; on the housing
    ordinance, 150; job placement
    success of, 122; March on
    Washington cochaired by, 154;
    McCoy's meeting with, 142; threats
    from rioters, 155; on ULP finances,
    161; on the ULP's conservative
    reputation, 141; on the ULP's
    early priorities, 68; on the War
    on Poverty, 151–53; on work
    programs for black youth, 172
education: "alternative" high schools,
    143–44; black children encouraged
    to stay in school, 172; black
    counselors, 101, 209–10n25;

black-history curriculum, 101; black
    school-age population, 47; black
    teachers, 50–51, 54, 95, 99–101,
    134, 144–45, 209–10n25; busing,
    144, 146, 164; charter schools,
    173–74; college grant program,
    134, 172, 215n67; curriculum
    reform, 146; desegregation of public
    schools, 100–101, 111, 132–34,
    144–46, 164; discrimination in, 48,
    50–51, 100–101, 164; Epstein's
    study of educational programs, 47;
    equal access to public education,
    98–102, 143–44; graduation parties,
    49; graduation rates for black
    students, 49; "Great Schools"
    integration plan, 144; health
    education programs, 42–43, 46–47,
    194n4, 194n7; integration of blacks
    into a previously all-white system,
    48; lecture series on health
    challenges, 43, 194n8; for middle-
    class/professional vs. working-class
    blacks, 181; in the new social service
    regime, 95–102; scholarships, 48,
    100–101, 134–35, 172, 210n30;
    school superintendents, 145–46;
    school-to-employment pipeline, 49;
    segregation in public schools,
    resurgence of, 159; of students in
    public housing, 164–65; ULP
    library on African American life and
    history, 194n4, 195n12; ULP
    programs for black youth, 171–74,
    221n54; unequal support for/
    treatment of black students,
    164–65; voucher program, 173;
    Workers School, 85. See also
    vocational training
Educational Medical Program for
    pregnant teens, 143–44
election by districts, 177
Elizy, Robert J., 31
Elkins, Myrtle Hull, 78

Elks Lodge #115, 134
Elliott, Elizabeth, 14
Elliott, S. E., 46
Ellis, David E., 116
Ellison, Marechal-Neil, 74, 100–101, 209n24
Emancipation Day, 55
Emergency Shelter Program, 214n50
Employers' Association of Pittsburgh, 30
employment. *See* jobs
entrepreneurship, 26, 32, 38, 148, 167
Epperson, David, 142, 150, 152, 155–56, 178
Epstein, Abraham, 11–12, 41, 47
Equitable Gas, 141
Ethiopian liberation, 90
ethnicity. *See* race/ethnicity
Evans, George E., 80
Executive Order 8802, 102

Facts, 120
fair employment legislation, state and local, 119–21
Fair Employment Practices Commission. *See* FEPC
Fair Housing Partnership, 163
Fair Housing Program, 214n50
Fair Labor Standards Act, 84
Family Welfare Association, 72
farmwork, 19
FAT (Forever Action Together), 140
Federal Emergency Relief Administration, 76
Federal Housing Administration (FHA), 126–28
federal poverty programs, 152
FEPC (Fair Employment Practices Commission), 102–4, 108, 119, 121
FHA (Federal Housing Administration), 126–28
fine arts department (ULP), 77
Finkelstein, Miss, 46
Finley, Irving, 117–18, 123

Fitts, William S., 88
Flanigan, John, 150
Flood, Edgar Wright, 108
folk medicine, 46–47
food programs, 43–44, 170–71
Ford Foundation, 147–48, 153
Forever Action Together (FAT), 140
Fort Pitt Brewing, 72
Fort Pitt School Play Group, 87
Foster, Bill, 166
Foster, William Z., 13, 22
Fowles, Richard M., 89
Fraser, John D., 12, 188n14
Frazier, James T. G., 147–48
Frederick Douglass Memorial Hospital (Philadelphia), 209n13
Freeland, Wendell G., 128, 134, 142, 144–45, 152, 155–56, *158*
Frenz, Reverend, 89
Frick Training School for Teachers, 50–51, 54, 209–10n25

Galbreath, Robert F., 206n71
Gammage, Jonny, 176
gangs, 174
Garrison, Oswald, 31, 66
Garvey, Marcus, 55
Garvin, Roy, 93–94
General Electric, 119
ghettoization, 129–30
Gimbel's Department Store, 72, 143
Ginzberg, Eli, 133
girls' clubs, 52–53, 87
Girl Scouts, 53, 86–87
Glasco, B. F., 99
Goldberg, Anthony, 99–100
Golden Triangle (Pittsburgh), 4, 125, 159
Gould, Howard D., 78, 101
Granger, Lester, 85, 153–54
Grant's Five and Ten Cent Store, 74
grassroots civil rights organizations, 145–46. *See also under* Urban League of Pittsburgh

Graves, Dorothy, 148
Great Depression. *See* Depression
Greater Allegheny and Monongahela
    Housing Corporation (*later*
    Allegheny Housing and
    Rehabilitation Corporation),
    148–50
Greater Pittsburgh Convention and
    Visitors Bureau, 166
Greater Pittsburgh Fair Housing
    Movement (1966), 128
Greater Pittsburgh Fair Housing
    Movement, 147, 150
Greater Pittsburgh Improvement
    League, 128, 138
Greater Pittsburgh Literacy Council,
    170
Greater Pittsburgh Multilist, 129
Great Migration (1910–1920), 2, 10,
    23–24, 41, 46
Green, Cyrus T., 49, 194n8
Green, Dianne, 164, 172, 174
Greenlee, William A. ("Gus"), 111
Gruber, J. A., 19
guilds, 153–54

HACP. *See* Housing Authority of the
    City of Pittsburgh
Haley, Leon, 127, 147, *158*, 162, 177
Hall, Wylie A., 79
Haller Baking, 94
Hampton Institute, 99
Harlem (New York City), 96–97
Harlem Hospital (New York City), 96
Harris, Abram L., 78; *The Black Worker*,
    79
Hatcher, James S., 89
HDCC (Hill District Community
    Council), 73, 79–80, 203n37
Health Advisory Council (Community
    Action Pittsburgh), 221n45
health and medical care: black doctors,
    131–32; black hospital, proposed,
    46; black hospital movement,

96–98, 208n11, 209n13; black
    medical students, 132; black nurses,
    46, 95–96, 131; blacks vs. whites,
    health of, 163–64; in coal towns,
    42; death rate among blacks, 46;
    discrimination against black health
    professionals, 45–46; equal access
    to, 117, 131–32; first black public
    health nurse, 46; food support
    projects, 170–71; Health and
    Housing Committee, 53; health
    clinic, 97–98; health education
    programs, 42–43, 46–47, 194n4,
    194n7; health screenings, 43, 170;
    health surveys, 131; hospitals, 96,
    208n11; infant mortality, 41–43,
    163; lecture series on health
    challenges, 43, 194n8; in the new
    social service regime, 95–102;
    pneumonia deaths among blacks,
    41; racial disparities in, 45–46;
    southern black medical beliefs and
    practices, 46–47; study of hospital
    employment/training practices,
    131; ULP health/nutrition
    initiatives, 170–71; ULP ties
    with hospitals and health care
    organizations, 194n4; well-baby
    clinics, 43
health and welfare department (ULP),
    130–31
health committee (ULP), 43, 95, 97,
    131–32, 194n4
Health Education Office (HEO), 170
Healthy People, 164
Heineman, Kenneth J., 153
Heinz, 15, 27, 104–5
Helping Hand Society for Homeless
    Men, 75
Hemphill, James, 26
HEO (Health Education Office), 170
Herron Hill Community Center, 102
Highland Park pool (Pittsburgh), 139
Hill, Dave, 152

Hill, T. Arnold: black women's employment promoted by, 49; Clark's letter to, 13; on Ethiopia's liberation, 90; on Reginald Johnson, 103; on the Labor Relations Act, 84–85; vs. Maurice Moss, 102; and the NNC, 86; as NUL secretary of industrial relations, 90; ULP visited/supported by, 22, 66, 190n31; on the Wagner Act, 83–84

Hill, William E.: background of, 78; boycott movement renewed by, 93–94; and Homer Brown, 100; departure from ULP, 103; at the National Conference of Negro Organizations, 86; in the National Negro Congress, 85; socioeconomic survey of poor and working-class life by, 90–91, 207n82; as ULP industrial secretary, 77–78, 107; visits Soviet Trade Unions, 86, 205n60

Hill District Community Council (HDCC), 73, 79–80, 203n37

Hill District Protest Committee, 51–52

HIPPY (Home Instruction Program for Pre-school Youngsters), 174

Hofer, Marguerite, 156

Holden, Matt, 152

home and school visitor program, 54, 64, 101

home economics unit (ULP), 20, 36–38, 43–44, 49, 59–60, 62–64

Home Instruction Program for Pre-school Youngsters (HIPPY), 174

Homeless and Transient Bureau (Allegheny County), 76, 79

homelessness/homeless shelters, 4, 20, 75–76, 169–70

Homes Registration Office, 106

Homestead Grays, 67–68

Homewood-Brushton neighborhood (Pittsburgh), 125, 148

Homewood Civic Club, 54

Homewood Civic Improvement Association, 128

Hospital Council of Western Pennsylvania, 131

Hospitality/Leisure Training Institute, 166

household workers. *See* domestic service

Housewives Cooperative League, 94–95, 208n6

housing: AHRCO-built homes, 148–50; black construction workers/electricians, 148–50; black-owned real estate and construction firms, 37–38, 129, 214n43; blockbusting, 129, 150; Carnegie Steel's policies on, 36–37; in coal towns, 38–39; cooperative ownership projects, 128; counseling program, 168–69; dilapidated, 106–7; discrimination in, 107, 126–30, 150, 156, 159, 163; establishing black middle-class neighborhoods, 127–28; fair housing legislation, 127; first black home owner, 129; Health and Housing Committee, 53; home economics unit's reports/recommendations, 37–38, 193n64; home ownership, 125–29, 151, 169–70, 214n43; Inspection Day, 43; for low-income black communities, 148–51; map of black communities, *149;* in mill towns, 37; patterns, study of, 129–30; productivity tied to, 38; rental assistance, 169; rent exploitation, 36, 126–27, 147; segregated, 37–38, 130; shortages of, 36–37, 106, 126–27 (*see also* urban renewal); slum landlords, protests against, 147; studies of conditions for blacks, 194n7; tenants' rights, 107; ULP housing programs, 214n50; unsanitary, 36–37; wartime, 106. *See also* public housing; urban renewal

Housing Act (1954), 125, 128
Housing Assistance Program, 214n50
Housing Authority of the City of
    Pittsburgh (HACP), 80, 110, 125,
    130, 150–51, 170
Housing Counseling Services, 214n50
housing department (ULP), 147
Housing Information Program,
    214n50
Hovde, Bryn, 80, 129–30
Howard, G. B., 10, 12
Howard Heinz Endowments, 133
Howell, William, 74
Hubbard, 105
Hubert, James H., 31
Hughes, Langston, 67
"Human Values" series (KDKA), 88
Hunger Services, 170–71

ICC (Interstate Commerce
    Commission), 84
Illery, Alma, 94, 121
immigrant workers, poverty of, 187n1
Incentives to Excel and Succeed, 172
Independent Brewery, 72
industrial era, end of, 159–65
industrial relations department (NUL),
    33–34
industrial relations department (ULP):
    closing/reopening of, 20–21, 35;
    establishment of, 14, 192n57;
    industrial employers' resistance to
    placements, 15–16; industrial loan
    fund, 84; management luncheon
    organized by, 119; placement of
    black women by, 16; placement rates
    for, 14–16, 72; registration efforts
    by, 103; under Tyson, 12; union-
    dues fund, 211n36; vocational   ·
    training work by, 81, 99–100
inequality: fighting against, 115–35;
    in education, 132–35, 143; in
    employment, 115–23, 140–41; in
    health care, 130–32; in housing,
107, 126–30; literature on racial
    equity, 118–19; and the ULP's
    efficacy, 180–81. *See also*
    discrimination, gender;
    discrimination, racial; segregation
infant mortality, 41–43, 163
Informer, 90–91, 121
Inspection Day, 43
Institute for the Study of the Black
    Family (University of Pittsburgh),
    162
Interdenominational Social Action
    Alliance, 177
International Brotherhood of Red Caps,
    84
Interracial Action Council, 137
Inter-Racial Commission (Federal
    Council of Churches in America),
    89
Interstate Commerce Commission
    (ICC), 84
intraracial class relations, 30–31, 59–61,
    110–11
Invincible Club of Ten, 189n24
Iron Valley Coal, 26
Irvis, Leroy Kirkland, 108, 137, 152,
    154–55
"It Takes a Whole Community to Raise
    a Child," 174

Jackson, Ella, 152
Jackson, Jim, 171
Jacob, Walter, 150
Jacobs, John, 180
Jeffries, Christina ("Miz Jeff"), 34,
    58–59, *92,* 109–10, 153, 201n9
Jewish agencies, 119–20
Jim Crow: black community's assaults
    on, 3–4; black women's efforts to
    abolish, 94; at CCC camps, 75;
    collapse in Pittsburgh, 159; in
    hospitals, 97–98; NAACP's fight
    against, 68, 98; ULP's fight against,
    39, 68, 157. *See also* segregation

jobs: in breweries, 72; at the Civic
Arena, 138–39; clerical, 73, 122; in
coal mines, 22, 25 (*see also* coal
miners, black); and day care, 53;
in the defense industry, 103;
Depression's impact on black
women's employment, 72;
discrimination in, 19–20, 49–50,
115–21, 156–57; in domestic
service, 5, 16, 19, 82–83, 204n46;
for elevator operators and bellman,
72, 81; fair employment legislation,
state and local, 119–21; in health
care, 166; industrial, 14; for light- vs.
dark-skinned blacks, 61; in
manufacturing, 21–22, 159–60;
married vs. single men, recruitment
of, 22, 25–26; for middle-class/
professional vs. working-class blacks,
181; for physicians, 97; placement,
3, 14–16, 72, 117–19, 122, 166;
political empowerment tied to job
creation, 165; promoting black
workers and expanding available
jobs, 22–25; for relief workers,
72–73; school-to-employment
pipeline, 49; skilled, for black
women, 104, 117–18; for skilled
workers, 15–16, 21, 23–25, 39,
148; for social welfare workers,
28–30, 35, 38–39; state employment
offices, 82, 103; summer, for college
students, 17, 24; for teachers,
50–51, 54, 95, 99–101, 134, 144–
45, 209–10n25; ULP employment
projects/services, 166–68; for
waiters, 81; wealth building tied to
job creation, 165; welfare-to-work
programs, 167; at Westinghouse, 8,
15, 121–22; white-collar jobs open
to blacks, 49–50, 140–41; work
programs for black youth, 172. *See
also* entrepreneurship; industrial
relations department

Job Training and Partnership Act
(JTPA), 167–68
Johnson, Charles S., 67, 117, 133
Johnson, G. M., 26
Johnson, Mrs. H. L., 192n57
Johnson, James Weldon, 45
Johnson, John, 17–18
Johnson, Mordecai, 88, 90
Johnson, Ralph, 108
Johnson, Reginald, 74, 103, 107–8
Johnson, Mrs. Toki Schalk, 154
Johnstown (Pennsylvania), 17–18
Joint Committee on Social Crisis, 73
Joint Congressional Committee to
Investigate Housing, 126–27
Joint Welfare Initiative, 167
Jones, Eugene Kinckle, 21, 58,
190n31
Jones, Julia B., 109
Jones, Richard F., 99, 129–30
Jones and Laughlin Steel, 26, 52, 63,
74, 121
Joseph Horne Department Store,
22–23, 143
JTPA (Job Training and Partnership
Act), 167–68
Junior League of Pittsburgh, 173
juvenile justice system, 54, 101,
175

Kaufman, Mrs. Raymond, 208n11
Kaufman's Department Store, 20,
143
KDKA radio station, 88
Keith, Harold, 123
Kennywood Amusement Park, 55
KIDS II, 173
King, Martin Luther, Jr., 146,
155–56
King, T. J., 89
King Edward Apartment House, 28
Kinner, Marie, 43, 46
Kroger Baking and Grocery, 76
Kuhn, David W., 131

labor movement, 13, 31–32. *See also* unions
Labor Relations Act (Pennsylvania), 84–85
Lampkin, Daisy, 37, 51, 57–58, 65, 94, 101, 208n6, 209–10n25
Larimer neighborhood (Pittsburgh), 125, 148
Lauw, Valerie, 168
Lavelle, Robert R., 129
Lavine, Harold, 203n37
Lawrence, David, 138, 154
Layton, Mrs. S. W., 31
Leavitt, Frank, 50, 81, 99–100
Lee, J. R. E., 90
Leech, Earnest, 17
Lemington Home, 154
Lepera, Vincent, 161
Lett, Harold: boycott movement led by, 93; on the CCC, 75; Citizens Committee promoted by, 73–74; committee/board work of, 73; on the CWA, 75–76; departure from the ULP, 77; on the Helping Hand Society for Homeless Men, 75; socioeconomic survey of poor and working-class life by, 90–91, 207n82; training course for black waiters by, 81; as ULP industrial secretary, 73, 107, 201n9; unemployment relief efforts of, 74; on unions, 76; on vocational training for black youth, 99–100; "What Is Happening to the American Negro," 88
Lewin, A. W., 51
Life magazine, 87
Lincoln Hospital (New York City), 96
Lincoln Play Group, 87
Lincoln Scout Troop No. 37, 87
Linkages, 174
Livingston Memorial Association, 46
Lockhart Iron and Steel, 29, 63, 123, 126

Logan, Robert H., 56–57
Lower Hill (Hill District, Pittsburgh), 53, *114,* 124–25, 138, 148
Lowndes, Grace: on attitudes toward light- vs. dark-skinned black women, 61; black women's employment promoted by, 49; on black women's preparedness for employment, 28; black women's socioeconomic conditions surveyed by, 27; boycott movement led by, 93; contribution to the ULP's success, 193n61; on the Depression's impact on black women's employment, 72; girls' clubs organized by, 52–53; and Jeffries, 201n9; and Mrs. H. L. Johnson, 192n57; Julia B. Jones on, 109; as a Morals Court worker, 27, 52, 86; on neighborhood improvement groups, 86–87; on relief for unemployed workers, 72; resignation/retirement from the ULP, 52, 64
Lucy Stone League of Republican Women Voters of Allegheny County, 57

Magee-Women's Hospital (Pittsburgh), 144
Management Council, 3, 117
Mandela, Nelson, 176
Manley, A. L., 31
Mann, Margaret, 30, 43–44, 59, 64
manufacturing, 16, 21–22, 159–60
March of Dimes, 173
March of Dimes Premature Birth Impact Summit, 170
March on Washington movement (MOWM), 3, 5, 102, 154
Marcy, C. Howard, 95
Marland, Sidney, 144, 146
Marshall, W. G., 22
Martin, Edward, 120
Mason, Louis, 108–9

Master Builders Association, 142
May, Edwin C., 21, 27, 45, 54, 62–63, 65
May, Walter A., 10, 12–13, 19, 62, 188n14
McCann's stores, 74
McConway and Tarley, 105
McCoy, Jim, 141–45
McCreary, Mrs. A. H., 82
McDonald, Valerie, 176
McDowell, John B., 150
McDowell, Mary E., 88, 206n71
McIlvane, Donald, 147, 156
McKay, Claude, 67
McKinney, Earnest, 16–17, 99
Meadow Gold, 94
Mellon National Bank, 124, 126
Mercy Hospital (Philadelphia), 132, 209n13
Metropolitan Baptist Church, 67, 170
Metropolitan Pittsburgh Crusade for Voters, 177
Metropolitan Tenants Organization (MTO), 140
migrants, southern black: biased perspective on work habits of, 23; farmwork sought for, 19; Great Migration, 2, 10, 23–24, 41, 46; job-search assistance for, 14; medical beliefs and practices of, 46–47; mistreatment of, 14; resumption of migration, 20; single men, bias against, 60–61; from Tennessee, 13–14; traveler's aid assistance for, 14, 20, 29–30; ULP bias against, 59–60
Milgram, Morris, 127
Mini Corporation, 148
Minority Elderly Outreach Program, 166
Montefiore Hospital, 46, 72
Moon, Mollie, 154
Moore, Jesse T., Jr., 180
Moore, M., 17

Morals Court, 27, 52, 59, 62–64, 86
Morawska, Ewa, 187n1
Morgan Community House, 30, 52–53
Morris, Gertrude Clark, 48, 78
Morsell, Samuel R., 10–12, 65
Moss, Maurice, 103; background of, 73; as Baltimore Urban League director, 73; bathhouse promoted by, 45; on the black community in Pittsburgh vs. other cities, 96–97; on black women protesting discrimination, 138; Citizens Committee promoted by, 73–74; committee/board work of, 73, 77; conferences organized on welfare of mill/mining towns, 74; on curative vs. preventive work, 86; on desegregating public schools, 99; on discriminatory housing practices, 107, 126–27; on employment of blacks in Pittsburgh, 77; on equal access to public education, 98; on fair employment legislation, 120; on gender discrimination, 109; HDCC led by, 79; vs. T. Arnold Hill, 102; Irvis fired by, 154; on NYA-trained workers denied employment, 105; public housing supported by, 80; Race Relations Day co-organized by, 89; on relief funds tied to voting, 57; scholarship committee promoted by, 210n30; as ULP executive director, 73, 201n9; on urban renewal, 124–25; on wartime defense plans, 103–4
Moss, Winnifred, 100
Mother's Assistance Fund, 72
Mowbray, Paul F., 13–14
MOWM (March on Washington movement), 3, 5, 102, 154
MTO (Metropolitan Tenants Organization), 140
Mucha, Frank R., 126
Mullen, J. R., 105
Murray, Philip, 90

NAACP: fair employment legislation promoted by, 119–20; in the Interracial Action Council, 137; interracial housing developments supported by, 128; on jobs at the Civic Arena, 138; on segregated hospitals, 98; and the UBPC, 142–43; ULP's collaboration with, 35–36, 41, 55, 68, 125; urban renewal supported by, 125

National Achievers Society, 172

National Alliance of Postal Employees, 88–89

National Casket, 208n6

National Conference of Negro Organizations, 86

National Conference of Social Work (Philadelphia), 91

National Council of Jewish Women, 174

National Council on Household Employment (*formerly* National Committee on Employer-Employee Relationships at Home), 82

National Education Association (NEA), 100

National Housing Agency, 106

National League for the Protection of Colored Women (New York City), 2, 11

National League on Urban Conditions among Negroes. *See* National Urban League

National Negro Congress (NNC), 85–86, 90, 95

National Negro Health Week, 42–43

National Park Service, 88

National Recovery Administration (NRA), 76–77, 103

National Urban League (NUL; *formerly* National League on Urban Conditions among Negroes): annual conferences of, 31, 90, 132–33, 178; consumer pressure groups studied by, 94; education advocacy work, 70;

founding of, 2, 11, 180; gender discrimination in, 109; goals of, 11; growth of, 2, 11; guilds of, 153–54; housing-equality work of, 147–48, 153; organized labor movement supported by, 83; social-service vs. civil-rights mission of, 140, 155; ULP's ties with, 66, 122, 132–33, 199n64; Vocational Opportunity Campaign, 73. *See also* industrial relations department (NUL)

National Youth Administration (NYA), 70, 87–88, 105

NEA (National Education Association), 100

NEED (Negro Education Emergency Drive), 134, 172, 215n67

Negley Run East End (Pittsburgh), 37

Negro American Labor Council, 138

Negro Education Emergency Drive (NEED), 134, 172, 215n67

Negro Girl Scout troops, 53

Negro Health Education Campaign, 42–43

"Negro History and Achievement" (Larimer School, Pittsburgh), 101

Negro League baseball, 67–68

neighborhood councils, 80, 152

neighborhood improvement groups, 86–87

Neighborhood Rehabilitation, 148, 150

New Castle (Pennsylvania), 17–18, 36, 189n24

Newcomb, Robert E., 38

New Deal, 2, 4–5, 71, 75–77, 160, 168, 172. *See also* welfare state; WPA

Newer Thrusts in Health Care, 170

New Futures Initiative, 168

Newmyer, W. W., 49

news reporting, racially biased, 51

New York School of Social Work, 54

Nickens, Oswald J., 128, 150

Ninth Annual Institute on Human Relations, 118

NNC (National Negro Congress), 85–86, 90, 95
North Side Bidwell Presbyterian Church, 67
North Side neighborhood (Pittsburgh), 148
Northview Heights (Pittsburgh), 168, 172, 174
Northview Heights Family Support Center, 168
NRA (National Recovery Administration), 76–77, 103
NUL. *See* National Urban League
nurses, 46, 95–96
NYA (National Youth Administration), *70*, 87–88, 105

Obama, Barack, 179
Office of Economic Opportunity, 144
Office of Substance Abuse and Prevention, 175
Oliver Iron and Steel, 72
On-the-Job Training Program, 166
Operation Dig, 139–40, 142
Operation Equality, 147–48, 153
Operation Home, 169
organized labor. *See* labor movement; unions

PACE (Program to Aid Citizen Enterprise), 153
Pace, Mrs. Franklin, 146
Painters, Decorators, and Paper Hangers of America, 122–23
Pangburn, Virginia, 101
Parker, Harold, 104
Parris, Guichard, 32–33, 118, 181
Passavant Hospital, 96
Patrick, LeRoy, 144, 150
PCASA (Pittsburgh Coalition against Substance Abuse), 175
PCSSN (Pittsburgh Council for Social Service among Negroes), 10–12

Pearce, Georgine (Brown), 51, 54, 72, 101, 193n61, 194n8
Peck, Fannie B., 95
Pennsylvania capital-labor conflicts, 13
Pennsylvania Equal Rights League, 128
Pennsylvania Railroad, 84, 104
Personal Responsibility and Work Opportunities Act ("welfare to work"; 1996), 160
Peterson, C. A., 105
Peterson, Carlos F., *114*
PHA (Pittsburgh Housing Association), 106, 126, 130, 147
Philadelphia Company (Pittsburgh), 22, 81
Phoenix Rise Homeless Prevention and Rapid Re-housing Program, 169
Pickens, William, 48–49
Pilot Placement Project, 3, 117–19, 122
Pittsburgh: black population decline in, 160; black population growth in, 2, 3*t*, 163; fair employment law in, 120–21; fair housing legislation in, 127–28, 150; hostility toward organized labor in, 13; metropolitan area of, 17, *18*; open housing law in, 128
Pittsburgh Alliance for District Elections, 177
Pittsburgh Board of Education, 101–2, 143–46, 168, 174
Pittsburgh Board of Realtors, 127, 147
Pittsburgh Brewery, 72
Pittsburgh Chamber of Commerce, 107
Pittsburgh Civic Club, 45
Pittsburgh Coal, 33, 74
Pittsburgh Coalition against Substance Abuse (PCASA), 175
Pittsburgh Commission on Human Relations, 150
Pittsburgh Council for Social Service among Negroes (PCSSN), 10–12

Pittsburgh Courier: as advertising medium for the black community, 94; on Berry, 108; black political candidates promoted by, 56–57; on Clark, 12; Community Sing co-sponsored by, 111; on discrimination by the Board of Education, 51; on education/ training for jobs, 140–41; health education programs promoted by, 42; on the Housewives League, 95; on Jeffries, 58; on labor and industry, 118; on NUL annual conferences, 90, 133; on protecting jobs for blacks, 81; on Richardson, 147; on Tanneyhill, 108; on training course for black waiters, 81; on the ULP, 35; on the ULP art exhibit, 66–67; on the ULP as a health advisory resource, 221n45; on ULP desegregation work, *136;* ULP publicity by, 12–13; on the ULP's membership drive, 65; on the ULP's role in protests against discrimination, 138; on the ULP theater production, 67; on union steel workers, 86; "Urban League Said to Be in Dire Straits," 64; urban renewal supported by, 125; under Vann, 10; on the Workers' Council, 85

Pittsburgh Cracker Bakery, 121
Pittsburgh Crawfords, 67–68
Pittsburgh Gazette Times, 29
Pittsburgh Hospital (Philadelphia), 132
Pittsburgh Housing Association. *See* PHA
Pittsburgh Labor College, 85
Pittsburgh League for Social Justice, 13
Pittsburgh Plate Glass, 17, 63
Pittsburgh Post-Gazette, 3, 121–22, 125–26, 176
Pittsburgh public schools. *See* education
Pittsburgh Railway, 15, 133

Pittsburgh Railways, 108
Pittsburgh Survey, 10, 187n1
Pittsburgh Terminal Coal, 35
police brutality/harassment toward blacks, 51–52, 56, 175–76
police reform, 176
political empowerment of blacks, 56–57, 165, 177–79
postindustrial era, 159–65
poverty: and access to education, 49; benchmark studies of, 162; of blacks in Pittsburgh vs. other cities, 162; of blacks vs. whites, 159; after deindustrialization, 4; extent of, 20, 162; of immigrant workers, 187n1; War on Poverty, 144, 151–53
Powell, Adam Clayton, Sr., 66
Prattis, Percival, 124, 129
Price, Hugh, 122, 176, 180
Proctor, Ralph, 140–41, 145, 154–55, 216n14
Program to Aid Citizen Enterprise (PACE), 153
prostitution, 52, 61
public assistance, termination of, 160
public housing: controlled occupancy of, 130; education of students in, 164–65; equitable integration of blacks into, 130; Northview Heights, 168, 172, 174; proportion of black tenants in, 151; quota system in, 130, 150–51; scattered-site units, 151; and slum clearance, 79–80; St. Clair Village, 129, 164–65, 174–75; tenant selection criteria, 110; the ULP's interest in/ promotion of, 76, 80, 127, 129–30, 150–51
Public Housing Improvement Program, 169–70, 214n50

Quimby, W. E., 49–50

race/ethnicity: Allegheny County Race
    Relations Committee, 107;
    Allegheny County survey of race
    relations, 115–17; biological vs.
    social view of, 170; Chicago race
    riot (1919), 34; interracial conflicts/
    assaults, 51, 55–56, 63, 89, 107;
    presentations on racism, 89; Urban
    League programs undermined by
    racism, 181; Wood on race relations,
    31. *See also* discrimination, racial;
    Jim Crow
Race Relations Day, 89
railroads, discrimination by, 55, 83–84,
    104
Randolph, A. Philip, 102
real estate industry, 36–38, 68, 126–28,
    147, 169, 214n43
recreation department (ULP), 81, 87
Reed, H. M., 16–17
Reed, Touré, 180–81
Re-entry Assistance Management
    Program, 167
Reeves, Robert, 169
refugee assistance, 171
Reid, Ester Moore, 67
Reid, Ira deAugustine, 133; "A Study of
    200 Negro Prisoners in Western
    Penitentiary," 79
Republican Party, 179
Reynolds, T. A., 105
Ricco, Orleans, 156
Rice, Charles, 80
Richardson, Dorothy Ann, 147
Ridge, Tom, 176
Robinson, John Carter, 192n57
Robinson, Selma, 82–83
Robinson, William Russell, 128, 155
Rogers, Clarence, 123
Roosevelt, Franklin Delano, 102
Rosalia Maternity Hospital, 72
Rose, Payton, 46
Routzahn, Mary Swain, 91
Ruck, Rob, 68

Salvation Army, 72
Sanders, Levi, 154
Satleroe, Hilma, 46
Schatz, F. C., 22–23
School of Industrial Administration
    (Carnegie Institute of Technology),
    121
School of Nursing (University of
    Pittsburgh), 170
School-to-Industry Program, 167
Scully, Mrs., 27, 63–65
Sears, 142–43, 216n19
segregation: desegregation promoted by
    the ULP, 98, 111, 144–45, 164,
    182; in education (*see under*
    education); in homeless shelters, 20;
    in housing, 37–38, 130; in
    medicine, 97–98, 132; militants'
    response to, 135; resistance to
    desegregation, 146; of swimming
    pools, *136,* 139; systemic, Urban
    League programs undermined by,
    181. *See also* Jim Crow
Self-Employment Training (SET)
    Program, 166–68
Self-Sufficient, Trained, Active and
    Resourceful (STARS) Program, 169
Seniors in Community Service Program,
    166
SET (Self-Employment Training)
    Program, 166–68
Shadyside Hospital (Philadelphia), 132
Shaw, Margaret ("Peg"), 59–60
Shoemaker, Samuel M., 118–19
"skills registration month" campaign,
    119
slum clearance. *See* urban renewal
Smith, Alfred, 57
Smith, Templeton, 35, 74
SNAP (Supplemental Nutritional
    Assistance Program), 171
social service regime, new, 93–111;
    boycott movement, 93–94;
    community building, 110–11;

"Don't Buy Where You Can't Work" campaign, 5, 93–94; health and education in, 95–102; Housewives Cooperative League, 94–95, 208n6; wartime programs, 102–7

Social Service Row (Hill District, Pittsburgh), 79, 91

social welfare workers: jobs for, 28–30, 35, 38–39; networks of, 31

social work fellowships, 29, 31, 39, 48, 78–79

social work's professionalization, 10

Soho and Gazzam Owners and Tenants League, 80

Soho Community Center, 53

South Africa, 178

Sperber, Robert I., 144–45

Spero, Sterling, 35; *The Black Worker*, 79

sports, 67–68, 87

Springer, Eric, 132

Spurlock, Edith (Sampson), 10

Staisey, Leonard C., 142

Standard Cigar Factory, 27

Standard Sanitary Manufacturing, 16–17

Standard Steel Car, 17–18

Stanton Land, 128

Stark, Mrs. H. D., 82

STARS (Self-Sufficient, Trained, Active and Resourceful) Program, 169

State Emergency Relief Board, 76

state employment offices, 82, 103

State of Black Youth in Pittsburgh, The, 171

St. Clair Village (Pittsburgh), 129, 164–65, 174–75

steel industry, 16, 23, 25, 31–32, 50, 86

Steel Workers Organizing Committee, 86

Steiner Manufacturing, 121

STEM (Technology, Engineering, and Math) Program, 221n54

Step Down, 171

Stevens, Tim, 177

Stewart, Frances, 51–52, 88, 94

Stewart, Howard R., 139

stock market crash (1929), 72

Stoner, Aluvia, 19, 192n57

Street Academy (Pittsburgh), 143–44

Strickland, Arvarh E., 181

strikebreakers, black, 32–33, 83, 106

"Study of 200 Negro Prisoners in Western Penitentiary, A," (I. Reid), 79

summer camp, 44–45

Supplemental Nutritional Assistance Program (SNAP), 171

swimming pools, 44–45, 53, *136,* 137, 139, 156, 182

Tabor, Edward O., 89

Taggert, Joseph P., 55

Tanneyhill, Gertrude, 108

technological changes' impact on employment, 21

Technology, Engineering, and Math (STEM) Program, 221n54

teen pregnancy, 143–44, 173

Teller, Sydney, 56

Tennessee, black migration from, 13–14

Terrace Village (Hill District; Pittsburgh), 80

Thanksgiving food distribution, 171

Thayer, Alonzo: and Gerald Allen's thesis on coal-camp life, 192n58; background of, 34; on black union vs. nonunion workers, 34–35; at the Chicago Urban League, 35; on conditions for black coal miners, 35; on Democratic blacks, 57; departure from the ULP, 35; efforts to expand black membership in unions, 32; efforts to expands jobs available to black workers, 22; labor movement supported by, 34–35; at the NAACP, 35–36; on race relations,

56; ULP social service work under, 35–36, 43; on unemployment among blacks, 72

theaters, discrimination in, 55

Thieman, Frederick, 174

Thomas, Jesse J., 66–67

Thomas, Julius A., 119

Thompson, F. Marie, 104

Thornburgh, Richard, 160

Three Rivers Stadium (Pittsburgh), 142

Thurgood Marshall Achievers Society, 172, 173

TNT (Transitionally Needy Training) Program, 166–67

Tolliver, H. R., 89

tourist trade, 166

trade schools. *See* vocational training

Transitionally Needy Training (TNT) Program, 166–67

Traveler's Aid Society, 29–30

Trigg, C. Y., 12, 188n14

Truman, Harry S., 118, 123

Trump, Donald, 179

Tuberculosis League, 95

Tuskegee Institute, 99

Tyson, Francis, 11–13, 20, 31, 33, 46, 62–64, 81, 192n58

Tyson, Helen Glenn, 54

UBPC (United Black Protest Committee), 142–43

ULP. *See* Urban League of Pittsburgh

UMWA (United Mine Workers of America), 33

unemployment: of blacks, 71–72, 160, 162–63; of blacks vs. whites, 160; compensation for, 85; discriminatory layoffs, 19–20; escalation in Depression years, 72–73; and manufacturing's decline, 159–60; relief during the Depression, 71–74 (*see also* New Deal; WPA); after World War I, 19

Union Construction, 37–38

unions: black members of, 9, 32, 84, 105–6, 122–23; and black strikebreakers, 32–33, 83, 106; Brotherhood of Railroad Station Porters, 84; building trade, 32; coal strikes, 32–34; discrimination by, 16, 32, 76, 83–85, 106, 116, 123; education for members of, 85; hostility toward, 13; International Brotherhood of Red Caps, 84; in wartime, 105–6. *See also* AFL; CIO

Union Station (Pittsburgh), 14, 22, 30

United Black Protest Committee (UBPC), 142–43

United Mine Workers of America (UMWA), 33

United Negro Protest Committee (UNPC), 139–42, 151

United Steel Craft, 150

United Way, 161

University of Pittsburgh: African American education studied by, 99; fellowship programs of, 29, 31, 39, 48, 78–79, 134

University of Pittsburgh Medical Center (UPMC) Health System, 166

UNPC (United Negro Protest Committee), 139–42, 151

UPMC (University of Pittsburgh Medical Center) Health System, 166

Upper Hill (Hill District, Pittsburgh), 53

Urban League movement: and the black freedom movement, 135, 140–41, 154–55; class and gender biases of, 1; debate over impact on poor and working-class blacks' lives, 1; middle-class image of, 1; social science goals of, 1–2; ULP's influence on, 111, 178; white supremacist thought challenged by, 180–81

Urban League of Pittsburgh (ULP):
area served by, 17–19, *18;* art
exhibit, annual, 66–67, 88; black
professionals/businesspeople
programs, 3, 117–19, 122; black
strikebreakers opposed by, 32; black
vs. white contributions to, 65, 156;
bridge-building by, 66–68, 181;
casework vs. referral approach of,
54–55, 116–17; on CCC camps,
76; civil rights strategies of, 142;
conservative reputation of, 141–42;
corporate support of, decline in, 9;
curative vs. preventive work of,
86–87; data collection/research by,
78, 90–91, 162, 202–3n32;
Department of Labor's collaboration
with, 15, 34, 188n19; desegregation
promoted by, 98, 111, 144–45,
164, 182; discrimination
documented/fought by, 2–4,
45–46, 49–51, 55, 58, 68, 75;
education advocacy work (*see*
education); employment advocacy
work (*see* industrial relations
department [ULP]; jobs);
entrepreneurship promoted by, 26;
executive director vs. board
members, 62–64; fair employment
legislation promoted by, 119–20;
fair housing legislation promoted by,
127; fellowship programs of, 29, 31,
39, 48, 78–79, 134; finances of, 21,
59, 64–65, 153, 156, 161; founding
of, 2, 9–14, 58; fundraising by, 153,
161–62; gender, class, and racial bias
within, 58–66, 68, 109–10; goals of,
12; and grassroots civil rights
organizations, 3–5, 93, 115, 137,
139–40, 155–57; as a health
advisory resource, 170, 221n45
(*see also* health and medical care);
housing advocacy work (*see*
housing); housing counseling

services of, 168–69; housing
programs of, 214n50; 100th
anniversary of, 179; influence of,
nationwide, 89–90, 122, 178; in the
Interracial Action Council, 137;
interracial alliances built by, 156;
interracial housing developments
supported by, 128; labor
movement's ties with, 31–32,
34–35, 39, 83–86, 105–6, 181;
leadership of, 12, 188n14; legacy of,
debates about, 180–81; loan fund
of, 167; membership drives by, 65;
militants, collaboration with, 141–
42, 216n14; movie viewings by, 67;
NAACP's collaboration with,
35–36, 41, 55, 68, 125; NUL's ties
with, 66, 122, 132–33, 178,
199n64; offices of, 15, 34, 79, 91,
161–62, 188n19; Porter Prize
awarded to, 175; on proper
behavior, 60; racial barriers in the
workplace fought by, 16; relief
advocacy work, 20, 189n27; on
single black men, 60–61; skilled
black workers as focus of, 21, 148;
social service/social justice work of,
2–4, 9, 35–36, 39, *40,* 68, 78, 91
(*see also* home economics unit;
housing; jobs; social service regime,
new; *and specific programs*); sports
promoted by, 67–68; staff salaries,
64, 109–10; standing committees
of, 62; state contracts of, 153; steel
industry studied by, 16, 23–24;
tensions within, 154–55; theater
promoted by, 67, 77, 90–91;
turnover in, 107–9; unemployment
relief work of, 73–74; white
members of, 61–62, 64; women's
contribution to, 58–59, *92,* 109,
193n61 (*see also* Jeffries, Christina;
Lowndes, Grace; Mann, Margaret;
Pearce, Georgine; Woodson,

Virginia); women's resignation from, 64; World War II's influence on, 2
Urban Redevelopment Authority, 160
urban renewal, 76, *114,* 115, 124–25, 130, 138, 151
US Census of Occupations, 19
US Council of National Defense, 43–44
US Steel (*later* USX), 116, 121, 123, 133, 159–61

vagrancy, 29
"Value of the Urban League in Pittsburgh, The" (essay contest), 48
Vann, Robert L.: black political candidates promoted by, 56–57; on black school counselors, 101; and Camp James Weldon Johnson, 87–88; capital-labor conflicts navigated by, 13; on discrimination by the Board of Education, 51; fundraising for the YMCA by, 56; on the Housewives League, 95; judgeship campaign of, 57; on the PCSSN, 10; *Pittsburgh Courier* edited by, 10, 64; political leanings of, 57; role in NUL annual conference in Pittsburgh, 90; ULP social service agenda promoted by, 12–13, 56
Veterans Administration hospital, 132
vice, 52. *See also* Morals Court
Villard, Oswald Garrison, 190n31
violence by black youth, 174–75
vocational committee (ULP), 101–2, 210n28
vocational conference, 74
vocational guidance program, 102
Vocational Opportunity Campaign, 73, 102–3, 108, 134
vocational training, *70;* vs. academic education, 47, 98–99; for black youth, 98–100; in CCC camps, 76; for household workers, 82;

industrial relations department's work on, 81, 99–100; studies of trade school graduates, 50
voter registration, 176–77
voting, relief funds tied to, 57

Wagner Act (1935), 83–84
Wagner-Costigan antilynching bill, 89–90
Wagner-Steagall Act (1937), 80
Ward, C. A., 89
Ware, Carl, 147–48
War on Poverty, 144, 151–53
wartime labor recruitment, 19
wartime programs, 102–7
Washington, Booker T., 42, 180–81
Washington, Charles W., 108
Washington, Jeanette, 43, 46
Washington, Milton, 148–49, 160
Weaver, Robert, 103
Webber, June, 203n37
Weinbert, Mary D., 203n37
Weiss, Nancy, 11, 180
Welfare Conference, 73
welfare state, 91, 111, 160–61, 165–66, 168–69. *See also* New Deal
welfare-to-work programs, 167
Werner, Jackie, 55–56
West, Alice, 58
Westinghouse, *8,* 15–16, 63, 121–22, 159
Westmoreland, Antoinette, 74
"What Is Happening to the American Negro" (Lett), 88
Wheeling Mold and Foundry (West Virginia), 19, 39
Wilkerson, Herbert, 154
Williams, J. A., 194n8
Williams, Lettie B., 189n24
Willie, Charles V., 164
Wilson, Boyd, 123
Wilson, Robert Lee, 90
Women's Bureau, 52
Women's Court, 52

Wood, L. H. Hollingsworth, 31, 66,
    190n31, 199n64
Woodson, Isaiah, 17
Woodson, Virginia, 53, 87, 193n61
Workers' Council, 85, 105–6
Workers School, 85
Works Progress Administration. *See* WPA
World War II, 2, 9, 71
Worthington Pump and Machinery, 38
WPA (Works Progress Administration),
    3, 75–77, 82, 87–88, 202n29

Yarbrough, Dean, 79
Yellow Cab, 122
YES (Youth Employment Services), 168
YMCA, 16, 52, 56, 67–68, 99, 194n4,
    201n9

Young, Marechal-Neil Ellison, 74, 100–
    101, 209n24
Young, Whitney, 155
Young, William Arthur, 209n24
Young, W. P., 29, 81, 123, 126, 130
Young Women's Committee for Fair
    Employment in Pittsburgh, 138
Your Future, 103
Youth Crime Prevention Council, 174
youth development department (ULP),
    172
Youth Employment Services (YES),
    168
Youth Opportunity Conference, *70*
YWCA, 82, 90, 99, 194n4

Zahniser, Charles R., 10

CIVIL RIGHTS AND THE STRUGGLE FOR BLACK EQUALITY IN THE TWENTIETH CENTURY

Series Editors

Steven F. Lawson, Rutgers University
Cynthia Griggs Fleming, University of Tennessee
Hasan Kwame Jeffries, Ohio State University

Freedom's Main Line: The Journey of Reconciliation and the Freedom Rides
Derek Charles Catsam

Gateway to Equality: Black Women and the Struggle for Economic Justice in St. Louis
Keona K. Ervin

The Chicago Freedom Movement: Martin Luther King Jr. and Civil Rights Activism in the North
edited by Mary Lou Finley, Bernard LaFayette Jr., James R. Ralph Jr., and Pam Smith

The Struggle Is Eternal: Gloria Richardson and Black Liberation
Joseph R. Fitzgerald

Subversive Southerner: Anne Braden and the Struggle for Racial Justice in the Cold War South
Catherine Fosl

Constructing Affirmative Action: The Struggle for Equal Employment Opportunity
David Hamilton Golland

An Unseen Light: Black Struggles for Freedom in Memphis, Tennessee
edited by Aram Goudsouzian and Charles W. McKinney Jr.

River of Hope: Black Politics and the Memphis Freedom Movement, 1865–1954
Elizabeth Gritter

The Dream Is Lost: Voting Rights and the Politics of Race in Richmond, Virginia
Julian Maxwell Hayter

Sidelined: How American Sports Challenged the Black Freedom Struggle
Simon Henderson

Becoming King: Martin Luther King Jr. and the Making of a National Leader
Troy Jackson

Civil Rights in the Gateway to the South: Louisville, Kentucky, 1945–1980
Tracy E. K'Meyer

In Peace and Freedom: My Journey in Selma
Bernard LaFayette Jr. and Kathryn Lee Johnson

Democracy Rising: South Carolina and the Fight for Black Equality since 1865
Peter F. Lau

Civil Rights Crossroads: Nation, Community, and the Black Freedom Struggle
Steven F. Lawson

Selma to Saigon: The Civil Rights Movement and the Vietnam War
Daniel S. Lucks

In Remembrance of Emmett Till: Regional Stories and Media Responses to the Black Freedom Struggle
Darryl Mace

Freedom Rights: New Perspectives on the Civil Rights Movement
edited by Danielle L. McGuire and John Dittmer

This Little Light of Mine: The Life of Fannie Lou Hamer
Kay Mills

After the Dream: Black and White Southerners since 1965
Timothy J. Minchin and John A. Salmond

Faith in Black Power: Religion, Race, and Resistance in Cairo, Illinois
Kerry Pimblott

Fighting Jim Crow in the County of Kings: The Congress of Racial Equality in Brooklyn
Brian Purnell

Roy Wilkins: The Quiet Revolutionary and the NAACP
Yvonne Ryan

James and Esther Cooper Jackson: Love and Courage in the Black Freedom Movement
Sara Rzeszutek

Thunder of Freedom: Black Leadership and the Transformation of 1960s Mississippi
Sue [Lorenzi] Sojourner with Cheryl Reitan

For a Voice and the Vote: My Journey with the Mississippi Freedom Democratic Party
Lisa Anderson Todd

Pittsburgh and the Urban League Movement: A Century of Social Service and Activism
Joe William Trotter Jr.

John Hervey Wheeler, Black Banking, and the Economic Struggle for Civil Rights
Brandon K. Winford

Art for Equality: The NAACP's Cultural Campaign for Civil Rights
Jenny Woodley

For Jobs and Freedom: Race and Labor in America since 1865
Robert H. Zieger